The Brezhnev
Politburo and the
Decline of Detente

The Brezhnev Politburo and the Decline of Detente

HARRY GELMAN

Cornell University Press

Ithaca and London

First published 1984 by Cornell University Press.
Published in the United Kingdom by Cornell University Press Ltd., London.

International Standard Book Number (cloth) 0-8014-1544-6
International Standard Book Number (paper) 0-8014-9280-7
Library of Congress Catalog Card Number 83-45963

Printed in the United States of America

Librarians: Library of Congress cataloging information appears on the last page of the book.

The paper in this book is acid-free and meets the guidelines for permanence and durability of the Committee on Production Guidelines for Book Longevity of the Council on Library Resources.

To Shirley,
David, Peter, and Pam

Contents

Preface

This book is the product of many years of watching the internal and external struggles of the leaders of the Soviet Union, and of observing the somewhat discouraging spectacle presented by successive American administrations in their interaction with those leaders. The reader will find that I attempt a synthesis of three aims. In part, the book seeks to illuminate what I believe to be the reality at the center of Soviet politics, and the driving assumptions of the Soviet oligarchy. In this respect, I am struck by the extent to which the conclusions reached by Nathan Leites in his seminal work of more than thirty years ago, *The Operational Code of the Politburo,* seem to continue to be valid. In part, the book is a conscious effort to advance Western Kremlinology, and to build upon the work begun late in the Stalin era by Robert Conquest and continued in Khrushchev's time by Myron Rush, Carl Linden, and most notably, Michel Tatu. And finally, through the discussion of Soviet policy toward the United States in the Brezhnev era, I hope to shed some light on our own dilemmas.

Chapter 1 and most of Chapter 4 of this book are drawn from work sponsored by the Director of Net Assessment, Office of the Secretary of Defense, and originally published by the Rand Corporation in April 1981 as a Rand Report.* That Rand study was prepared under the aegis of Richard Solomon, director of Rand's

---

* Harry Gelman, *The Politburo's Management of Its America Problem,* R-2707-NA (Santa Monica: The Rand Corporation, 1981).

research program on national security policy issues, as part of an effort to develop more effective approaches for managing America's long-term competition with the Soviet Union. I wish to express appreciation to Rand for its permission to use this material, which appears here in considerably revised form. The views expressed in this book are not necessarily shared by the Rand Corporation or by any department of the United States government.

I am also grateful to colleagues who read parts of the book manuscript and furnished helpful suggestions: Abraham Becker, Thane Gustafson, Grey Hodnett, Arnold Horelick, Kay Oliver, and particularly Myron Rush, at whose suggestion I began the project of enlarging the Rand paper into a book. I hasten to add the customary disclaimer that I alone am responsible for any faults and errors that may exist. Indeed, much of what I have to say about the Soviet leadership—and also about the United States—is controversial, and it is unlikely that any two Sovietologists, or any two Americans, will agree on all the points raised.

My thanks go, also, to my wife, for all her encouragement and support through this long and arduous effort. Finally, I would like to express gratitude to the many former colleagues in the American bureaucracy whose insights have helped me over the years.

HARRY GELMAN

Santa Monica, California

The Brezhnev
Politburo and the
Decline of Detente

Introduction

During the 1970s, as Soviet-American relations entered and left the era of detente, Western views of the Brezhnev leadership and its attitudes toward the Western democracies tended to become increasingly polarized. By the end of the decade, those at one extreme of the spectrum of opinion saw the Soviet leaders as perpetually threatening crude military aggression in the manner of Hitler. At the other extreme, particularly in Europe, there were many who continued to believe that these same leaders showed an unrequited desire for permanent accommodation. Between these extremes, there were opposing tendencies. One current of thought assumed that the events in the Third World during the latter part of the decade had alarming implications for the West, and that these events signaled a steady growth in the Soviet propensity to expand. An opposing trend of opinion argued that such events were part of a natural process, unpreventable and fundamentally un-threatening, through which the USSR was emerging as a great power on the world scene. One view stressed Soviet gains; the other, Soviet setbacks.

In general, the first viewpoint perceived a purposeful pattern of Soviet behavior hostile to Western interests in widely separated places; the other saw no pattern, but only a series of fragmented and coincidental regional events. The first perspective considered this worldwide Soviet behavior incompatible with the maintenance of good bilateral relations with Moscow; the second was interested primarily in maintaining these bilateral relations and, on the whole, accepted the Soviet intimation that detente should be insulated from Soviet efforts to promote the erosion of the West's position around the world.

Looking at Europe, one perspective held that the Soviet leadership was striving rather cynically to perpetuate a military imbalance it had established unilaterally; the other either denied that Moscow had a significant net local military advantage or found the proposed Western response more threatening. The first viewpoint saw the Politburo as seeking to play on strains within the Western alliance in order to maximize Soviet leverage on the alliance's component parts and thereby hasten its disruption. The second saw Soviet policy as primarily defensive, intended to shore up a Soviet economic and political position that was menaced by a deteriorating economy and a fragile East European empire.

The contrast between these two interpretations was particularly sharp in regard to the Soviet posture toward the United States. One view held that the Soviet leaders were continuously striving, within a gradually receding limit of tolerable risk, to nudge a long-term process of world change along paths that were congenial to Soviet interests and more and more inimical to those of the United States. Those who subscribed to the other view tended to see the USSR essentially as a bystander or, at most, as a mere protector of an entirely autonomous process of change. Three-fourths of the way through the decade a leading exponent of this second view maintained that the Soviet Union was "more likely to assign its military power the task—beyond defense—of preventing others from interfering with change than of imposing change." [1]

Finally, whereas one view saw the Politburo's intense pursuit of military strength throughout the 1970s as deeply disturbing, destabilizing, and fundamentally threatening to the United States, the other was much more sanguine, believing that "it is inevitable and, frankly, desirable that both sides maintain their defenses." Furthermore, this latter view held that "we both have—or believe we have—an interest in holding these forces to a minimum," even if in practice both sides have tended to "move constantly the other way." Consequently, there was nothing strange or different or "sinister" in the Soviet pursuit of military power in the era of detente. This view implied that there was no asymmetry between Soviet and American attitudes toward military spending in the 1970s; and in any case, we should understand that "a Soviet speaker would say that detente is the process by which his country capitalizes on its growing power to curb American excesses." [2]

It seems evident that America's Vietnam experience helped to influence many of the assumptions about the Soviet Union harbored by those, in the United States and elsewhere, who maintained the second set of views described. If one argued a priori that the major threat to peace stemmed from American "excesses" in resisting a process of international change, then one naturally tended to believe that Soviet motives were essentially defensive and, if not praiseworthy, at least readily understandable and certainly no worse than our own. Moreover, some felt more dangerous tendencies might come to the fore in the Soviet leadership and in Soviet policy if American policy were overly provocative. According to this reading, Americans should empathize with Soviet perceptions of a hostile and dangerous United States and not provoke dangerous confrontations by contesting Soviet policy too vigorously.

Although some in the West who inclined toward this view during the 1970s have modified their assumptions in response to events, others have not. Some have maintained this perspective whether the Soviets have acted close to home or at great distances, whatever the nature of the regimes the Soviets have supported, and whatever the force ratios the Soviet leaders have sought to achieve. Inevitably, this viewpoint has conferred a certain legitimacy upon the process through which the Soviets have incrementally added to their geopolitical strength, and through which the position of the West and of the United States has gradually been diminished.

At the same time, however, some of those who take a more somber view of Soviet policy, and who share the first perspective described above, may be inclined toward rationalizations of a different kind. While denying—correctly, in my view—that the Soviets are merely innocent beneficiaries of radical international change, they attempt to uphold the dubious proposition that the Politburo not only actively exploits and encourages but also creates virtually all those trends on the world scene harmful to Western interests. While focusing on the real military vulnerabilities of the West, they have tended to speak and act in a manner that heightens rather than reduces its political vulnerability to the Soviet Union. And while emphasizing the hostile implications of Soviet behavior, they have not responded adequately to those who continue to see Soviet policy as essentially defensive.

The premises underlying this book are much closer to the first view of Soviet foreign policy than to the second, but they do not deny the existence of a defensive element in the behavior of the Soviet leadership. In the discussion that follows I argue that throughout the Brezhnev era a profound sense of vulnerability—over both the legitimacy of party rule and the stability of Soviet gains—powerfully reinforced the leadership's felt need to keep pressing for incremental gains within the scope of available opportunities and the limits of prudent risk. In consequence, I contend that from start to finish the consensus of the Brezhnev Politburo was highly pessimistic about the compatibility of Soviet interests with those of the United States. For various reasons, this predisposition was further reinforced by the process of political struggle within the Brezhnev leadership. As a result, conservative ideological assumptions and a heightened sense of the priority to be given Soviet military power dominated the leadership's thinking from the earliest stages of the Brezhnev regime. Unfortunately, these views did not change greatly during the period of detente with the United States in the early 1970s. Eventually, these Soviet patterns of thought and action, the American reactions they fostered, and the Soviet responses to those reactions combined to put an end to any sense that the two superpowers were probing for mutuality of interest. The legitimacy of detente was one of the casualties of this process.

Against this backdrop, the death of Brezhnev and the advent of a new regime has once again raised questions about the assumptions that underlie Politburo policy toward the United States. My discussion considers whether the domestic and external environment surrounding the post-Brezhnev Politburo is likely to permit a fundamental change in these assumptions.

This book is divided into five chapters. The first seeks to reconstruct thematically the Soviet leadership's goals and fears in its worldwide interaction with the United States, and to isolate those factors that drove the evolution of Politburo conduct in the Brezhnev era. The second examines certain structural characteristics of the internal Soviet political environment that helped determine the course of the political struggle within the Brezhnev Politburo. The third traces certain events in that internal struggle and their effects upon the attitudes the Brezhnev leadership brought to detente. The fourth then discusses the evolution of the Soviet detente relationship with the United States within the historical competitive context of external Politburo behavior from which it first emerged in the 1970s, and into which it eventually returned. Finally, the fifth chapter considers the prospects for Soviet-American relations in the post-Brezhnev era against the background of the asymmetrical vulnerabilities of Soviet and American societies.

1 / Soviet Postulates, Concerns, and Priorities

THE SOVIET WORLD HORIZON

In the last years of the Brezhnev regime, a member of the aging and ailing Soviet leadership had occasion to allude to the fact that the regime was undergoing a broad "counterattack" from its chief opponent.[1]

It has always been somewhat unusual for a Politburo member to use this word in this context, for to do so implies that he acknowledges a preceding, equally broad, and hostile Soviet stimulus. It is thus hardly surprising that having used this term to characterize U.S. policy toward the USSR at the start of the 1980s, A. P. Kirilenko did not follow up on his hint that a long-standing Soviet offensive posture toward the American position in the world might have helped to precipitate Washington's response to the invasion of Afghanistan. Instead, Kirilenko argued that in seeking to isolate the Soviet Union, the United States was trying to rebel against objective, self-propelled phenomena that were incrementally and inevitably eroding American influence and in the process advancing that of the Soviet Union. In reacting against "the profound consequences of detente and the objective process of progressive social change taking place in the world," the United States was vainly seeking to turn back "the laws of history," which, Kirilenko implied, both necessitate and legitimize Soviet advances.[2]

19

Moreover, in trying to carry out this policy, the U.S. leadership was said to have given vent to "whim, caprice, emotional outbursts."[3] It was alleged that these reactions contradicted American self-interest, which required graceful adjustment rather than foolish resistance to historical necessity. Soviet pronouncements on this subject were calculated to impress upon foreign audiences a certain anger and contempt at this amateurish yielding to emotion. The Brezhnev Politburo had no intention of acting in the same manner.

Confronted with such an attack, the first imperative for the party leadership was to respond vigorously yet appropriately, without allowing itself to be "provoked" into abandoning the line that was believed to optimize Soviet interests.[4] "No one will succeed in provoking us," insisted Brezhnev; "No one will push us off this course."[5]

In the Politburo's view of the world, pugnacious struggle so shaped and channeled has a dual advantage: it continues, even intensifies, that universal offensive against American influence which has been so much resented by unrealistic circles in the United States, and at the same time it earns whatever political rewards may result from professed moderation towards states other than the United States.

With the Soviet–U.S. bilateral relationship at a standstill, Soviet competitive strategies for dealing with the United States in the world arena today thus retain an essential continuity. An overview of the interacting spheres of Soviet concern will suggest the nature of the offensive and defensive tactics that were developed over the last decade, and show how they have been adapted to the new challenge.

In Regard to the Capitalist Industrial World. By appealing to the perceived self-interest of U.S. allies in maintaining their separate economic and security relationships with the USSR, by pressing on the lines of cleavage opened up by the multiple disparities among Western interests, by encouraging and playing upon allied perceptions that U.S. policy is dangerously unpredictable, immoderate, and inconsistent, and by attacking the domestic base of those individuals and groups most supportive of the United States, the

Soviet leadership since the last year of the Carter administration has sought to escape the isolation Washington has tried to impose on it and endeavored to isolate the United States in its turn.

In Regard to China. Confronted since the late 1970s with the prospect of an increasing Sino-American security alignment against them, the Soviet leaders now see trends as somewhat more reassuring. They have searched assiduously for a means of separating their two antagonists without paying a significant price to either. The Politburo has concentrated on efforts to split the weaker opponent from the stronger by combining intimidation—the conventional and nuclear threat assembled on China's northern borders—with blandishments. To this end, the Brezhnev leadership repeatedly offered China improvement in selected aspects of the bilateral relationship, while refusing to give up the geopolitical gains it had made in Asia at Chinese expense, notably in Indochina. Although these efforts were long unsuccessful, the Soviet leadership now believes it has made progress. Gratified that Chinese differences with the Reagan administration have led to some cooling in Sino-U.S. relations, the new Andropov Politburo seeks to cash in on what the Soviet leaders see as a Chinese inclination to conciliate them.

In Regard to Its Own Sphere. While pursuing uninhibited efforts to consolidate its new position in Afghanistan, the Politburo has managed to halt the decay of its position in Poland at moderate political cost, and regards this as a significant accomplishment. The Soviet leaders are well aware that over the long term the political situation in Poland will probably remain volatile and precarious, and that the economic situation there is also likely to be grave for many years. Nevertheless, they are highly gratified that they have been able to arrange for the Polish military regime to cap popular pressures, at least for the time being obviating the need for a Soviet military intervention that might have severely damaged Soviet dealings with Western Europe. They are also gratified, although hardly surprised, that the adverse Western reaction to this change has proved both weak and ephemeral in its effects on the Soviet

Union. Meanwhile, the Politburo continues to tighten the screws at home, accelerating the consolidation of domestic ideological conformity, disposing of the remnants of the dissident intellectual forces that had been emboldened by the Soviet Union's Helsinki pledges, and thus creating a fait accompli to be incorporated into the revised definition of detente.

In Regard to the Third World. The Soviet leadership perseveres in its long-term effort to extend the Soviet political presence into more and more nooks and crannies throughout the world which were previously dominated by Western influence. To this end, the leadership adjusts and modulates what was already a highly diverse set of policies so as to meet the defensive needs and offensive opportunities created by the new U.S. posture. Exploring avenues of opportunity as they are opened up by the interaction of unpredictable variables, the Politburo accepts major setbacks as inevitable incidents in its gradually broadening advance through the enemy's hinterland. A few representative examples suggest the flavor of the whole:

1. To African and Latin American radicals, to the Arab rejectionists, to the Europeans, and to the Chinese, the Soviets stress with redoubled vigor the paramount importance of the particular grievances each of these audiences harbors against the United States. The Soviet leadership thus seeks to intimate to each audience that the Soviet offense in Afghanistan is, in comparison, of trivial consequence for its interests.

2. While employing various diplomatic expendients to reassure those audiences the Politburo wishes to soothe—such as India and the Arabs—that the ongoing effort to crush resistance in Afghanistan poses no threat to them, the Soviets seek tacitly to convey the opposite impression to those audiences for whom intimidation is thought useful, such as Pakistan.

3. While playing upon the misgivings of some (such as India and Kuwait) over U.S. efforts to strengthen its local military presence and capabilities, the Soviets quietly take steps to

enhance the USSR's own naval presence in the Indian Ocean and its military readiness in the Caucasus.

4. While intensifying efforts to defend and consolidate those political and military bridgeheads achieved through a Soviet security relationship over the last five years (in Angola, Ethiopia, South Yemen, Afghanistan, and Indochina), they adjust to what they believe will prove only transitory disappointments in other arenas.

5. Although chagrined at their inability to affect the course of events in Lebanon in the summer of 1982, the Soviet leaders patiently await the emergence of new opportunities in the Middle East, and see little reason to doubt that they will materialize. The Politburo remains confident that Israeli intransigence will indefinitely prevent any solution of the Palestinian issue brokered by the United States. It is equally confident that the Western powers will never be able to restore predominant Western influence throughout Lebanon. It is hopeful that Egypt without Sadat will eventually gravitate away from American influence, and sanguine that fresh instability will sooner or later present the Soviet Union with a new opening in the Gulf region. The Soviet leaders see a considerable possibility that the Iran-Iraq war may further such fruitful instability in the Persian Gulf. Meanwhile, they continue to be encouraged by the long-term, open-ended possibilities created by the expulsion of American influence from Iran, and they remain alert for sudden changes in the Iranian internal situation that may present an opportunity to advance. Despite the worsening of their relations with the Khomenei regime, they believe they remain better positioned than the United States, both institutionally and geographically, to take advantage of such changes when they come.

6. Meanwhile, the Soviets seek to preserve and develop their existing arms-supply relationships with a variety of African states by making use of the potential offered by the South African bogey. They strive to build upon resentments evoked in Black Africa by the Reagan administration's posture toward South Africa. And they confidently await major long-term

benefits from exploitation of the eventual racial explosion they expect in South Africa, assured that the American relationship with that country will guarantee fresh opportunities for Soviet policy in Black Africa.

7. At the same time, the Soviets cautiously begin to cultivate a new relationship on the main enemy's decaying periphery—with Nicaragua—while loudly anticipating the eventual harvest of further fruit in El Salvador. Greatly encouraged by the recent acceleration of U.S. difficulties in Central America, they now regard this area as the most active front in the broad process that has eroded U.S. influence in different parts of the Third World over the last decade. They believe that the polarization of local social forces will exacerbate these American difficulties over time regardless of the U.S. response. They also expect to profit as the growing turmoil in Central America intensifies strains within the United States and increases friction between Washington and those European social forces sympathetic to the Central American left. At minimal risk to themselves, they therefore support and encourage Cuba in its long-term effort to assist and stimulate this process.

8. Accordingly, the Soviet leaders see an ongoing need to reinforce their geopolitical stake in Cuba. They continue quietly to expand the multiple military and political uses they have found for this oldest Soviet bridgehead in the Third World. While continuing to value Castro as a major instrument of attack on American interests in Africa and Latin America, they seek to pacify his annoyance at the Afghanistan embarrassment and to encourage him to repair the damage it has done to Soviet and Cuban interests in the nonaligned movement—and thus, gradually, to help revive the temporarily diminished intensity of anti-American sentiment in that movement.

This brief tour of the Soviet world horizon suggests that the current leadership's strategy toward the United States is both defensive and coercive. The defensive aspect of Soviet behavior responds to what the Soviets see as unprecedented U.S. efforts to isolate and surround them. The coercive core of the Politburo's policies reflects the Soviet hope to so shape the international environment as to compel the United States to restore those elements of the bilateral relationship which the Soviets still deem useful, but to do so on terms favorable to accelerated Soviet exploitation of competitive advantages. This Soviet stance has been inherited from the Brezhnev regime.

Viewing the world as a single interrelated, many-faceted battlefield, the Soviet leaders have for many years regarded the management of their direct bilateral relationship with the United States as but one aspect, albeit a very important one, of a much broader, indeed universal interaction with the United States. This interaction involves a multitude of engagements, sometimes open and sometimes hidden, sometimes sharp and sometimes subdued, between interests that in most cases are assumed a priori to be incompatible. Although, as we shall see, the Politburo's priorities across the wide canvas have shifted over time with changing circumstances, a very large proportion of the Soviet energies devoted to coping with the United States was always channeled through Soviet dealings with others. After 1975, for reasons to be explored below, this proportion grew steadily. With the drastic downturn of the bilateral relationship in 1980, the competitive thrust of the Brezhnev Politburo's policies affecting the United States, long dominant in Soviet thinking, became all-embracing.

This does not mean that the increasingly decrepit members of the Brezhnev leadership in its final years at last acquired a "master plan" for further advance in the world at U.S. expense, a plan magically able to anticipate the interaction of all the myriad variables they previously had been unable to foresee. On the contrary, despite the obligatory obeisance all Soviet institutions must make to paper plans, the practical decision-making horizon of the Soviet leadership, particularly in foreign affairs, most of the time remained remarkably short.

Instead of a blueprint, the Soviet leaders under Brezhnev had a consistent world view centered on the unblinking expectation of lasting struggle with the main antagonist—a view that furnished them with a sense of self-justification under all circumstances and provided a stable framework from which to assign priorities as decisions and events emerged. They were isolated within a network of advice and information shaped to confirm this attitude of pugnacious righteousness. Although different points of view did exist among the foreign policy experts who surrounded them, in no case was the Politburo confronted with advisers who had the treasonous temerity to interpret ambiguous phenomena in a fashion that might challenge the fundamental preconceptions of these old men. In the military sphere, where the General Staff and a few closely associated functionaries enjoyed a virtual monopoly of esoteric information and advisory rights,* the view of Soviet needs and interests which could be voiced was even more closely circumscribed.

Thus informed and supported, the members of the Brezhnev Politburo explored new avenues of opportunity as they arose, forming tentative expectations and discarding them with great dexterity, sometimes blundering, but always subordinating this shuffling of expedients to a central purpose.[6]

THE ELUSIVE CORRELATION OF FORCES

The Soviets now say that the United States is attempting to reverse the trend of the world "correlation of forces." They imply that any such attempt is illegitimate.

Within this amorphous concept the Soviets have subsumed, in extremely vague fashion, all the political, social, economic, and military factors they perceive as involved to some degree in their worldwide competition with their chief antagonists. On the positive side of the ledger, the Soviets thus include not only their attainment of an edge in ICBM throw-weight but also such trends of the 1970s as the successive humiliations of the United States in Vietnam and Iran, the baneful effect of the OPEC cartel upon Western economies, the successful Soviet-Cuban operations in Africa, American difficulties in Central America, the internal political and economic disarray in the United States, and the decline of the moderating

* Through the mechanism of the joint Politburo-military committee known as the Defense Council, discussed in Chapter 2.

Yugoslav influence and the rise of that of Cuba in the nonaligned movement. Thus all trends, nonmilitary as much as military, which affect the relative status of the United States and the Soviet Union are used in measuring the correlation of forces. In this equation, events that further weaken the antagonist are often as important as Soviet victories.

The Soviet leaders have also long been aware that there is another side to this ledger. Among the negative trends in the correlation of forces, an objective Soviet observer would list such factors as the fragile, dangerous, and unreliable Soviet relationship with Poland; the grave and growing Soviet economic difficulties and the long-term decline in the rate at which the Soviet economy has been overtaking that of the United States; Chinese opposition to the consolidation of Soviet geopolitical gains in Asia; the negative reaction in the Moslem world to the invasion of Afghanistan; the Soviet inability to end resistance in that country; and most worrisome, the prospect of a revival of military expenditures and deployments in the West.

As a result of the tension between the two sets of phenomena, the Soviet leadership is at once confident and increasingly assertive in exploiting the opportunities created by favorable trends, and indignant and defensive about threats to Soviet interests evoked by the reactions to that exploitation.

There is in Moscow no objective standard by which to weight the factors involved in the correlation of forces, and different Soviets almost certainly measure them differently. But whereas the frequent assertions of Soviet propaganda must to a certain extent be discounted,* it is probably true that most Soviet leaders saw favorable trends as considerably outweighing unfavorable ones in the 1970s, and since then have perceived the United States as frantically seeking to reverse this ratio.

* Soviet media have over the years regularly proclaimed that the correlation of forces was changing to their advantage, making such claims in periods of Soviet good fortune and bad fortune alike, including periods (such as that of the illusory missile gap) when the Politburo has wished to convey a misleading impression of strength. The manipulation of this concept is, in fact, an instrument of Soviet political warfare, but this does not mean that the Politburo does not believe in its underlying reality.

The more rapid accretion of favorable developments in the second half of the decade reassured the Soviet leadership that notwithstanding many Soviet defeats, difficulties, and dangers, basic trends were working in their favor. The members of the Politburo, no less than the leaders and populace of the United States, are sensitive to the emotional impact of symbolic events. The replacement of Batista by Castro has been followed two decades later by the replacement of Haile Selasse with Mengistu; the humiliating U.S. flight from Saigon has been followed by Soviet entry into Cam Ranh Bay; the Shah and Somoza have fallen. The Soviet reaction left no doubt of the Politburo's view of the meaning of these symbols for the U.S. position in the world. The overthrow of the Shah, exulted Andrey Gromyko in an election speech in February 1980, has created "a gaping hole in American foreign policy."[7] Though these images of U.S. disaster were counterbalanced to a considerable degree by the misadventures and worries of Soviet policy, particularly the ongoing crisis in Poland, the Soviet leaders were probably quite confident as to who was in retreat over the last decade and who was pressing ahead.[8]

Soviet assumptions on this score were strongly reinforced by the opinions of others. The Soviet leaders surely agreed with the often-stated Western assessment that the USSR had emerged as an increasingly important actor on the world scene during the 1970s. They were well aware of the view, widespread in both Western Europe and the United States, that American leverage and influence in Europe has been eroding since the late 1970s, partly because of personality differences between leaders and different perceptions of national interest, but also because of underlying secular shifts in relative economic strength.[9] And they were equally were aware of the common American perception that the second half of the 1970s was characterized by a succession of momentous U.S. disasters in the Third World, beginning with the humiliating flight from Saigon.[10]

The Soviet leadership regarded this train of U.S. misfortunes as invigorating to observe and important to encourage not only for its own sake (the weakening of the U.S. position being an objective good in itself, since it changes the *relative* correlation of forces), but also because of the possibilities, however chancy, thereby opened up for the implantation of Soviet influence. The Politburo takes it for granted that such influence, particularly in areas not contiguous to the Soviet Union, may be relative, conditional, possibly ephemeral, but at the same time it discounts this circumstance. Painfully aware that not every American loss produces an immediate Soviet gain, and that not every Soviet gain endures, the Soviet leaders share a perspective that renders these realities patiently supportable. If any given trends are not immediately and obviously zero-sum in their effects, there is reason to believe they will be so in a broader or longer-term perspective.

These Soviet considerations were reinforced by one Soviet achievement which the Politburo assumed was not fortuitous. Side by side with the contraction of American influence and the emergence of unprecedented opportunities for the projection of Soviet power abroad, during the 1970s the Soviet leaders witnessed favorable changes in the relative Soviet position in the three chief military arenas: the strategic balance with the United States and the regional confrontations with NATO and China. Moreover, the Soviets believed that these favorable modifications in military balances were facilitated not merely by the energy and determination of the USSR but also by the various social and economic weaknesses of its antagonists—underlying factors that again testified to a changing correlation of forces.

Among some Soviets who had an institutional vested interest in pursuing a maximum advantage in the arms competition, this heady experience tended to diminish even the customary awe of the superior size, technological level, and productive potential of American industry. As one Soviet writer asserted, in the areas of production that really matter in military terms—that is, heavy industry—the American advantage was rapidly dwindling. In fact, he alleged it had almost vanished and that the United States was frittering its undoubted economic advantages away in areas of self-indulgence which contribute nothing to the correlation of forces.

In analyzing the economic potential of a state it is necessary to consider also the characteristics of the country's industrial production. In the U.S.A. the production of such items as objects of luxury, means for advertising, automobiles, household appliances, etc., which cannot be converted in practice to satisfy military needs or have limited significance in this area, makes up a significant proportion of total industrial output. If industrial production in the USSR currently comprises more than 75 percent of the American level (in 1950 it comprised less than one-third of the USA level), the [annual output of all Soviet heavy industry] is not less than 90 percent of comparable production in the USA. It is clear that this has not only tremendous general-economic but also military-economic significance. . . . The coefficient of superiority of the socialist commonwealth over the aggressive imperialist bloc in the area of assuring the material needs of military construction is currently considerably more weighty than the corresponding index of the USSR in comparison with Hitlerite Germany during the past war.[11]

Although these assertions were probably regarded as one-sided and tendentious even by other Soviets,* the hint of a certain contempt for the lagging and frivolous behavior of the competitor was probably reflected to some degree in Kremlin attitudes during the 1970s.

Thus, a Soviet leader might say it was not for the sake of our blue Russian eyes that the Americans froze their ICBM and SLBM launcher totals for a decade while we rushed past them; not for us that they relied instead upon qualitative advantages that we have now also largely eliminated. Nor is it a matter of goodwill that the West failed to attempt to halt the growing preponderance of Warsaw Pact tanks in Europe during the last decade, and had no deployment programs in train to anticipate and compensate at the time for the installation of the SS-20. Certainly it is not because of Chinese goodwill that the pace of modernization of Chinese conventional forces facing the USSR fell behind the rate at which the Soviet Union continued to strengthen its own forces on the Chinese border.

---

* The presentation cited, published midway through the 1970s, was clearly meant as an argument for maximum Soviet perseverance in the allocation of resources in the desired direction, and for avoiding temptations to fall into the American consumerist trap. Some Soviets today would disagree with certain of its assumptions, especially the tacit suggestion that there is no competition for resources in the USSR between military industry and heavy industry, as well as the intimation that the American standard of living has no significant effect upon the world correlation of forces.

All these historic omissions were instead the result of specific deficiencies in the Politburo's antagonists. In the U.S. case these deficiencies reflected the enervating effects of the Vietnam War upon the American will to compete, even in weapons production. In the case of NATO, the failure to compete reflected the members' extreme reluctance to make sacrifices commensurate with Soviet force improvements, and their inability to agree on any counter-measures until long after the particular Soviet stimulus had materialized. And in the Chinese case, profound and enduring economic and technological weakness impeded the development of Chinese military strength. All these developments were surely very encouraging to the Politburo.

And yet, a note of less than complete assurance about the continuation of these trends can be detected in much Soviet commentary since 1978. The reality of the United States' large new military programs, the prospect of European theater nuclear deployments, and the threat of American transfers of military technology to China undoubtedly created a Soviet sense that new dangers which the leadership must fight to overcome were emerging even as the USSR entered a prolonged period of increasing economic stringency. Such factors as the revival of American nationalism, the heightened threat of encirclement, and the extreme volatility of the Third World forces the leadership sought to manipulate in the 1970s have multiplied the latent uncertainties with which the Politburo must now contend. Clearly, more arduous struggle is in prospect if the advances of the 1970s are not to be surrendered.

THE OFFENSIVE ESSENCE OF SOVIET
DEFENSIVE CONCERNS

A note of righteous grievance permeates the Soviet reaction, both public and private, to the U.S. response to the invasion of Afghanistan. The Americans, it is implied, are unreasonably trying to deprive the Soviet Union of that which rightfully belongs to it by virtue of geopolitical achievement and historical mission.

What is the United States perceived as seeking to wrest from the Politburo, and what do the Soviet leaders see themselves as defending? Three sets of claims are at stake: the legitimacy of an expandable Soviet empire, the Soviets' right to play a continuously growing role throughout the world, and the legitimacy of asymmetrical Soviet rights in the field of military security.

The Legitimacy of the Expandable Empire

First, the Politburo is determined to ensure the "irreversibility" of its authority—defined as "socialist gains"—inside the Soviet Union, in Eastern Europe, and also in such other areas, particularly those adjacent to the USSR, as history and the balance of forces may from time to time reveal. In defending this dual claim, the Soviets on the one hand appeal for recognition of the Politburo's right to maintain internal stability within the established boundaries of its empire. On the other hand, they demand respect for those natural changes dictated by geography—that is, for what are intimated to be the Soviet Union's natural gravitational rights as a great power to force a small neighbor into its orbit.

The Politburo thus expects its adversaries to acquiesce in its right to use force if necessary to preserve Soviet domination over Poland, and also to accept a similar Soviet right to employ force in consolidating and extending Soviet domination over Afghanistan.

An Expanding (Supplanting) World Role

Second, the Politburo wants the United States to acknowledge the legitimacy of its intention to make incremental use of emerging opportunities and capabilities in order to become a fully global actor.

The Right to Emulate. Soviet spokesmen generally defend this demand by arguing that the Soviets have the right to play a role that the United States has heretofore reserved for itself. This argument is sometimes supplemented, particularly in private conversations, with the accurate observation that even now the Soviet

Union has not yet achieved either the far-flung political presence or the far-reaching power-projection capabilities long enjoyed by the United States. U.S. objections to Soviet overseas operations are therefore said to reflect a continuing and hypocritical refusal to accept the Soviet Union as a real equal. Some sympathetic non-Soviet observers similarly suggest that the U.S. stance exacerbates historical Russian feelings of inferiority and wounds the Politburo's *amour-propre,* thereby encouraging Soviet bad behavior (behavior that is thus actually the fault of the United States).

This line of justification and self-justification generally ignores the fact—incessantly cited in other contexts—that America's global role, which the Soviet Union sometimes professes to emulate, is widely perceived as gradually declining. Indeed, the Politburo sees the USSR's efforts to expand its own role as heavily dependent on just this trend. The corollary of this fact is that the Soviet leadership in practice seeks not merely to match but incrementally to supplant the American presence and influence. Although the Politburo takes for granted that the erosion of American influence does not guarantee a corresponding Soviet gain, or ensure the permanence of any such gain, such an erosion is seen as a prerequisite. The effort to expand the Soviet global role and to prevent the evaporation of recent Soviet gains is therefore interwoven with an incessant effort, involving very large Soviet resources, to encourage and play upon anti-American sentiment in every part of the world.

For the Soviet leadership, the decisive test of the antagonist's readiness to accept the inevitability and legitimacy of the emerging Soviet role is his willingness to maintain a mutually profitable bilateral relationship with the USSR even as the supplanting process advances. The Politburo believes that the United States never fully accepted the need to separate Soviet-U.S. dealings from Soviet policies that affect the United States elsewhere in the world, and concludes that it seized upon the invasion of Afghanistan as a pretext to reject such compartmentalization explicitly.

"You Do the Same to Us." In private Soviet representatives argue that this American stance is also hypocritical because the United States, in their view, has never ceased striving to undermine

Soviet interests abroad. Among the examples cited are the Middle East, where the United States was instrumental in facilitating a major reduction in Soviet influence after the 1973 war; and China, with whom the United States in the late 1970s sought to construct a security relationship, allegedly to "encircle" the Soviet Union.

It is indeed possible that some Soviet leaders have seen this argument as additional justification for what they felt impelled to do in any case. The Politburo, however, has had a highly asymmetrical view of these matters. Thus, even as it has insisted on isolating the bilateral relationship from the consequences of its competitive operations against American interests in the Third World,* it has refused to accept the U.S. association with China as a matter that can be separated from its bilateral dealings with Washington. On the contrary, the Brezhnev leadership responded to the unfolding of the U.S.–Chinese relationship with repeated warnings that it could have major effects upon U.S.–Soviet bilaterals, including arms control negotiations.[12] In this case, the Soviet leaders professed to believe in "linkage."

More fundamentally, the Politburo has never provided reason to believe it would respond to major American concessions in areas of relative Soviet weakness—such as briefly appeared possible, for example, at the time of the October 1977 Soviet-U.S. communiqué on the Middle East—by making comparable concessions to American interests elsewhere. Still less has it given evidence that it would condone a general relaxation of its offensive posture against the United States throughout the Third World in general. In obedience

---

* These operations are generally justified in lofty terms as reflecting the unalterable and inevitable Soviet duty to come to the aid of "revolutionary and national liberation movements." This justification is taken much more seriously by some Western observers than by the Soviet leaders themselves. The Politburo has, to say the least, a highly selective sense of this obligation, which in practice is measured almost exclusively in terms of realpolitik and the net Soviet advantage in the worldwide struggle with its main antagonists. Even the ideological leanings of a given movement are significant to the Soviets only to the extent that they promise to serve the larger geopolitical interests of the USSR. Thus while the Marxist MPLA in Angola and the less radical ZAPU of Zimbabwe were deemed worthy of Soviet support, such movements as ZAPU's more radical (but Chinese-contaminated) rival ZANU were not, nor were assorted Kurds in Iraq, Eritreans in Ethiopia, and Biafrans in Nigeria (to say nothing of the Afghan tribesmen and the Cambodian ultra-Marxists).

to the taboo against "unprincipled" fundamental concessions that would constrict the Party's freedom of maneuver and reduce its room for future advance,[13] the Soviet leadership recognizes no region of the world—and no country within any region—as a sphere of influence of the United States exempt from Soviet efforts to supplant American ascendancy.[14]

Indeed, the Soviets are indignant at the notion that they might be asked to make such an exception. To do so, they argue, would translate detente into the "preservation of the status quo," whereby "imperialism could continue unhindered its tyranny in the areas remaining in its sphere of influence."[15] This Soviet position is also asymmetrical: the Soviets argue the opposite case when defending their inherent right to ensure continuation of a friendly regime in Kabul.

In sum, the merging of the ostensible quest for equality with the compulsion to seek to supplant is a constant motif in Soviet thinking, although it is fully verbalized only in rare moments of brutal candor:

> We want to be treated as equal partner in the world. What we want is equality, the status of equal rank. In the Middle East we are visualizing a draw. Sadat, however, is committing a grave mistake if he allies himself so closely with the losing party, the Americans. . . . The United States has no business in the Middle East.*

The Compulsion to Attack. The Politburo wishes the United States to accept this attacking *(nastupatel'nyy)* compulsion, the very essence of Soviet policy toward the American position in the world, as a fundamental reality fully compatible with detente. Such spectacular events as the combat deployment of Cuban or Soviet forces (in Africa and Southwest Asia) and the use of Soviet geopolitical strength to underwrite aggression by others (in Southeast Asia) are therefore not isolated aberrations in the Soviet interpretation of

---

* Statement by an unidentified "high-ranking official" of the Soviet Embassy in Washington who has been posted there continuously since 1960, in an interview in *Die Welt* (Bonn), January 14, 1980.

detente, but rather special manifestations of a continuous flow of policy. Although particular kinds of Soviet behavior may or may not be repeated, depending on circumstances, the propensity to seek to supplant, which drives the entire underlying process, is unabating and cannot be compromised.

In principle, then, the attacking compulsion is insatiable; it appears to deny the possibility of reaching any point of lasting equilibrium between the USSR and the United States. Periods of pause and retreat which may appear to imply the acceptance of such a balance are instead disturbing anomalies that must be justified, both to oneself and to one's associates, as interludes of consolidation within a broader framework of unabating offensive. It is for this reason that Brezhnev felt obliged to assure some militant followers in the spring of 1973 that the improvement of bilateral relations with the West was a stratagem that would enable the Soviet Union to improve its relative position to the point where by 1985 it could deal with the West more forthrightly.*

Since the sun may not shine forever, advantages must be pursued when they are at hand. It was not enough that the post-Shah regime in Iran sought to perpetuate Iranian hostility toward the United States by seizing U.S. diplomats. The Soviet leadership, lacking a good opening to that regime, felt it must seek one by fanning the flames of that hostility, and thus it hailed the takeover of the U.S. embassy, at first quite explicitly, in the broadcasts of an "unofficial" radio station under Soviet control.[16] After the United States vehemently protested, the Soviet leaders modified their support for the kidnapping of the American diplomats, but continued it implicitly. Thus, at a March 1980 luncheon for the visiting Hungarian foreign minister, Gromyko said Iran had recently "provided an example of staunchness in defending its national interests against imperialist pressure, blackmail, and threats."[17] The pressures in question, of course, had been organized by the United States in

---

* A credible account of this incident appeared in The *New York Times,* September 17, 1973. I shall defer to Chapter 4 a more detailed discussion of the peculiar factors that impelled Brezhnev to make this statement, and the extent to which he himself believed it.

an effort to secure release of the U.S. diplomats being held hostage, while what was being so staunchly upheld against those pressures was Khomenei's unwillingness to release the diplomats.

Similarly, it was not enough that the United States was ignominiously expelled from Vietnam in 1975 with the aid of Soviet-supplied materiel. To consolidate a position of advantage, the Politburo then felt it necessary to discourage Vietnam from pursuing a non-military solution to its border problems with Pol Pot's Cambodia—a solution that could reduce Vietnam's need for Soviet aid—and instead actively encouraged a military solution that would perpetuate Vietnamese dependence on the USSR. One manifestation of this Politburo policy was, of course, the signing of the Soviet-Vietnamese treaty of November 1978, which set the stage for the Vietnamese attack on Cambodia in December and eventually produced the Soviet military presence in the former American base at Cam Ranh Bay.

Nor is it enough that Washington has been forced to accept a permanent Soviet military alliance with, and military presence in, a close neighbor of the United States. In addition, the Cubans must be encouraged and discreetly assisted in their eagerness to seize emerging opportunities to further the erosion of the American position in Central America. The Soviet reaction to the progress of such erosion has been characteristic, providing striking testimony to the prevalence of the Politburo's zero-sum view of the world.[18]

The Danger of Falling Back. Underlying all such attitudes and behavior is the unspoken assumption that if the Soviet Union does not press ahead in its universal struggle against the United States, it may fall back. Given past Soviet experience and the economic power of the West, the Soviet leaders are acutely aware that their influence on noncontiguous clients, whatever their ideological makeup, is potentially fragile. (Indeed, except for those cases in which the Soviet hold can be enforced by military occupation, the same may be true for contiguous clients, as Tito, Mao, Kim Il Sung, Ceausescu, Dubček, and Amin have variously shown). Precisely because the permanence of both gains and opportunities must be considered uncertain, consolidation can be ensured only by pressing on.[19]

In sum, the Soviet offensive posture is dictated by a confluence of judgments, assumptions, and emotions: the sense of beckoning opportunities created by American misfortunes and a changing "correlation of forces"; the Leninist compulsion to pursue potential gains to the limit of prudence; an awareness of the emergence of strategic parity and of the growth of Soviet force-projection capabilities; the rationalization that the United States behaves similarly; and superimposed on all else, the fear that the gains of recent years may be reversed if not reinforced with new ones.

THE LEGITIMACY OF ASYMMETRICAL SECURITY

At the same time that the Soviet leaders see themselves as defending the legitimacy of their efforts to expand their world role at American expense, they sense that they are involved in the defense of certain favorable asymmetries in their security relationships with their antagonists which have evolved over the years. The Soviets have come to regard these asymmetries as prescriptive rights essential to the defense (and therefore to the advance) of their national interests, although they are simultaneously prejudicial to the interests of their opponents and in some cases have repeatedly been objected to as such.

The assumption of such unequal military rights and needs is often implied when the Soviet leaders invoke the term "equal security." Although the Soviets do not usually spell out their claim, they tend to suggest that because of the disadvantages imposed by the USSR's geography and other unique geopolitical burdens, the Soviet Union must deploy greater force levels in each sphere than its antagonists do in order to end up with equivalent security, or "equilibrium."

Occasionally, this contention has been made explicit. Most broadly, the overall size of the Soviet armed forces in comparison with those of the United States was publicly justified on the grounds of the Soviet Union's need to defend itself on two fronts, along the Soviet-Chinese frontier as well as in Europe.[20] What was not acknowledged was the conviction, apparently equally strongly held, that the Soviets must maintain a local advantage in each of these theaters.

In the case of China, from 1965 on, the Soviets gradually accumulated local forces and firepower that they considered sufficient to overmatch the Chinese at every step on the escalatory ladder. The Soviet measurement of sufficiency was heavily influenced by the need to offset their dependence upon a long rail line for reinforcement, but most Western observers believed that the Soviet buildup overcompensated even for the defensive needs this handicap created. The Chinese therefore concluded that the stationing of these powerful forces in Siberia and Mongolia was intended simply to intimidate them. The Soviets, however, saw this as justifiable, a necessary insurance-through-superiority, particularly because these forces could also be used to exert geopolitical leverage on Chinese behavior elsewhere, in Indochina, for example. In the late 1970s, the Politburo accordingly became indignant at the possibility that China might receive from the United States the wherewithal even to dilute this superiority.

The Politburo's underlying attitude toward sufficiency in Europe appears roughly similar. Although the Soviets have offered no justification for the Warsaw Pact's sizable advantages in manpower and tanks (since they do not even admit these advantages exist), it is conceivable that at one time they may privately have regarded them as necessary to compensate for what was then an important NATO advantage in tactical nuclear weapons. Despite the virtual elimination of this handicap in recent years, the Soviets continue to improve on their very large offensive advantage in tanks, unwilling to forego the measure of extra military insurance it confers, the bargaining advantage it presents in arms control forums, and the intimidating weight it gives the Politburo in dealings with West European states and populations.

At the same time, having sought and failed in SALT I and II compensation for the so-called Forward Based Systems (FBS)*— the French and British nuclear delivery systems and the U.S. carrier-based nuclear weapons in the European theater—the Politburo has proceeded to produce and deploy systems in Western Russia—the SS-20 IRBM and the Backfire bomber—which again, in the Western view, greatly overcompensate for this Soviet handicap. The Soviets have professed to believe that these systems have merely restored an "equilibrium," and to be indignant over the West's plans to respond by deploying nuclear systems capable of reaching the Soviet Union.† Having established a unilateral, non-negotiated fait accompli, they insisted on the right to participate in determining the Western response, and indicated their intention to take additional steps to preserve their advantage in reaction to a Western refusal to halt deployment. Once again, the Soviet leaders regard the United States as the chief cause of the Western failure to accept the legitimacy of the asymmetrical security established with the advent of the SS-20.

Finally, the Soviet leadership appears to believe that in the strategic sphere Soviet vital interests require them to pursue a war-fighting capability in excess of that required merely to deter the United States from launching an attack. The quest for this additional capability is evidently regarded as a search for insurance against the possibility that deterrence might fail and thus as a legitimate reinforcement of the Soviet sense of security, like the unacknow-

---

* The USSR probably received tacit, partial, and temporary compensation for FBS in the U.S. acceptance and legitimization of unequal SLBM ceilings in SALT I. This was obviously considered inadequate, however, particularly since those ceilings were to be rendered moot in the broader framework of the SALT II agreement, which permitted both sides to mix and match disparate systems to common ceilings.

† Thus, during Andrey Gromyko's visit to Germany in November 1979, he characterized the Western resolve to proceed with theater nuclear deployments as an unacceptable attempt to set "political preconditions" for negotiations. On the other hand, he suggested that the Soviet deployments to which NATO now finally proposed to respond did not represent such an effort to establish preconditions, precisely because they had been going on for some years without response. He appeared to be implying that the force ratio established with the advent of the SS-20 had been legitimized by Western inaction, and must be recognized as "equilibrium" (Moscow Radio, November 24, 1979).

ledged advantage in tanks and manpower maintained in Europe. At the same time, just as the Soviets are unwilling to acknowledge the degree of insecurity that their own pursuit of maximum security in Europe creates in the West, so they are unwilling to come to grips with the American perception that Soviet strategic overinsurance is a menace to its deterrent—and thus to U.S. security. Because the Soviets are unwilling to accept any formulation that would question the legitimacy of this overinsurance, they explicitly rejected the principle of mutual-assured destruction during the SALT negotiations.[21] They have thus, in effect, disowned any responsibility for the preservation of a sense of mutual deterrence.

In an attempt to compensate for this refusal, the Soviets have in recent years claimed that a strategic parity or "equilibrium" exists and have vigorously denied any intention of upsetting it by seeking superiority.[22] These statements bear a strong resemblance to the analogous Soviet assertions that the introduction of the SS-20 has brought about an "equilibrium" in Europe. Because such general reassurances do not address the destabilizing capabilities of the Soviet weapons deployments in question, they do not remove the insecurity that these Soviet actions create. As a result, Soviet overinsurance has evoked a reciprocal deployment response, including, in the strategic sphere, a reciprocal decay in U.S. adherence to the notion of mutual-assured destruction.

THE FAMILY OF DEFENSIVE-OFFENSIVE CONCERNS

A family resemblance in Politburo attitudes has thus existed in diverse spheres of Soviet policy. In the Brezhnev era, the determination to ensure adequate defense of Soviet interests was seen as simultaneously requiring and justifying the forcible addition of Afghanistan to the inner sphere of Soviet control, the continuous outward pressure against the American position in the world, the vigilant preservation of unequal security balances in regional theaters, and the pursuit of a strategic war-fighting capability against the United States.

In Politburo thinking, the adverse implications these attitudes hold for others have apparently been legitimized by the underlying assumption that Soviet interests can be adequately defended only at the expense of the antagonist and are fundamentally incompatible with his interests. It is thus taken for granted that if the Politburo allows constraints to be placed on its behavior by foolishly accepting the possibility of a real and lasting middle ground, such constraints must provide a unilateral advantage to the opponent.[23]

FACTORS IN THE EVOLVING SOVIET POLICY MIX

Despite the Politburo's strong proclivity to go to the limits of prudence in order to maximize gains, there is reason to believe that the leadership's evaluation of disparate alternative advantages has fluctuated somewhat with changing circumstances. Over the last decade, several interacting factors have to some degree affected the evolving Soviet calculation of costs and benefits.

THE SCOPE OF THIRD WORLD OPPORTUNITIES

Certainly the single most important factor has been the growing scope of opportunities for Soviet involvement in the Third World. This development is itself the product of both the shifting situations on the ground—in specific Third World arenas—and changing Soviet and American political and military capabilities. For reasons that will be enumerated later, changes in all of these respects began to accumulate rapidly in the second half of the 1970s, and taken together they greatly increased preexisting incentives for Soviet assertiveness. In the beginning of the 1980s, however, this wave of opportunities subsided somewhat, and Soviet behavior became perceptibly less assertive.

THE SCOPE OF ALTERNATIVE BENEFITS FROM DETENTE

Second, despite all its rhetoric about the impossibility of "linkage," the Soviet leadership has never been indifferent to the prospective payoff in bilateral benefits that might, in principle, flow from selective acts of restraint calculated to conciliate the American elite. In practice, however, the potential rewards of restraint have at no stage seemed commensurate with the gains to be obtained through seizure of competitive opportunities.

In retrospect, it is possible that none of the benefits the Soviet leaders originally sought from the detente relationship would ever have sufficed to constrain Soviet behavior in the Third World. Even the realization of the maximum, highly exaggerated Soviet hopes of 1971–1972—the hope for massive American and Japanese capital investments in Soviet energy production, for example— might not have induced the Politburo to refrain from exploiting those qualitatively new opportunities that emerged after 1975 in Africa and elsewhere. But in any case, this contingency never arose. With the rapid dissolution of these hopes, particularly after the passage of the U.S. trade legislation of December 1974, the issue became moot; the incentive was now far too small to constitute a motive for restraint which might have neutralized the Politburo's powerful imperative to maximize gains. Since the mid-1970s, the Soviet leadership has contemptuously dismissed Washington's periodic attempts to hold other aspects of the Soviet-U.S. relationship—such as arms control agreements—hostage to better Soviet behavior. The Politburo has made it clear that those efforts demonstrate a naive misconception of its view of the balance of Soviet interests.

THE TOLERABLE PRICE OF AVERTING SINO-U.S. COLLABORATION

Third, for more than a decade after the Soviet border clashes with China in 1969, the Politburo feared that the United States would seek to utilize Soviet vulnerability in the East as a point of leverage upon Soviet policy. From the moment that Sino-American normalization surfaced in 1971, the Soviet leadership was increasingly convinced that the United States was in fact attempting to apply such leverage, and it disregarded U.S. disclaimers, assuming (correctly) that they were not seriously intended.[24] In the earliest stages of this process, between the summer of 1969 and the spring of 1971, the Politburo's concerns about China were sufficiently great that the Soviet Union was in fact willing to make certain concessions to the United States—discussed below—in an effort to ensure U.S. neutrality and, if possible, to obtain some degree of alignment between the United States and the USSR against China. Later, and particularly after the Soviet leadership had simultaneously been disappointed with the practical fruits of detente and enticed by new opportunities for gain at America's expense in the Third World, the Politburo became adamant in its determination to avoid further such concessions to the United States at all costs. What in one context had been seen as a wise tactical adjustment to unfavorable circumstances was now, in another context, seen as unprincipled yielding to pressure, as allowing the Party to be "used" by the enemy.[25]

In the late 1970s, the Soviet leadership therefore responded to what it perceived as a growing Sino-U.S. alignment against the USSR with a combination of vague and inadequate threats to the major opponent (the United States), and equally vague inducements to the secondary one (China). The Brezhnev Politburo, though increasingly alarmed at the Sino-U.S. combination against it, for a long time evidently refused to acknowledge, even to itself, that its offensive policy of maximizing gains against the geopolitical interests of both adversaries had been largely responsible for driving them together. Instead, the Soviet leaders were inclined to ascribe these unwelcome developments to the blind, autonomous, and ultimately unappeasable malevolence of particular individuals: for example, Zbigniew Brzezinski in the United States and Deng Xiaoping in China. This view led the Soviets to the rationalizing conclusion that concessions would only encourage America's propensity to follow this baneful line—an assumption that meshed well with the Politburo's felt need to avoid any such concessions and instead to maintain an offensive posture. This pattern of Soviet thought was in turn facilitated by the continuing ambiguity of Washington's long-term aims toward China, an ambiguity that stemmed from the American failure to reach a consensus on how to coordinate its China policy with its policy toward Moscow.

Early in the 1980s, however, this frozen Soviet posture began to shift somewhat in response to changing circumstances. As already suggested, the major change was the interruption in the growth of the Sino-American security alignment which occurred in 1981, largely although not entirely as a result of the emergence of major Chinese frictions with the new Reagan administration over Taiwan. The resulting coolness between Beijing and Washington helped influence the Chinese to begin a process of incremental improvements in their posture toward Moscow. By late 1982, this process, in turn, had at last induced the Politburo to advertise the possibility that it might eventually make significant concessions to Beijing. The Chinese remained skeptical of these hints, and continued to regard the Soviet Union as the primary threat to their security. Despite its differences with Washington, Beijing therefore was careful to maintain its connection with the United States, and to allow some improvement in 1983. Nevertheless, the small, step-by-step improvements in the atmosphere of Sino-Soviet relations begun in 1981 also went on, and seemed likely to continue indefinitely.

In sum, the Soviet leaders, having weathered what they saw as a decade of American efforts to use the Chinese connection to exert leverage on Soviet policy, at last emerged into a period of greater ambiguity in the strategic triangle.

THE BALANCE OF PERSONAL AND INSTITUTIONAL INTERESTS

The fourth factor in the evolving mix of Soviet policies, the internal dimension, was of a different order. One should not imagine that Soviet policy toward the United States was thrashed out by a Politburo divided between "hawks" and "doves." Rather, policy emerged from the interplay of subtle shadings of difference among the leaders and institutions represented in the informal Politburo consensus—a consensus to which all have felt it wise to conform even as events moved it in a direction more highly prized by some than by others. The evolution of that consensus and the complex way in which it was affected by the struggle among the oligarchs under the Brezhnev leadership are discussed in some detail in Chapters 2 and 3. We may note here, by way of anticipation, three interactive tendencies among the institutions upon which the leadership relied.

The Growing Military Effects within the Regime. There is little doubt that over time the Politburo's growing confidence in the political rewards to be obtained through the military instrument influenced the relationships among the institutions that surround it. Above all, the prestige of the Soviet military establishment and its leaders, already greatly enhanced by the political effects of growing Soviet strategic strength, rose further with successive demonstrations of how Soviet power-projection capabilities could augment the Soviet political position in the Third World. This enhancement of the political position of the Soviet military, in turn, had policy consequences. It appears likely that Soviet military leaders, particularly Marshal Grechko, were important participants in the political coalition that favored an increasing Soviet engagement in such Third World enterprises regardless of the effect on American attitudes.

The point is not, of course, that the military could dictate to the Party. Rather, the total political environment, both inside and outside the Soviet Union, gradually impelled party leaders toward the consensus that this line of policy was in the net Soviet interest. As a result, each Politburo member was increasingly inclined to assume, particularly in marginal situations, that it was in his personal political interest to lean in the direction made more attractive by military endorsement.

One symptom of this changing political atmosphere was the party leadership's readiness to authorize Soviet military spokesmen to make increasingly explicit references to the legitimacy of the Soviet combat role overseas. Marshal A. A. Grechko's statement at the 24th Party Congress in 1971 was one of the first such assertions:

> The outstanding succeesses of the country of socialism and our military victories have exerted tremendous influence on the world's destiny and promoted the growth of the peoples' liberation movement and the development of the world revolutionary process. The Soviet Army has demonstrated convincingly its historical mission as the defender of everything which is advanced and progressive, against the forces of reaction and aggression.[26]

Such pronouncements continued and grew stronger throughout the era of detente. By 1974, for example, Grechko declared:

> At the present stage the historic function of the Soviet armed forces is not restricted merely to their function in defending our Motherland and other socialist countries. In its foreign policy activity, the Soviet state actively, purposefully opposes the export of counterrevolution and the policy of oppression, supports the national liberation struggle, and resolutely resists imperialist aggression in whatever distant region of our planet it may appear.[27]

By the close of the decade, such assertions had assumed an extraordinarily defiant tone:

> From the very first day of its existence the army of the land of the Soviets was an army of friendship and fraternity among peoples, an army of internationalists. The entire 60-year-plus history of the Soviet state and its armed forces is evidence of this. Soviet people did all they could to support the revolutionary struggle of the working class of Germany, Austria and Hungary in 1918–1919 and to help Mongolia and China in their struggle against the Japanese militarists. Many Soviet volunteers fought in the international brigades in Spain. Loyal to their international duty, Soviet servicemen, together with the servicemen of other socialist countries, went to the assistance of fraternal Czechoslovakia in 1968. At the request of Afghanistan's revolutionary government, a limited contingent of Soviet troops is now fulfilling its international duty on the Democratic Republic of Afghanistan's territory.[28]

Another, more subtle symptom of this change was the apparent upgrading of the importance of military as opposed to countervailing political considerations in Soviet decision making, even in some cases when it could be predicted that results would play into the hands of the United States. The decision to proceed with the invasion of Afghanistan may have been such a case, although the Soviets may have underestimated the scope of the negative political consequences as they weighed them against the powerful imperatives to act. A clearer example was the decision late in the decade not merely to persist in adamantly refusing to discuss the Japanese claim to the southern Kurils but to enlarge the garrisoning and fortification of those islands in a highly visible manner. Although there are probably important military reasons for this conduct (the desire to deny U.S. entry to the Sea of Okhotsk in wartime and to ensure Soviet egress), many outside observers thought the price paid—in terms of increased Japanese hostility toward the Soviet Union and the Japanese propensity to increase military cooperation, as desired by the United States—was disproportionate, and almost certainly foreseeable.*

The International Department of the Party.   Aside from the military, the Central Committee apparatus, particularly its International Department under party secretary and candidate Politburo member B. N. Ponomarev, was probably the most important Soviet institution supporting the more forward line in the Third World as it unfolded in the 1970s.

In what has evidently been an ongoing rivalry with the Foreign Ministry over the management of different aspects of Soviet foreign policy and the rendering of policy advice to the Politburo, the International Department seems to enjoy certain advantages in dealings with major portions of the Third World. In particular, it has had ongoing, frequently publicized contacts with leaders of the so-called national liberation movements—contacts the Foreign Ministry has evidently lacked.

This bureaucratic or operational advantage, discussed in detail below, has probably been more important in influencing Soviet policy toward "liberation movements" in the Third World than have the relative positions of Andrey Gromyko, a full member of the Politburo since 1973, and Ponomarev, still merely a candidate member. In general, the Central Committee apparatus probably possesses a more direct channel of influence to the Politburo than does the Foreign Ministry, although this is probably outweighed by the foreign minister's personal stature in those policy areas in

---

* Some observers suggest that in this instance Soviet calculations of their political interests reinforced their military motives, and that Soviet decision makers assumed that using such deployments to intensify pressure upon Japan would eventually be profitable. Some sentiment of this kind undoubtedly exists in important Soviet circles. The Soviet leadership consensus cannot have felt high confidence in this thesis, however, nor can it have been unaware that these deployments might have seriously adverse effects upon Japanese attitudes toward rearmament. Therefore, professional military views on Soviet force disposition needs were probably decisive.

which he has primary operational responsibility, such as dealings with the capitalist industrialized world.

This circumstance may have played some role in the Soviets' watershed decision to take decisive action on behalf of the MPLA during the civil war in Angola in 1975–1976, despite the angry American reaction.

The Foreign Ministry and the Institutes. It is conceivable that some sections of the Foreign Ministry and some of the leaders of the advisory foreign policy institutes may initially have been unenthusiastic about the priorities displayed in this trend of Soviet policy. In addition, they may have resented the attitudes and influence of the Defense Ministry and been somewhat more concerned about the consequences for the Soviet bilateral relationship with the United States than were other sections of the foreign policy elite. If so, this lower-level lack of enthusiasm for Soviet military adventures in the Third World had virtually no effect on the Politburo's policy choices in the second half of the 1970s.*

Foreign Minister Gromyko's speeches, as well as his travels and the pattern of his contacts, suggest that he has always given dealings with the United States and Europe much more personal attention, and a higher priority, than he has given most of the underdeveloped world. But if he shared any initial lower-level misgivings about the regime's priorities, they probably dissipated in the face of the general hardening of Soviet policy as the decade went on and as relations with the United States decayed.

---

* Galina Orionova provides a vignette that illustrates the reaction in the USA Institute to this shift in Soviet priorities:

> There was a conference or a closed meeting [in] . . . April, 1975, [on] the invasion of North Vietnam into South Vietnam. And the question was raised whether it was worthwhile, because there were too many losses in foreign policy. . . . But then Zhurkin was present and he shut up those who spoke in these terms. Such thinking is not allowed even at the closed seminars. . . . Another point was made at the seminar that maybe it would be better not to intervene or to support national liberation movements. . . . But the person who spoke for it was shut up too.

(Barbara L. Dash, *A Defector Reports: The Institute of the USA and Canada,* Delphic Associates, May 1982, p. 188.)

THE "NEW CLASS" AND DETENTE

Finally, some observers—notably Alexander Yanov[29]—have stressed that large sections of the Soviet privileged classes have had a vested interest in the preservation of those personal economic advantages that the "New Class" derived from detente. Since this vested interest appears real enough, one may ask why this consideration had so little visible effect on the Soviet policies that eroded the Soviet-U.S. relationship over the last decade. Several factors seem to have been responsible.

First, the cooling of U.S.-Soviet relations has not yet severely curtailed the advantages members of the subelite derive from greater opportunity for contacts and travel and increased access to Western consumer goods. This is partly because some intercourse with the United States still goes on, but largely because detente with Western Europe has thus far been affected only marginally.

Second, the posture of the regime has in any case been well calculated to deflect any resentment within the Soviet aristocracy over the demise of detente with America. As noted earlier, the Soviet regime has never ceased to assert its support for the notion of improved economic and political relations with the United States, while simultaneously insisting that Soviet actions elsewhere in the world must be isolated from the bilateral relationship. In effect, then, the United States is forced to assume immediate responsibility for the decay because it insists on linking the bilateral relationship to Soviet behavior in the Third World. If Moscow simply refused to do business with the United States, the Soviet elite would find it much easier to hold the regime responsible for the consequences of detente's demise.

Third, the regime derives countervailing support within the Soviet aristocracy for its Third World military activities as a result of the considerable pride many Soviets take in the USSR's new role as a superpower and world actor.

And lastly, I also submit that the decision-making oligarchs of the Politburo were in any case considerably less susceptible to pressure from below than is sometimes supposed. This theme is developed more fully in Chapter 2.

2 / The Political Mechanics
of the Brezhnev Regime

The tendencies sketched at the end of Chapter 1 were shaped by the protracted political struggle that went on within the regime from the day of Nikita Khrushchev's removal. They were influenced, above all, by the perceived personal political interests of the twenty-five or so individuals who at any given moment constituted the Politburo and Secretariat of the Central Committee. The composition of this group of key players altered spasmodically throughout the Brezhnev era, with intervals of quiescence. Before reviewing, in Chapter 3, the events within this group which conditioned Soviet behavior, we shall consider certain of the characteristics of the leadership environment which helped determine who rose and who fell.

First, the Soviet leaders existed in a highly private world. Their jostling, combining, recombining, as they inched their way up the Politburo hierarchy or were expelled, was of course continuously affected by what was simultaneously happening in the world below and the world outside—that is, by the constant struggle in secondary officialdom over Soviet internal policies and by the course of events abroad. But although the leaders all interacted in complex ways with the teeming life below them, one should not underestimate the degree to which they were also separated from it. The supreme party leadership in the Brezhnev era did not regard itself as part of a broad elite; it *was* the elite.[1] As Grey Hodnett has suggested, it was an oligarchy; and moreover, an oligarchy that was self-renewing, self-contained, and intensely conscious of the wall between itself and the rest of the Party.[2] Indeed, the leadership spent much of its energies in wall maintenance.

THE KREMLIN WALL

It is well known that the post-Khrushchev oligarchs placed a high premium on stability, order, routine, and predictability; perhaps less widely recognized was their peculiar sense of political decorum. Early on they apparently agreed to minimize the public airing of Politburo policy disputes, and indeed, in the Brezhnev era public polemics were on the whole greatly diminished from what had been seen under Khrushchev. One aim of the rule of self-restraint was certainly to minimize the disadvantages the regime had incurred in Khrushchev's time from the public display of the leadership's dirty linen. But perhaps more fundamentally, this understanding was intended to protect the exclusivity of Politburo and Secretariat decision-making prerogatives and to shield the oligarchs from pressures from below, and most particularly from the manipulation of such pressures by one of their number.

This rule applied in particular to the airing of Politburo disputes at plenary sessions of the Central Committee. Contrary to a myth that has become fairly widespread in the West, the Brezhnev leadership did not regard it as natural for Politburo disagreements over momentous policy or personnel issues to be transferred to the Central Committee for resolution. Indeed, the oligarchs saw the rare and unavoidable exceptions as pernicious anomalies.[3] What was normal, in their view, was to stage-manage Central Committee plenums by having the Secretariat select speakers to support the Politburo's consensus view as announced to the plenum in the report of the party leader.[4] When the Politburo could not come to agreement on an issue, normal and proper behavior was to defer the issue to another plenum, or, if necessary, to defer the plenum itself. Thus, on one notable occasion in July 1970 the members of the Central Committee, who had already assembled in Moscow, were left to cool their heels for two weeks while the Politburo wrangled over whether Premier Aleksey Kosygin would retire, and if so, who would replace him.[5] There could be no question of bringing the matter to the Central Committee's attention unresolved.

In the Brezhnev era, violations of the rules governing Politburo prerogatives were usually punished sooner or later in the political process. If a Politburo member chose to make explicit his solitary dissent from the Politburo consensus on the floor of a Central Committee plenum—as V. M. Molotov, for example, had done on a notable occasion in 1955[6]—his action would be considered, in the new, post-Khrushchev atmosphere, an extraordinary and shocking event. If a *non*-Politburo member attacked leadership conduct at a Central Committee plenum—and the only known occasion since the 1920s occurred when Nikolay Yegorychev, the Moscow city party first secretary, did so in June 1967—retribution, as we shall see, was drastic indeed. We shall also see that even Brezhnev sometimes found himself in political difficulties when he took actions that in the view of his colleagues went beyond the framework of Politburo consensus.

When Brezhnev's various leadership opponents took their quarrels with him outside the Politburo walls, they generally found that they had assumed a grave political liability, increasing their vulnerability to Brezhnev's machinations within the oligarchy. Werner Hahn has shown that RSFSR Premier Gennadiy Voronov, already in a weak position within the Politburo in 1970, probably sealed his political fate by continuing publicly to oppose large agricultural investments in the next five-year plan and to espouse controversial alternatives after the Politburo had decided to ratify such investments.[7] As we shall see, when Alexander Shelepin tried to bring pressure on the Politburo from below in order to unseat Brezhnev in 1965, he probably greatly assisted Brezhnev's ability to muster a Politburo coalition against him later in that same year. Similarly, there is reason to believe that Ukrainian Party First Secretary Petr Shelest's attempt to use strident public statements to pressure Brezhnev and the Politburo consensus to maintain an overtly pugnacious posture toward Western Europe in the late 1960s was ultimately disastrous for Shelest personally. That is, Shelest's behavior engendered very strong resentments that cumulatively increased his personal vulnerability to reprisal on other grounds once his colleagues changed their view of the optimal Soviet tactics toward the capitalist powers.*

In sum, in the Brezhnev era the oligarchs appear to have been highly jealous of their special decision-making status, and their conduct suggests great sensitivity to the importance of the barrier separating them from the cadres immediately below, who merely suggested, informed, and executed. They sought to ensure, insofar as circumstances permitted, that in practical terms admission to the Central Committee conferred a personal rank, but not membership in a functioning body with decision-making powers. At the same time the Brezhnev leadership thoroughly accepted the need for an expanded circle of expertise both within and alongside the central party apparatus in order to enrich Politburo decisions. But the record suggests that this same leadership was highly resistant to any suspected efforts from below to modify its prejudices, let alone to alter those policy postulates—in particular, the policy role given the military establishment—which were deeply intertwined with personal power relationships. And finally, as I have suggested, the leadership tended to be suspicious and resentful of attempts by any of its members to play upon public opinion in order to lever policy. It exacted revenge upon those who attempted this whenever the perpetrator was sufficiently isolated politically (as in the case of Voronov), represented a sufficiently broad threat to all (as in the case of Shelepin), or was, for special reasons, already vulnerable (as in the case of Shelest, who had long been viewed by his colleagues as tending to foster Ukrainian nationalism).[8]

LEADERSHIP GRADATIONS

The leadership of course imposed upon itself sharp gradations of status, and status was measured in different ways. Perhaps most

---

*I do not mean to deny the view of many scholars that Shelest fell over the issue of Ukrainian nationalism but merely to stake out a position I shall defend below: Ukrainian nationalism was the issue used to destroy Shelest as a leader, not the issue that estranged him from the consensus and provided the broadly shared animus necessary for his destruction.

obvious was the considerable distance between the junior members of the Secretariat, who did not have seats on the Politburo, and the senior members who did. The former—men such as I. V. Kapitonov, in charge of cadres, and M. V. Zimyanin, in charge of propaganda and ideology—served in positions of great functional responsibility, and their broad authority in these matters over party officials below the leadership group contrasted with their secondary status within the leadership. Even these, the weakest and most junior members of the oligarchy, were nevertheless oligarchs in the sense that they were authorized inhabitants of the special world that ruled the remainder of the party. At the same time, they were themselves broadly supervised by senior secretaries who were Politburo members; in the two areas cited, these were, through most of the Brezhnev era, Kirilenko and Mikhail Suslov respectively.

Within the Politburo itself "candidate" members nominally differed from full members in that they did not have a vote. But since, according to Brezhnev, the Politburo strove for consensus and avoided votes whenever possible, the distinction was mainly one of rank, with the "candidates" bearing a special sign of juniority.[9] Probably more important, as many observers have noted, was the distinction between those Politburo members who were Moscow-based and those who were not. The latter, including such full members as the Ukrainian, Leningrad, and Kazakhstan party bosses V. V. Shcherbitskiy, G. V. Romanov, and D. A. Kunayev, did not attend the weekly Politburo meetings and thus probably missed much important business—business to which even those candidate members stationed in Moscow, such as RSFSR Premier Mikhail Solomentsev, had access.* It is also somewhat unlikely that out-of-town Politburo members normally received the many routine decision memoranda that, according to one source, were

---

* When it was known in advance that particularly important decisions were to be made, however, it appears that out-of-town Politburo members would normally come to Moscow. It is also conceivable that such members were polled by telephone on occasions when momentous ad hoc decisions were being taken. Nevertheless, it is obvious that other things being equal, those stationed outside of Moscow were at a vast disadvantage.

circulated between Politburo meetings for leadership signature or comment.[10]

Most important of all, the Politburo was informally divided throughout the Brezhnev era between a changing group of four or five at the top and all the others, a distinction signaled by many of the symbols of special status so important in the Soviet Union. This top echelon always included the Premier (first Kosygin, then N. A. Tikhonov) and the president (N. V. Podgornyy until Brezhnev usurped his position in 1977). Throughout the Brezhnev period, the other three members of this top echelon were the leaders of the Secretariat: first, Brezhnev, Podgornyy, and Suslov; then, Brezhnev, Suslov, and Kirilenko; then Brezhnev, Suslov, and K. Yu. Chernenko; and at the end, Brezhnev, Chernenko, and Yu. V. Andropov.

SOURCES OF BREZHNEV'S AUTHORITY

The continuing presence in the top circle of the oligarchy of the Secretariat's leading figures was a natural consequence of that body's powerful multiple functions. Chaired by the general secretary—or, in his absence, by the next-ranking secretary on hand—the Secretariat served as managerial organ for the party machine, and thus, to a large extent, for Soviet society as a whole. It was the steering committee for the Politburo's weekly Thursday meetings.[11] It was also the appointing body[12] for all the senior positions in Soviet society subject to the leadership's personal approval, except those reserved for Politburo decision (those on the so-called Politburo *nomenklatura*).*

---

* At every level of the party hierarchy, the corresponding party committee decides who is to occupy key positions of the local party and administrative structure immediately below, subject to confirmation by the next highest party authority and, sometimes, to certain other constraints. At each level, the lists of posts to be filled and the pool of authorized names on which to draw are together known as the *nomenklatura*. At the top, the party leadership fills designated senior posts in all sectors of Soviet society, and the list of such posts and corresponding pool of names is the so-called Politburo *nomenklatura*. In practice, the Politburo itself apparently decides only the most senior of these appointments, and the Secretariat chooses the remainder. It is not entirely clear where this line is drawn.

The Secretariat was also the general secretary's major instrument for dealing with the ministerial apparatus of the government and for grappling with the Soviet economy. Throughout his tenure Brezhnev therefore relied upon the Secretariat, as Stalin had done initially and as Khrushchev did in his turn, to expand his hold on the regime and his leverage on his colleagues.

It is true that Brezhnev also had other means of exercising his authority, in particular through his chairmanship of the Defense Council, the joint organ of the Politburo and the defense establishment for defense policy, which is discussed in some detail below. The evidence suggests that through much of the Brezhnev era, senior Secretariat members other than Brezhnev were *not* admitted to the Defense Council. Thus, until Brezhnev approached the end and the situation changed, the two sources on which he drew for his authority were quite separate.

In this way, Brezhnev interacted from the beginning with the Ministry of Defense, an organization that was nominally subordinate to the government Council of Ministers but that in practice was responsible only to the party Politburo and its organ, the Defense Council. From the onset of the Brezhnev regime, much the same was true of the other two major foreign affairs bureaucracies, the KGB and the Foreign Ministry. Although both were represented on (or attached to) the Council of Ministers, they worked not for Premier Kosygin but for the Politburo and its chairman. From the start, therefore, and long before he emerged in a public foreign policy role in the early 1970s, Brezhnev could exercise personal policy supervision over both the state instruments of coercion (mainly the KGB and the Ministry of Defense) and the state foreign affairs apparatus (mainly the Foreign Ministry, the KGB, and the Ministry of Defense). This capability necessarily extended his authority well beyond what he achieved through the Secretariat.

It is also true that in the second half of his tenure, from 1973 on, Brezhnev relied increasingly for political support within the Politburo on personalities who had their organizational base outside the party Secretariat: in particular, the defense minister, the foreign minister, and (once Kosygin had finally been replaced), the premier.* Thus in his later years Brezhnev sought to broaden and diversify his political backing in the leadership.

Nevertheless, the Secretariat remained Brezhnev's primary base, and may well come to serve the same purpose for his successor, despite Andropov's initial weakness in this body. The Secretariat's rule as the key link to the party machine remains vital for the general secretary. It was here that Brezhnev placed the man on whom he relied most closely: Andrey Kirilenko for most of the Brezhnev era, and Konstantin Chernenko after the late 1970s. We shall see that when Brezhnev's grip on the leadership began to weaken in his final year of failing health, one of the decisive signs of the change was his inability to prevent an unwelcome force— Yuriy Andropov—from returning to the Secretariat.

THE CC DEPARTMENTS

As one consequence of the Secretariat's institutional role and political authority, the central apparatus supervised by the Secretariat—that is, the large departments of the Central Committee specializing in different aspects of Soviet economic and political life— as a rule occupied the political heights in dealing with the extra-party organizations they were designated to watch, guide, and harass. The degree of dominance apparently varied from arena to arena. The Department of Propaganda and Agitation, for example, has generally exercised godlike powers with respect to the work of most Soviet journalists,[13] but the Department of Science and Educational Institutions, under the reactionary leadership of S. P. Trapeznikov throughout the Brezhnev regime, sometimes encountered considerable resistance, in part because of the privileged status of the Academy of Sciences.[14] The various economic departments of the Central Committee apparatus were so much resented by the ad-

---

* Although KBG Chairman Andropov was elevated to full Politburo membership along with the defense minister and foreign minister in 1973, his attitude toward Brezhnev was from the start somewhat ambiguous, and it appears unlikely that Brezhnev relied upon him very long as a major source of political backing.

ministrators in the economic ministries of the Council of Ministers that early in the Brezhnev regime Premier Kosygin is credibly alleged to have made two unsuccessful—and rather quixotic—efforts to have this segment of the party apparatus abolished or curtailed.[15]

There were two departments of the Central Committee that had central substantive policy responsibilities with regard to the outside world and therefore interacted with the various Soviet institutions concerned with foreign policy.[16] One was the CC Department for Relations with Communist Parties of Socialist Countries. This was the regime's organ with central responsibility for supporting policy toward the Soviet-controlled Communist states and toward the Communist regimes that had either seceded from the Soviet bloc (Yugoslavia, Albania, China) or otherwise evolved outside of Soviet control (North Korea, Vietnam, Laos, and Cambodia). For the first three years of the Brezhnev regime, this department was headed by Yuriy Andropov.

The other was the International Department of the Central Committee, headed for many years by party Secretary Boris Ponomarev.

THE CENTRAL ROLE OF THE INTERNATIONAL DEPARTMENT

This department's orientation toward worldwide and eternal "struggle" with the United States was a natural consequence of its origin and its function, factors that were reinforced by the ideological proclivities of some of its leading personnel. As Leonard Schapiro has noted, the International Department inherited from the Comintern (dissolved in 1943) the responsibility for dealing with the Communist parties of the world and for ensuring that the various international mass organizations set up as auxiliaries—such as the World Peace Council—continued to serve the interests of the Soviet state.[17] Moreover, as the Western colonial empires dwindled after World War II and a "third world" of new states and nationalist movements arose, the International Department progressively expanded its functions. It became the regime's primary and authoritative organ for dealing with the so-called national-liberation movements. As such, the department was responsible for choosing, cajoling, funding, and helping to arm and train those factions in the Third

World deemed, for ideological or other reasons, most likely to serve Soviet interests. Unlike the many Soviet academic writers who advised them, the department's leading officials, such as Rostislav Ul'yanovskiy and Karen Brutents, were thus not only theoreticians but also practitioners. The new role in nurturing ersatz Marxist-Leninists where reliable Communist parties did not exist became an increasingly important supplement to the department's old role in attempting to guide and control an increasingly fragmented and heterogenous Communist movement in the capitalist world, a movement that was mostly remote from power and sometimes unresponsive to Soviet interests.

The department therefore naturally regarded itself as the point of the spear in the incremental, long-term Soviet effort to supplant Western, and particularly American, influence in the vast marginal ground between East and West. Although there were many disappointments along the way, it appears that when exceptional opportunities surfaced, as they did in Angola in 1975, the department's views and assumptions had a powerful influence on the Politburo's response.

Meanwhile, as the Soviet Union entered the period of detente with the West in the early 1970s, the scope of the department's work again visibly broadened to include dealings with Western political and economic leaders who hitherto had been the special province of the Foreign Ministry or the Politburo. Thereafter, throughout the decade, Secretary Ponomarev and department first deputy chief Vadim Zagladin paid multiple visits to the United States and Western Europe, conversing with senior government and business leaders, providing numerous interviews in the Western media, and polemicizing on behalf of Soviet trade goals or arms control positions. These activities went on separately from and in parallel to the department's accelerated efforts to promote the expulsion of Western influence from Third World areas that had once been totally oriented toward the Western powers.

In short, Schapiro is surely right when he suggests that the International Department during the Brezhnev regime became something "much more important" than an institution for relations with nonruling communist parties—although *inter alia,* it retained

that function. Its operations came to mirror the breadth and contradictory nature of Soviet policy toward the West much more than
the activities of the Foreign Ministry did. At the same time, like
other departments of the Central Committee, the International
Department retained important institutional advantages over the
government ministry whose work it paralleled. Despite the fact that
its leader Ponomarev was outranked by Gromyko after 1973, its
other functionaries continued to be given protocol precedence over
their opposite numbers in the Foreign Ministry. As a staff office
of the party Secretariat, the department was at the center of the
structure of power, whereas the ministry stood to one side. Consequently, even after Foreign Minister Gromyko's promotion to
the Politburo, the department in its everyday work probably enjoyed
a much more direct pipeline to the Brezhnev leadership than did
the ministry. Schapiro has, in fact, contended that the department
came to exercise *the* central role in "coordinating intelligence" and
informing the leadership. "It seems therefore beyond dispute," he
asserts, "that the International Department is the element in the
Soviet decision-making process which gathers information on foreign policy, briefs the Politburo, and thereby exercises, subject to
the Politburo, decisive influence on Soviet foreign policy." [18]

This judgment appears to be largely true, although it must be
qualified. On the one hand, it appears that the department does
have some responsibility for synthesizing information. Accounts
received in the West about the work on foreign policy subjects
which academic institutes of the Academy of Sciences perform on
commission from the International Department make clear that
the department uses the results of such work as background raw
material in its ongoing labors for the leadership.[19] It is reasonable
to suppose that the department, in view of its privileged position,
also uses inputs of information from other, more esoteric Soviet
organizations, as Schapiro suggests. Indeed, to the extent any element in the Soviet decision-making process does serve as a central
focal point to supply information and policy analysis, it seems
likely that element is the International Department.

On the other hand, it also is evident that the department did
not have a monopoly and that the Brezhnev Politburo obtained

some information and assessments through other channels. Although it appears safe to conclude that the Politburo was never even aware of the vast majority of the materials that the USA Institute and other academic institutions produced for the Central Committee apparatus, personal assessments requested from a very few senior experts, such as USA Institute director Yuriy Arbatov, may have reached the Politburo undigested by the International Department.[20] Moreover, it seems obvious that cables from at least some Soviet ambassadors must, at least on occasion, be read verbatim by senior Politburo members. This was evident, for example, during the 1968 Czechoslovak crisis, when Ambassador Stepan Chervonenko's reporting from Prague was widely alleged to have played a major role in alarming the Soviet leaders;[21] and again in the early 1970s, when Ambassador Anatoliy Dobrynin in Washington served as a key link in the "back-channel" SALT negotiations.[22] It is also conceivable that Gromyko, particularly since his entry into the Politburo in 1973, has found it possible to circulate occasional Foreign Ministry assessments directly to his peers, thereby somewhat diminishing the International Department's institutional advantage.

On the whole, however, it does appear that the department's role has been predominant. While the Brezhnev Politburo had some alternative sources of political information and analysis—some very important in a given context—none is likely to have approached the breadth and long-term continuity of influence on the leadership created by the daily, intimate work of Ponomarev's organization. Given the strong ideological bias of many of the department's personnel and the combative focus of its efforts, this influence is likely to have continuously reinforced the leadership's underlying assumptions.

The one important gap that appears to exist in the International Department's purview is military policy. As Edward Warner has observed, although the Central Committee apparatus includes several departments to deal with such important matters as military loyalty and security, military morale and ideological rectitude, and defense industry,* neither the International Department nor any other segment of the CC *apparat* seems to have been given broad, central support responsibility for defense policy making.[23] Since it is apparently considered unique, this realm is uniquely reserved to the joint administration of the Politburo and the military leadership.

BREZHNEV, THE LEADERSHIP, AND THE DEFENSE COUNCIL

One of the perquisites Brezhnev apparently inherited from Khrushchev, along with his title of first secretary, was chairmanship of a joint Politburo–military leadership committee to deal with defense matters, a committee that in Brezhnev's time came to be called the Defense Council. Leaving the details of this institution to one side for the time being, it should be noted that its *political* significance rested in a separation of authority: that is, in the Politburo's tacit consent to allow a few of its members to conduct regular business with the military, on behalf of the leadership as a whole, in order to reach decisions on defense and defense-related matters.

This arrangement had two major political advantages for Brezhnev. First, it segregated information within the Politburo, and thus, to some extent, power. The fact that the Politburo delegated to certain of its members responsibility for closely supervising the evolution of Soviet defense programs and for absorbing military secrets and expertise meant a real, if always unacknowledged, diminution of the oligarchy's collective authority over those members. This arrangement resembled, in some respects, Stalin's practice— bitterly complained about in Khrushchev's February 1956 secret

---

* These are the responsibility, respectively, of the Administrative Organs Department (assisted by the KGB); the Main Political Directorate of the Soviet Army and Navy (a Central Committee department permanently imbedded in the Ministry of Defense); and the Defense Industry Department (which works in close collaboration with the Military-Industrial Commission of the Council of Ministers—both broadly supervised, through most of the Brezhnev era, by party Secretary Dmitry Ustinov).

speech—of subdividing the Politburo into unofficial "quintets" or "sextets," each privy to information on a specific subject which was not shared with the others.[24] Brezhnev was well aware that this segregation of functions and information both reflected and fortified the primacy of the man who stood at the apex of the pyramid and acted in all spheres.*

The extent to which Defense Council decisions have been subject to Politburo ratification remains quite obscure. Under Brezhnev, it is easily conceivable that some decisions of an ostensibly technical nature but with important political consequences (on deployment, for example) may not have been presented to the Politburo at all. Many others surely were, particularly when they touched on broad questions of resource allocation or on foreign policy (as in the case of arms control negotiations). Even then, however, Politburo members who were not regularly briefed on the technical background were probably at a great disadvantage in dealing with colleagues who customarily monitored such matters with the experts. Moreover, as some observers have noted, the seniority of the Politburo representatives on the Defense Council would itself often tend to deter opposition to council decisions when they were presented for Politburo ratification.[25]

This institutional arrangement also benefited Brezhnev by spreading responsibility and thus providing some political insurance against recriminations from key actors. Since the Politburo members present on the Defense Council with Brezhnev broadly shared both credit and onus for its work with the party leader,[26] they could not easily

* A certain degree of specialization within the Politburo is almost inevitable for the expeditious handling of business, and the periodic creation of ad hoc "commissions" of the Politburo to deal with specific problem areas has been confirmed by the Soviets and discussed by several Western writers. T. H. Rigby has speculated that beyond this, there existed under Brezhnev permanent and formalized Politburo subgroups concentrating on such matters as foreign relations, agriculture, and cultural-ideological affairs (T. H. Rigby, "The Soviet Government since Khrushchev," (*Politics* 12 [May 1977], 15). It is probable, however, that if they have existed, none of these has had a subversive effect upon the collective authority of the Politburo comparable to that of the Defense Council. Because of the extraordinary innate sensitivity of its concerns, the council—far more than any other subdivision of the Brezhnev Politburo—is likely to have had political effects that approach those of the Stalinist groupings about which Khrushchev complained.

evade supporting him should any attack on his stewardship of defense questions be mounted in other leadership bodies. This was probably of considerable importance in June 1967, when, as we shall see, such an attack apparently occurred.

By the same token, the one political disadvantage of this arrangement for Brezhnev was that it increased the potential leverage that could be brought to bear on the party leader by those colleagues who did sit with him on the Defense Council. It probably became quite important for Brezhnev to reach an accommodation of views with these colleagues on matters raised by the defense minister before those matters were brought to the Politburo. This circumstance, in turn, may occasionally have assisted the defense minister in his dealings with Brezhnev.

From this perspective, the identity of the Politburo members selected for the Defense Council was necessarily of major political importance to Brezhnev. It is therefore significant that membership in the Defense Council clearly did not remain constant throughout the Brezhnev regime. Moreover, the nature of the changes to be made was probably a matter of some tension and negotiation within the leadership. There is evidence to suggest two sets of such changes, one early in the regime, the other much later.

THE BREZHNEV DEFENSE COUNCIL, MARK I

When the oligarchs overthrew Khrushchev, they inherited an ongoing leadership institution which, according to the testimony of Oleg Penkovskiy, had been called the Supreme Military Council. During the early 1960s, two or three years before Khrushchev's fall, this body was said to have contained Khrushchev, who was chairman, and the three other most senior members of the party leadership (Suslov, F. R. Kozlov, and A. I. Mikoyan), along with Defense Minister R. Ya. Malinovskiy. In addition, according to Marshal S. S. Varentsov, Penkovskiy's friend who as commander of Soviet rockets and artillery was a frequent participant in meetings of the Supreme Military Council and who supplied Penkovskiy's information, each of the service chiefs apparently attended only those sessions in which matters involving his services were to be discussed.[27]

Within the first few years of the Brezhnev regime, this inherited body was renamed the Defense Council and apparently reconstituted to reflect a somewhat modified assortment of political figures.[28] The most authoritative and credible descriptions of this body as it existed in the first half of the Brezhnev era agree that it was chaired by the party leader and now included, as *ex officio* members, the Soviet premier (initially, Kosygin), the Soviet president (between 1965 and 1977, Podgornyy), the defense minister (in this period, first Malinovskiy, then Grechko), and the Central Committee secretary in charge of defense production (between 1965 and 1976, Ustinov).[29] It has been suggested, and it is reasonable to assume, that in addition to these five men, the chief of the General Staff and the chairman of the Military-Industrial Commission were participants, in view of their central responsibilities for the matters likely to have been discussed.[30] And in view of the KGB chairman's military functions—particularly in operating the large corps of militarized border guards—it is also plausible that he was an occasional participant.[31] Finally, there is little reason to doubt that a variety of other officials, including service chiefs, participated on an ad hoc basis when their interests or responsibilities were involved.

Thus the Defense Council under this original Brezhnev-era dispensation appears to have reflected, to a greater degree than was the case under Khrushchev, a conscious and formalized effort to bring together the key institutional representatives in the overlapping realms of Soviet defense. This policy was consistent with the new regime's increased stress on order, organizational symmetry, "scientific" process, and formality.

What was even more striking, however, were the apparent initial Politburo omissions. There is reason to accept the suggestion of some Western writers that Brezhnev, Podgornyy, Kosygin, and defense industries tsar Ustinov were the only original Politburo representatives on the Brezhnev Defense Council, and thus the implication that Brezhnev's most senior colleagues on the party Secretariat—for most of the era, Suslov and Kirilenko—were originally excluded.[32] This was a significant change from the arrangement under Khrushchev, when the senior secretaries Kozlov and Suslov had participated.

These exclusions received tacit public confirmation on the first of the two occasions when the Brezhnev regime publicized a formal reception of the entire military leadership by what seems to have been the Defense Council. This reception occurred in early April 1967, during the brief interval between Defense Minister Malinovskiy's death and Marshal Grechko's appointment to replace him. The Soviet press reported that Brezhnev, Podgornyy, and Kosygin received a large group of the leading commanders, who heard Brezhnev talk "about certain questions of military development." No other Politburo members were reported present.[33]

THE BREZHNEV DEFENSE COUNCIL, MARK II

In sharp contrast was the situation on the second such occasion, fifteen years later. In October 1982, a month before his death, Brezhnev addressed a similar broad gathering of the military elite, this time accompanied by five Politburo members: Premier Tikhonov, Defense Minister Ustinov, Foreign Minister Gromyko, and the senior party secretaries Chernenko and Andropov.[34] It seems reasonable to conclude that these men were now the Politburo contingent on the Defense Council.

It is thus probable that during the intervening years—embracing the 1970s and the rise and fall of detente—a number of changes had occurred, both shifting and broadening Politburo representation on the Defense Council. Certain of these changes were subtractions, and seem clear enough. When Brezhnev in 1977 finally succeeded in easing President Podgornyy out of office in order to usurp his title, the chair in the Defense Council reserved for a separate president was perforce removed. When party Secretary for defense industry Ustinov became defense minister in 1976, his function in the Secretariat was apparently filled for a time by a new junior appointee named Yakov Ryabov, who may then have been temporarily admitted to the Defense Council.[35] But this appointment—for reasons we shall examine later—was evidently politically controversial; three years later, Ryabov was transferred out of the

Secretariat, and for the remainder of the Brezhnev era it was not apparent that any secretary performed Ustinov's old job of supervising the defense industry. If this function was for the time being removed from the Secretariat, the corresponding seat in the Defense Council was probably vacated as well.

The vanishing from the Defense Council of separate representatives of these two offices was evidently more than compensated for, as other senior Politburo members were added. On the one hand, there was a return to the Khrushchev-era pattern of Defense Council participation by the party leader's two most senior colleagues from the central party Secretariat. It is not clear whether this institutional change occurred just before it was made public, or whether the accession to the Defense Council of the second- and third-ranking secretaries of the Central Committee—by October 1982, Chernenko and Andropov—flowed naturally from a precedent established at some point in the second half of the 1970s by their respective predecessors, Suslov and Kirilenko.

More remarkable still was the admission to the Defense Council of Foreign Minister Gromyko. In view of the Defense Ministry's notorious reluctance to allow the Foreign Ministry access to its secrets, this was a radical change from the institutional pattern that had apparently been followed by the USSR through at least the early 1970s. This event surely was made possible by two changes in Gromyko's position in the 1970s: his admission to the Politburo in 1973, and his emergence in a more and more prominent role as SALT negotiator and spokesman while the negotiations leading toward the SALT II agreement went forward in the middle and late 1970s and while Brezhnev's health deteriorated. As his role grew, it was apparently no longer politically feasible for the military to exclude him from the Defense Council, where the Soviet defense interests that were defended in the SALT process were discussed and planned in detail. It is also possible that the Defense Ministry became more pliant in this regard when Marshal Grechko, a professional soldier, died in 1976 and was replaced as defense minister by Dmitry Ustinov, a professional party official.

In sum, during the Brezhnev era the Politburo's presence in the Defense Council apparently first contracted and then expanded.

From Brezhnev's perspective, the eventual effect of this expansion was to dilute the political advantage he had at first enjoyed over most of his colleagues because of their distance from this arena. As compensation, the political insurance Brezhnev derived from shared responsibility for Defense Council decisions was increased.

Over time, the Politburo was able to bring considerably greater political weight to bear in its Defense Council dealings with the marshals. In part, this change seems to have reflected the effect of the arms control negotiation experience of the 1970s, which politicized internal decisions that hitherto had been the sole responsibility of the military and increased pressure within the leadership for access to esoteric data. At the same time, however, the trend toward wider Politburo participation in the Defense Council appeared to be a function of the increasing political tension in the leadership as the succession to Brezhnev drew closer and as the economic costs of the growth of Soviet military spending mounted. We shall return to this matter below in another context.

In this chapter we have examined certain aspects of the decision-making machinery used by the leadership in the Brezhnev era. I have placed particular emphasis on the effects of these governing rules and mechanisms in setting a framework for the political struggle among the oligarchs and also for the foreign policy that evolved during that struggle. I draw four conclusions:

First, the jealously guarded centralization of decision-making powers by the two dozen leaders was associated with conventions of behavior intended to inhibit attempts to attack collectivity by manipulating pressures from below, and intended to punish such attempts when they were made.

Second, this armor around the leadership policy consensus also inhibited the diffusion into that consensus of notions that challenged either the political interests or the policy prejudices of the leadership's dominant forces.

Third, the traditional internal mechanisms used by the leadership in establishing and applying policy, particularly the prominent roles assigned to the Secretariat and the International Department, provided the Politburo with powerful filters that protected the orthodox foreign policy views of the leaders from contamination by a heretical perspective. In the Brezhnev era, these filters remained more important than the elements of pluralism created by the expanded use of foreign policy expertise from outside the party machine.

Finally, defense policy was the one important aspect of foreign affairs where the Politburo's decisions were not directly influenced by the work of the International Department. The special body created to deal with defense policy—the Defense Council—proved to be by far the most important offshoot of the Politburo, and the particular exclusivity of its work was long a major source of the party leader's political strength. Late in the Brezhnev era, Politburo membership on the Defense Council changed significantly, probably reflecting both changes in the balance of forces within the party leadership and the strains created by the military priority.

Against this background, we can now consider how, given this institutional framework, Brezhnev's policy choices were conditioned by his evolving political needs.

3 / The Politburo as Battleground

BREZHNEV'S PREDICAMENT AT THE OUTSET

It should not be forgotten that Brezhnev was severely hemmed in when he began his struggle to expand his authority after Khrushchev's fall. At the outset he was constrained by the makeup of the leadership inherited from Khrushchev, since in the party Presidium (after 1966, Politburo) that assembled after the coup he could count with certainty on only one close ally, Andrey Kirilenko. The remainder of his first set of colleagues was a heterogeneous group including independent senior figures such as Suslov and Kosygin; outright rivals for his own job such as Podgornyy; allies of those rivals such as Podgornyy's friend party Secretary Vitaliy Titov; vulnerable party elders such as N. M. Shvernik and Mikoyan; personal protégés of Khrushchev's who would soon be swept away such as Secretary V. I. Polyakov; and a variety of smaller fry who were mostly prepared to gravitate toward the man who proved to be strongest. It was by no means clear at once to the would-be opportunists that their best choice was to throw their support to the first secretary.

Brezhnev's position was rendered still worse by the inevitable distribution, in the immediate aftermath of the coup, of the political rewards that had evidently been promised to certain of the conspirators. Brezhnev himself, as the most senior *apparatchik,* received the first secretaryship, but Nikolay Podgornyy, his close rival on the Secretariat, benefited from the promotion to full Presidium membership of Podgornyy's associate Petr Shelest, the party boss of the Ukraine who was later to cause many difficulties for Brezhnev. More important, a month after Khrushchev's fall Aleksandr Shelepin, the man who through his friends in the KGB had provided the "muscle" for the palace revolt,* collected the debt owed to him and entered the party Presidium.

By mid-November 1964, then, Brezhnev was joined at meetings of the Secretariat by no less than three senior party princes who were full members of the Presidium and whose interests were not subordinated to the first secretary's. One was Mikhail Suslov the Kingmaker, supporter and dethroner of Khrushchev, the man who had delivered the key address to the 1957 Central Committee plenum that had defeated the first attempt to depose Khrushchev[1] and who had also read the long list of charges against Khrushchev at the 1964 plenum that deposed him.[2] Although Suslov did not himself aspire to be first secretary, his long tenure and great prestige throughout the Party—and his tacit role as principal Defender of the ideological Faith—gave him powerful leverage upon all the other major actors. He was also the most formidable defender of the rights of the oligarchy against its leader. In the years before Khrushchev's fall Suslov had fought tenaciously to slow Khrushchev's erosion of the powers of the collective leadership, and Brezhnev could only expect him to feel similarly about his own ambitions.

Next to Suslov sat Podgornyy, a senior *apparatchik* whose experience in party administration was second only to Brezhnev's. Like Brezhnev a product of the Ukrainian organization, Podgornyy was now feudal patron of a party faction in the Ukraine which was struggling for ascendancy over a rival faction aligned with Brezhnev.[3] Podgornyy had been brought into the central Secretariat together with Brezhnev in 1963 to bolster Khrushchev's position, but had then lost out to Brezhnev in the competition for seniority among Khrushchev's lieutenants. Now, with Khrushchev gone, he remained at Brezhnev's elbow, conspicuous to the Party as the

---

* That is, the KGB had evidently escorted and guarded Khrushchev and ensured that he could take no step to undo the leadership's decision to depose him.

conventional, logical alternative should Brezhnev falter. Because of Podgornyy's important party standing, Khrushchev's heirs initially treated him with some care. He, rather than Brezhnev, was allowed to deliver the Presidium's report to the Central Committee plenum of November 1964, a month after the coup, giving the assembled party barons the welcome news that Khrushchev's highly unpopular bifurcation of the regional party apparatus into agricultural and industrial organizations was being undone. The fact that he had been chosen to deliver this speech led some Western commentators to conclude that he had secured the very important Secretariat portfolio for supervision of cadre policy. At the outset he also received some concessions on patronage: his associate Shelest was promoted and Podgornyy was apparently allowed to nominate another old associate, the liberal *apparatchik* A. M. Rumyantsev, as the initial post-Khrushchev editor of *Pravda*.

It later became apparent, however, that some of his colleagues saw Podgornyy as lacking steel in his makeup, and even, perhaps, regarded him with a certain derision. He also had the liability, as shall be seen below, of espousing policies during the first year after Khrushchev's fall which Soviet ideologues and the Soviet military regarded as unacceptably "soft." Podgornyy therefore was not Brezhnev's most dangerous initial rival.

It was instead Shelepin, a considerably younger man, who constituted the main early threat to Brezhnev. Shelepin was in several respects in a unique position. He was the only post-Khrushchev Presidium member with a foothold in both the government Council of Ministers (as deputy premier) and the central party apparatus (as a member of the Secretariat). At the same time, Shelepin had emerged from the Khrushchev era as the Khrushchev lieutenant entrusted with the chairmanship of the Party-State Control Commission, which Khrushchev had set up as an intrusive instrument to use against his factional opponents throughout the party structure. Now this commission was Shelepin's instrument. One of his long-time personal associates (Sergey Pavlov) ran the Komsomol, the Communist youth organization; another (Vadim Tikonov) ran the uniformed police, or MOOP; and a third (Vladimir Semichastnyy) ran the secret police, or KGB. Shelepin had many other friends in the second level of officialdom, and apparently he did not hesitate to encourage them to spread the word that his rapid rise would soon reach its logical climax. This was a mistake.

In addition to being forced to deal with these three senior colleagues in the Secretariat, Brezhnev at the outset had very limited direct influence within the Council of Ministers. This government apparatus, headed by the austere technician Aleksey Kosygin, ran the Soviet economy under the indirect supervision of the party oligarchs, at one level, and of the economic departments of the Central Committee apparatus, at another. Brezhnev's weak hold on this body in 1965 contrasted sharply with the situation seventeen years later, when one aged Brezhnev crony, Nikolay Tikhonov, had taken Kosygin's place as premier, and another, Ivan Arkhipov, had become Tikhonov's first deputy.

Finally, at the beginning and for several years thereafter, Brezhnev's public role as foreign policy spokesman was seriously limited by the dictates of collectivity. Like Khrushchev in the first few years of his rule, Brezhnev was forced to share this function with the Soviet premier and the Soviet president. He was frequently obliged to yield the spotlight entirely to Kosygin (who arranged the Tashkent Agreement between Pakistan and India in 1965, went to Glassboro to meet President Johnson in 1967, and traveled to Beijing for key talks with the Chinese in 1965 and 1969). This allocation of external responsibilities changed radically in the next decade, when Brezhnev was increasingly able to arrogate such activities to himself.

Thus, in the fall of 1964 Brezhnev appeared to be constrained in many important ways, leading many Western observers to conclude that he was gray, colorless, weak. Like Khrushchev in 1953— or Stalin in 1920—he seemed less imposing than some of his colleagues. He was frequently appraised as a temporary, transitional figure.[4]

THE SEIZURE OF THE SECRETARIAT

During the first eighteen months of his regime, however, Brezhnev undertook a series of clearing operations that gave him working control of the Secretariat and major elements of the central party machine. A combination of factors enabled him to extend and consolidate his power base, among them the power of initiative inherent in the first secretary's office. Gradually, the man who chaired the Secretariat and Presidium meetings was able to take the lead, first in proposing and brokering personnel changes in the central party apparatus, and then, by degrees, in seizing control of the policy agenda.

At the outset, the Politburo consensus to vacate certain jobs held by people regarded as creatures of Khrushchev (the most extreme example being A. I. Adzhubey, editor of *Izvestiya*) gave Brezhnev the opportunity to insert cronies in key secondary posts in the center. In filling such vacancies, Brezhnev was of course forced to bargain, make deals, and accept trade-offs against the claims of his senior Presidium colleagues—a procedure that never ceased completely, even after Brezhnev had grown much stronger. In some cases agreement proved impossible, and important slots were left vacant for months or years.[5] But from the beginning, Brezhnev was able to ensure that the compromises and the central patronage concessions that were made did not damage his own interests critically. And as time went on, he managed to promote further turnover in the central apparatus and to secure an increasing advantage in the bargaining over replacements.

Moreover, in the first eighteen months of his regime Brezhnev was able in this bargaining to secure a number of "strategic heights" in the central party machinery for himself, two of which proved especially important in the further extension of his authority. He acquired the first of these strategic positions in July 1965, when his longtime personal associate Konstantin Chernenko was named to head the General Department of the Central Committee, the organization that, among other things, controlled the flow of Secretariat and Presidium documents, staffed the meetings of these bodies, and recorded the formal and informal votes.[6] The second was secured in April 1966, when the Presidium member Andrey Kirilenko, a more senior Brezhnev associate, was appointed to the central Secretariat. One of Kirilenko's responsibilities was to act as Brezhnev's watchdog in the Secretariat for personnel matters. He supervised the junior Secretary Ivan Kapitonov, the compromise figure chosen in 1965 to run the Organizational Party Work Department, home of the dossiers of the top few thousand Soviet functionaries.

Thanks to the latent powers of his office, then, Brezhnev in only eight months was able to get a grip on the mechanism of the Party's top two decision-making bodies; and after eighteen months, he had established an important although somewhat looser hold on the party's personnel office. At the same time, however, there were other, more fundamental factors that enabled Brezhnev to advance and, in particular, to neutralize his two major initial rivals on the Secretariat, Shelepin and Podgornyy. These factors involved both the personal fears and the policy prejudices of the Presidium majority.

THE SHRINKING OF SHELEPIN

So far as Shelepin was concerned, it is clear that the leadership's fears were uppermost. Shelepin had emerged from his betrayal of Khrushchev with a combination of functions and associations which obviously intimidated his colleagues, yet not so much so as to prevent them from forming a decisive coalition against him. The anti-Khrushchev conspirators were well aware that Shelepin's alliance with Semichastnyy's KGB had been vital to the execution of the anti-Khrushchev coup; and Shelepin's success in this effort, however gratifying, could also be regarded as ominous. Twice before in post-Stalin history—in the cases of Lavrenty Beria in 1953 and of Marshal Zhukov in 1957—the oligarchs had reacted quickly when one of their number seemed to threaten their safety because of his hold over the instruments of coercion.

In this atmosphere of fear and suspicion, Shelepin did not hesitate to advertise his ambitions to audiences outside the decision-making organs. In the spring and summer of 1965 both Western and unofficial Soviet sources reported persistent rumors in Moscow, almost certainly spread by Shelepin's lieutenants, to the effect that Brezhnev would soon be replaced "by a man with a little more dynamism and natural authority." [7] These contrived rumors bore a certain resemblance to the anti-Brezhnev rumors disseminated in Moscow seventeen years later by adherents of another aspirant to Brezhnev's position, Yuriy Andropov.[8] In 1965, the Presidium oligarchs undoubtedly interpreted this airing of Shelepin's ambition as an attempt to place pressure on them "from below"; that is, as a violation of their prerogatives and the rules of the game. In the Soviet Union, as in the United States, the use of the inspired leak for factional purposes represents a tacit appeal to the influence of pluralistic outside forces, and is bitterly resented by those in control of the citadel. As I have suggested earlier, one of the measures of the difference between the two societies is the fact that in Moscow, unlike Washington, such tactics are most often counterproductive.

Instead of catapulting Shelepin to power, this gambit therefore apparently increased his isolation within the Presidium, enabling Brezhnev to build a broad Presidium coalition in support of a piecemeal reduction of Shelepin's position. At the close of 1965, the leadership took decisive measures against him. His most important instrument was destroyed when the Party-State Control Commission was stripped of jurisdiction over the Party and assigned to someone else. Shelepin was also now deprived of his deputy premiership in order, as the announcement explained, to "concentrate" on his work in the party Secretariat.[9] This was an important accomplishment for Brezhnev. Such was the party leader's success in dividing his rivals that it seems likely that Podgornyy, whose position was simultaneously being undermined by Brezhnev, sided with the Presidium majority to act against Shelepin.

Although Shelepin's followers defiantly disseminated more leaks in the winter of 1965 to the effect that this change had really been a promotion,[10] his fortunes were now permanently on the decline. His remaining strength was gradually whittled away in subsequent years through a methodical series of steps familiar in Soviet politics. In September 1966, his associate Tikonov was eased out of his position as head of the uniformed police; in May 1967, the Soviet leadership took the major step of ousting Shelepin's friend Semichastnyy from the KGB;[11] and the next month, another important Shelepin supporter, Moscow city party first secretary Nikolay Yegorychev, was summarily fired in a dramatic encounter to be discussed below. Shortly thereafter, Shelepin himself was removed from the party Secretariat and placed at the head of the trade union organization, a significant demotion. In June 1968, it was the turn of his follower Sergey Pavlov, who was removed as head of the Komsomol; in April 1970, some of Shelepin's friends in the party administration of the media were removed; and in April 1975, Shelepin himself was at last dropped from the Politburo.

Shelepin did not accept the gradual erosion of his position without a fierce political resistance that contributed to several confrontations within the leadership: in June 1967, in early 1970, and possibly in December 1974. In each case, the leadership dispute that Shelepin helped to precipitate appears to have centered on a policy issue on which Brezhnev was momentarily vulnerable. Although these struggles did not rescue Shelepin's political fortunes, we shall see that they had an important effect on Brezhnev's relationship with his lieutenants and colleagues, as well as on the tone of the leadership's policies toward the Soviet military and toward the United States.

THE NEUTRALIZATION OF PODGORNYY

Whereas fear was the primary motive in the neutralization of Shelepin, policy alignments in the leadership were the decisive factor when Podgornyy was removed from the Secretariat and hence eliminated as a meaningful challenger to Brezhnev.

The neutralization of Podgornyy was accomplished in stages, in the same period that the decisive check was administered to Shelepin. In April 1965, Podgornyy suffered a serious blow when Brezhnev persuaded the leadership to exile Podgornyy's longtime associate Vitaliy Titov to a party job in Kazakhstan, thus making it impossible for Titov to continue serving as a CPSU Secretary and as head of the Central Committee commission for party-organizational questions. Podgornyy was thus deprived of a major source of leverage on personnel appointments. In December, Brezhnev secured Presidium approval of the forced retirement of Soviet President Anastas Mikoyan, along with the transfer of Podgornyy to that prestigious but politically secondary job.* Four months later, at the 23d Party Congress in April 1966, the cycle was completed as Podgornyy was duly dropped from the party Secretariat and replaced by Kirilenko, who assumed the senior portfolio for supervisor of cadres.

How did Brezhnev put together a coalition in the party Presidium which was strong enough to accomplish these feats? Whereas a number of factors were probably involved—including the opportunism of some waverers who gradually recognized Brezhnev's growing strength—it is likely that the dominant consideration was that Podgornyy in 1965 had acquired a personal image (*oblik,* in Soviet parlance) on such issues as resource allocation, the role of Soviet defense expenditures, and the overall Soviet posture toward the world, and that this personal posture had offended the majority of his colleagues. Brezhnev, on the other hand, had pleased them on these matters.

THE "ALL-SERVICE" APPROACH TO
MILITARY FUNDING

The struggle for power just outlined took place in a period of transition and significant change both in Soviet foreign policy and in the division of the Soviet resource pie. The policy decisions made in 1965, taken together with the personal contests described, set patterns that were followed for many years.

Nineteen sixty-five was the year in which the Soviet military establishment and the Soviet political leadership reached the momentous decision henceforth to pursue the growth of Soviet military power on a much broader base than Khrushchev had permitted.

This was not merely a question of missiles. Although the Soviets were now probably beginning to reach decisions about the deploy-

---

* Although the position of president (literally, chairman of the Presidium of the Supreme Soviet) was a political dead end for a party *apparatchik,* it had major compensations. The incumbent shared considerable responsibilities in foreign policy, particularly in dealing with foreign visitors. More important, the presidency carried with it an *ex officio* seat in the Brezhnev Defense Council. Thus, for the next eleven years, Podgornyy was by no means a cypher.

ment rates of their upcoming third generation of ICBMs—rates that would so alarm the United States within the next few years—the development of these weapons was not a new phenomenon but one that dated from well back in the Khrushchev era. What was different and striking about the decisions reached in 1965 was that, in addition to their commitment to the expansion of their strategic programs, the Soviets decided to begin a long-term expansion of other forces on a multi-service front.

Throughout his years in office, Khrushchev, while generally encouraging strategic missile programs, had consistently sought, albeit with mixed results, to restrict spending for most of the other services. It is only a modest exaggeration to say that he took a dim view of everything but missiles, air defenses and submarines. He denigrated the value of the manned bomber, sneered at what he said was the vulnerability of most surface ships, and drastically cut back the expensive program for building surface ships which he had inherited from Stalin.[12] Although he envied the United States for its aircraft carriers, he insisted that the Soviet Union could not afford them.[13] Most important, he fought—successfully through 1960, unsuccessfully thereafter—to force the military to accept large cuts in the Soviet ground forces.[14]

THE FOREIGN POLICY CONSEQUENCES

The rejection of this attitude—largesse for the strategic forces, cheeseparing for most of the others—was one of the most important consequences of Khrushchev's fall. Brezhnev struck the new keynote in a speech in July 1965, when he called for "long, intensive, tenacious and disciplined work on a mass scale" to broadly strengthen Soviet conventional as well as nuclear military capability.[15] This new leadership consensus was to have momentous consequences in later years. In the 1970s, it brought forth not only the Soviet strategic deployments that erased American superiority but also, among other things, a several hundred thousand–man increase in the Soviet ground forces,[16] the revival of a significant manned-bomber program, and the building of much larger naval surface ships.

In time these changes had a major impact on Soviet foreign policy. The large growth in the size and firepower of the Soviet ground forces added weight to the various Soviet efforts of the 1970s to exert pressure and register geopolitical gains in the West, in the East, and to the South. The Brezhnev regime oversaw the rapid growth of Soviet air and sea military transport capabilities, the radical improvement in both firepower and deliverability of airborne forces, and the construction and deployment of a distant-venture surface navy. All these developments helped to facilitate the Soviet effort to expand Soviet leverage and influence abroad at Western and American expense, and to do so in places increasingly distant from Soviet frontiers.

The decision to adopt this "all-service" strategy in military resource allocation was apparently taken only after considerable acrimonious debate, not only within the political leadership but also within the military establishment itself.[17] The sparring over what was evidently a long-term readjustment of the shares of the military pie within the Ministry of Defense apparently interacted with simultaneous sparring outside the ministry over both the share to be allocated to the military as a whole and the division of the nonmilitary residue.

It appears likely that the growth of American involvement in Vietnam influenced the course of this debate to some degree. Probably more important, however, was the decision taken, after the failure of talks with the Chinese in November 1964 and February 1965, to begin a large-scale, long-term military buildup in the Far East. This buildup—which continued throughout the Brezhnev regime—came to consume a considerable portion of the ground force increase after 1965, and between one-seventh and one-ninth of all Soviet military resources.[18] Once this decision to commence the Far East buildup had been made, the pressures to allow a broad, multi-service expansion of resources apparently became irresistible, with consequences that extended far beyond the forces actually allocated to the East.

At the point when these decisions were taken, during the watershed 1965 struggle over resource allocation, Nikolay Podgornyy appears to have taken a position that was damaging to his factional interests in his personal struggle with Brezhnev. Podgornyy, along with Premier Kosygin, argued that other interests long sacrosanct for the Soviet Union must now give way to the needs of the Soviet consumer. But whereas Kosygin appears to have retreated somewhat in pressing this position in the summer of 1965 when he was confronted with a hardening leadership consensus for increased military expenditures,[19] Podgornyy continued publicly to insist on his position in terms that were exceptionally offensive to that consensus. In May 1965, he asserted that there was no longer any reason for the Soviet people to "suffer . . . material restrictions" in order either to develop heavy industry or even—specifically— "to strengthen our defense ability." [20] It was most unusual for any Soviet leader to attack the military priority publicly in this fashion. Although the consensus was in fact willing to increase spending for the consumer, it was emphatically unwilling to do so at the expense of the new military programs.

It was of considerable political importance to Brezhnev that Suslov the Kingmaker was unsympathetic to Podgornyy's views, and remained so throughout the rest of his career. Two weeks after Podgornyy had challenged the leadership's right to require the population to continue "to suffer" for defense, Suslov asserted— in his first major public statement since Khrushchev fell—that Soviet defense "*requires* considerable material sacrifices by the Soviet people," and that both "objective reality" and the Soviet Union's alleged "international duty" demand that "a considerable part of the national income be spent on defense" (emphasis added).[21]

Of almost equal importance to Brezhnev was the fact that Shelepin, who made no secret of his personal ambitions, set himself up from the beginning of the post-Khrushchev era as a bidder for the allegiance of both the military and the broad party constituency of ideological conservatives he shared with Suslov and Brezhnev. In his public utterances Shelepin demanded vigilance, internal discipline, the pursuit of military strength, and a rather pugnacious posture in the worldwide competition with the United States. Two months after Khrushchev's fall he told a foreign audience that the Soviet Union was not afraid of war, and called for Sino-Soviet rapprochement on the basis of common firmness in resistance to "imperialism." [22] In a June 1965 Navy Day speech, he called for strengthening defense in the face of what he alleged was the "constantly threatening danger of being subjected to a new military attack from the imperialist beasts of prey." His symmetrical theme, aimed at an internal and an external audience, was the demand for "revolutionary enthusiasm" and tighter discipline at home and "revolutionary watchfulness" and vigilance abroad. [23]

In sum, since Brezhnev was confronted simultaneously with temptation (Podgornyy's voluntary assumption of a vulnerable political stance),* positive incentives (the political rewards waiting in the form of support from the military and Suslov), and competition (the extreme rhetoric Shelepin offered the military and the ideologues), his reaction was a foregone conclusion.

BREZHNEV'S ODYSSEY IN THE RESOURCE STRUGGLE

Nevertheless, Brezhnev's economic policy choices were of course not simple, since other needs competed with military spending for his support. Indeed, his political life as Soviet party leader was burdened from start to finish by his simultaneous espousal of *two* "first priorities": one for military expenditures, the other for agricultural investment.

From March 1965, when he staked out his claim for a permanently heightened investment share for agriculture, through May 1982, when he announced a long-term and enormously costly food program, Brezhnev remained committed to using increased financial outlays to combat the production disasters repeatedly occasioned by bad weather and the Soviet system of agricultural management. The returns from this policy of throwing money at the problem became less and less satisfactory throughout his tenure in office,

---

* In subsequent years, after his assumption of the presidency, Podgornyy was a member of the Defense Council, and gradually appears to have mended his fences with the Soviet military. He acquired a reputation, in the late 1960s and early 1970s, as a very strong advocate of Soviet military assistance and general activism in the Third World. One might conclude that he spent the remainder of his career overcompensating for the events of 1965.

and the outlays more and more difficult to find. Nevertheless, it became very difficult to disembark from this course because of the dangerous political implications of food shortfalls, which were to be dramatically impressed on the Soviet leadership by the Polish disturbances of December 1970. Elements within the regime put forward alternative proposals to spur food production by greatly relaxing controls over the production activities of groups within the kolkhozes, but until the closing years of the Brezhnev era Brezhnev and the Politburo majority generally resisted these proposals on ideological grounds.[24]

This double yoke of permanent priorities forced Brezhnev to fight the recurrent resource allocation battles within an increasingly narrow framework. In the early years of the regime, through the late 1960's, the resource constraints, although already engendering fierce political infighting, were not yet nearly as severe as they later became. In the Eighth Five-Year Plan (1966–1970) the leaders made an attempt—much like their new all-service program of military funding—to advance the economy as a whole along a wider front than before. In effect, they sought to provide some concessions to all claimants on resources. They hoped that even after the share allocated to the military had been subtracted, the economic pie would grow fast enough (1) to permit the funding of Brezhnev's new agricultural program, which would consume about a quarter of all investment; (2) to maintain the customary growth in the rate at which investment capital was infused into heavy industry, thus sustaining rapid expansion in the output of producer goods; and (3) to accelerate the much smaller flow of investment allocated to industries producing consumer goods.

Thus, despite the political penalty Podgornyy was made to pay for explicitly urging that investment in consumer welfare be expanded even at the expense of military programs, the leadership decided to strive to raise the standard of living without touching this sacred cow. This decision in part reflected the implications of Brezhnev's agricultural program, which required an accelerated expansion of the output of the food industry to cash in on the anticipated larger crops. In part, it reflected a leadership consensus that some improvement in consumer goods supply was necessary in order to bolster incentives and raise productivity in both agriculture and industry. And in part, it may also have reflected the political influence of the "New Class" in the subelite that surrounded the leadership, a sector of society that was clamoring for consumer durables. In fact, the rapid rise in the production of consumer durables was to last longer than the spurt in any other aspect of personal consumption.[25]

For a few years in the late 1960s, for the first and last time in Soviet history to date, the Brezhnev leadership was able to satisfy almost all these competing claims. The new, broad military program was launched and protected, and so, on the whole, was Brezhnev's large agricultural program. Fewer funds were made available for agricultural investment than Brezhnev had hoped,[26] but exceptionally good luck with the weather compensated for this shortfall. Investments in heavy industry initially grew at the customary fast rate, resulting, at least at first, in the customary large production increases. Meanwhile, investments in consumer goods industries, which were only about 15 percent as large, grew nearly twice as fast as outlays for heavy industry.[27] Personal per capita consumption of food, soft goods, consumer durables, personal services, and communal benefits rose at the average combined annual rate of 5 percent between 1966 and 1970.[28] The greater part of the post-Khrushchev improvement in Soviet living standards occurred in this period.

In retrospect, this was the period of the free lunch for the Brezhnev regime; never again was the leadership able to cope with all these economic desires and demands simultaneously. In the 1970s, during the rise and fall of detente, constraints began to multiply. The weather grew worse in the first five years of the new decade, and worse still thereafter. In these same years the burden placed on the budget by the political necessity of subsidizing consumer food prices began to grow rapidly.* The reduction in new additions to the labor

* This burden of subsidization emerged and grew when the Brezhnev regime began to raise incentives for agriculture by increasing state procurement prices paid to collective and state farms for their products, yet found itself unable to recoup these increased expenditures by raising consumer prices for bread or meat because it feared the political consequences. The increasing budget gap that resulted represented a tacit, involuntary, and ongoing transfer of resources from investment to consumption.

force as a consequence of adverse demographic trends began to have a more and more serious effect. As time went on, industrial raw materials grew more difficult and expensive to procure. In particular, the decline in the rate of growth of oil production became increasingly ominous, and presently the effort to combat this flattening of the curve began to pull resources from the rest of the economy. Over a gradually widening circle of products, from grain to machine tools, the return on investment continued to go down. Most parts of the economy, and the Gross National Product, grew more and more slowly.

All these factors combined to increase the effective burden of defense, stimulating new political recriminations even before the end of the 1960s.[29] But the established rate of growth of military spending (3 to 4 percent) for many years continued to be untouchable.

Increasingly, this situation forced painful choices on the Brezhnev Politburo. The first response, in the early 1970s, was to cut the growth of industrial investment slightly, to curtail investment for the consumer somewhat more, and to maintain and even to increase the share of inputs into the languishing agricultural sector. The improvement of Soviet living standards now slowed, despite expectations to the contrary held out at the 24th Party Congress in 1971.[30]

Thereafter, as the pressures described began to grow more severe in the mid-1970s, the leadership responded with the radical decision to preserve the investment shares previously allocated to defense and agriculture by sharply reducing investment in industry as a whole. In the remaining years of the Brezhnev regime, the rate of growth of most key branches of both heavy and light industry dropped steadily. The slowdown of the expansion of heavy industry—particularly in sectors such as machine tools—threatened to make it increasingly difficult in future years for the civilian economy to supply the industrial inputs required by military industry.[31] The Soviet military leadership has traditionally been quite sensitive to this link between the current growth of heavy industry and the future needs of military production, and is likely to have become unhappy at the investment trend. Finally, as we shall note

in Chapter 5, by the late 1970s even the hitherto politically sacrosanct rate of growth of military spending may have finally begun
to be adversely affected to some extent. Thus, by the end of the
Brezhnev regime, the economic framework of the political alliance
Brezhnev established with the military in 1965 had at last become
unstable.

THE IMPACT OF THE STALINIST IDEOLOGUES

Interacting with the long-term economic effects of the new course
in military spending adopted in 1965 was a second political trend
within the Soviet regime. The revised Politburo posture toward the
military harmonized with the world view of powerful conservative
forces in the Party, released and activated by Khrushchev's fall,
who wished, to one degree or another, to heighten ideological
discipline within the Soviet Union. Some of these forces, described
below, were in Brezhnev's own entourage; others appear to have
been loosely associated with either Suslov or Shelepin. Although
not unanimous on how far they wished to pursue such specific
issues as restoring Stalin's prestige, cracking down on literary dissent,
or suppressing economic unorthodoxy, these people—and their
Politburo patrons—agreed in their general opposition to what they
saw as an enervating Khrushchevite liberalism in both domestic
and foreign policy.

Although the ideologues by no means had their way on every
issue, they tended, over time, to advance. In September 1965, the
political striking force available to this viewpoint within the leadership was illuminated, as by a flash of lightning, when A. M.
Rumyantsev, the new editor of *Pravda,* was abruptly dismissed
immediately after he had published an editorial espousing a moderate and tolerant line toward Soviet writers.[32] Undoubtedly engineered for ideological reasons by a phalanx led by Suslov and
Shelepin, this dismissal was obviously supported by Brezhnev, not
only because he shared their viewpoint but also because this was
another factional victory for the first secretary over Podgornyy,
who had worked with Rumyantsev in the Kharkhov organization

fifteen years earlier. At the same time, the episode may have further intensified the doubts that key actors harbored about Podgornyy.

THE IDEOLOGUES AND FOREIGN POLICY

As the ideologues gained ground, their views increasingly colored the premises of Soviet foreign policy. These adherents of the Party's more ideologically oriented tendency were also the guardians of its Manichean credo that the world is divided into two irrevocably opposed camps,—the credo that is the ultimate justification for the CPSU's authority. The ideologues therefore struggled tirelessly against those who wished to blur the image of a world divided between socialist good and imperialist evil. Even before the beginning of the active American intervention in Vietnam, leaders such as Shelepin were assiduous in emphasizing the perfidious and aggressive nature of imperialism and in discovering examples in U.S. policy.[33]

It should be emphasized that the political momentum behind this viewpoint was not weakened by the subsequent decline in Shelepin's personal standing. Despite some initial—and apparently controversial—efforts by Kosygin to hold open the lines of communication to Washington,[34] the leadership consensus soon decided to reverse Khrushchev's priorities in dealing with the Communist parties and regimes whose interests were hostile to the United States. Whereas the Khrushchev regime in its final months had grown increasingly cold toward North Vietnam as Hanoi turned toward China—and had, in fact, explicitly and publicly criticized Hanoi only a month before Khrushchev's fall[35]—the Brezhnev regime had another view of its primary interests, and increasingly set out to compete with Beijing in the display of "revolutionary" and "internationalist" credentials.

There was nothing inevitable about this choice. On the one hand, this reversal of priorities represented the triumph of what might be termed the "ideologically oriented" interpretation of national interest over the more "secular" interpretation. At the same time, it also reflected an underlying conviction of the incompatibility of Soviet and American interests in the Third World, a conviction that was gradually becoming manifest. Finally, the change in priorities implied acceptance of a permanent external rationalization for the exaction of great sacrifices to build Soviet military power.

BREZHNEV, THE STALINISTS, AND THE FOREIGN POLICY EXPERTS

As he reacted to the conservative current among his colleagues, Brezhnev's own posture toward Stalin and the Stalinist ideologues was somewhat ambivalent and inconsistent, reflecting multiple considerations and a complex balance of personal interests. In general, however, he leaned to the orthodox side.

To begin with, Brezhnev of course agreed with the consensus of the anti-Khrushchev conspirators that there must be an end to Soviet discussion of Stalin's crimes and no repetition of what they saw as Khrushchev's demagogic use of this issue against his rivals, that is, his efforts to exploit against them their shared role in the grisly past. Most of Khrushchev's colleagues and successors viewed his periodic offensives against Stalin's memory not only as attempts to blackmail the first secretary's opponents and to increase his own power, but also as so many wanton attacks against the apostolic succession through which power had been passed down into their hands, attacks that inevitably raised unanswerable questions about the legitimacy of their rule. This is one of the reasons why in Khrushchev's time majority coalitions hostile to his attacks on Stalin had tended to form and reform in the party Presidium despite its changes of personnel. It also explains why Khrushchev was periodically forced to retreat on the matter of Stalin,* and why after Khrushchev's ouster a fairly strong consensus arose among his successors to reaffirm the righteousness of the Party's reign during the Stalin period and ban further discussion of the crimes. The decisive step in this regard was taken in early 1966, when an article in *Pravda* issued a strident warning against any further use of the Khrushchevite expression, "the period of the cult of the personality." [36] The oligarchs were thus unwilling to allow the continued denigration of this major part of Soviet history. Mean-

---

* For example, in 1957, in 1960, and in the spring of 1963.

while, they took parallel steps to reverse Khrushchev's encouragement of Aleksandr Solzhenitsyn and to put an end to the flow of reminiscences about Stalin's concentration camps which had been tolerated until October 1964.

Second, Brezhnev apparently sensed that the manipulation of Stalin-era symbols could be personally useful in his effort to improve his position in the leadership. At the 23d Party Congress in 1966, he engineered decisions to rename the Presidium as the Politburo and to retitle the first secretary as the general secretary. Although these changes could be justified to his colleagues as enhancing the dignity and authority of the Party as a whole by harking back to an earlier tradition, the association of these titles with the Stalin era and with Stalin's personal authority also served to enhance the aura of uniqueness and special authority attached to Brezhnev's position. Similarly, Brezhnev's first public reference to Stalin after Khrushchev's fall was to praise the dictator's contributions as head of the State Defense Committee during World War II, a citation that was evidently meant to have useful connotations for Brezhnev's own position as head of the Defense Council.[37]

At the same time, Brezhnev's instinctive preference for a centrist position in the constellation of leadership forces imposed a certain caution. In the first eighteen months of the new regime, a variety of officials made vigorous attempts to induce the leadership to make a formal and public reappraisal of the adverse verdict rendered on Stalin by Khrushchev's 20th and 22d Party Congresses, and to reintroduce Stalin's works into the teaching syllabus.[38] Warned of the likelihood of violent reactions from foreign Communists, the Brezhnev leadership eventually decided that these changes would be inexpedient and unnecessary. At the 23d Congress Nikolay Yegorychev, himself one of the neo-Stalinists, was required to offer the regime's disclaimer of any intention to resurrect Stalinist methods.[39] Over the long term, the Brezhnev oligarchy settled on adherence to the formulation the Party had published in June 1956, which held that Stalin's accomplishments were more important than his errors, but that he had made serious mistakes in his later years. The oligarchs have since followed a policy of avoiding trouble by discouraging discussion of Stalin generally, while pursuing a gradual, intermittent tightening of the ideological screws—a policy that is itself a reflection of their Stalinist heritage.

Finally, Brezhnev's ideological course over the years was influenced by the contradictory inclinations of his lieutenants working in different spheres of policy. In addition to responding to the evolving political situation in the leadership and to the changing external environment, he had to work with a heterogenous set of personal clients, protégés, and advisers.

Certain of the old associates whom he appointed and kept in key posts in the central apparatus were among the most reactionary of all officials in their influence on Soviet foreign and domestic policy. The most notorious of these was the aforementioned Sergey Trapeznikov, head of the Science and Educational Institutions Department of the Central Committee, who throughout the Brezhnev regime was the *bête noire* of most Soviet intellectuals.[40] Another was V. A. Golikov, the long-established adviser for agriculture on Brezhnev's personal staff, a pugnacious defender of the purity of Stalin's collectivization of agriculture and a vehement opponent of any reformist tinkering with this Stalinist heritage.[41] A third was Stepan Chervonenko, a former *apparatchik* from the Ukraine who, as ambassador to Prague in 1968, is said to have played a major role in frightening the Politburo with his inflammatory dispatches about the Dubček danger and thus, in precipitating the crushing of the Czech experiment.[42] A fourth was Brezhnev's World War II associate General Ivan Pavlovskiy, who in 1968 carried out the invasion of Czechoslovakia and in 1979 planned (and apparently recommended) the invasion of Afghanistan.[43]

Other, more recent personal adherents to Brezhnev's coterie included such men as the journalist Konstantin Zarodov, whose 1975 chastisement of Western Communist parties for insufficient revolutionary ardor was publicly endorsed in a special gesture by the general secretary;[44] and Alexandr Yepishev, head of the Main Political Administration of the armed forces, whose rigid ideological views have on occasion had serious effects on Soviet life beyond the military sphere.[45] All of these people shared what might be termed Brezhnev's predominant inclinations.

At the same time, however, the post-Khrushchev leadership's expanded quest for "scientific" expertise exposed Brezhnev to a few persons with a different perspective, including Yuriy Arbatov, director of the Institute for the Study of the United States and Canada, and the one-time Central Committee consultants and journalists Aleksandr Bovin and Fedor Burlatskiy. These men appear to have shared a generally reformist outlook, and differed from Brezhnev's more reactionary subordinates in other respects, as well. Unlike most of the latter, Brezhnev's reformist consultants and speechwriters were not old, trusted political henchmen of the general secretary, with ties going back to the Ukraine or Moldavia. Some of them had worked in the central *apparat* in Khrushchev's time, but during Brezhnev's period of control, they were not allowed to place their hands on party or government administrative levers. They now existed on the fringe of the power apparatus, not within it. Although they had strong views on domestic issues, their access to the general secretary was based primarily on their knowledge of foreign affairs, and particularly of major industrialized countries such as the United States and West Germany. This Politburo did not regard them as experts on the Third World and the "national liberation movement," let alone on appropriate Soviet behavior in the competition with the United States in the Third World. This policy sphere was, on the whole, the domain of their opponents, the ideologues and ideologue-consultants of the Central Committee apparatus,[46] and, when action was required, of the military. Finally, the attitude of the reformist experts toward the interests and claims of the Soviet military establishment was one of coolness and barely disguised hostility, and in this respect they were of no help to Brezhnev in view of his felt need to maintain military support. In sum, their influence on him could only be highly fragmentary and ephemeral.

MARSHAL BREZHNEV

From the moment Brezhnev succeeded Khrushchev, his behavior toward the Soviet military establishment had thus been conditioned by the complexities of the internal political struggle. The line he took in 1965 and the choices he made on issues affecting the military—and not only in resource allocation—flowed partly from previous inclination but more particularly from his sense of the dynamics of political advantage in his evolving battle to expand his personal power.

In subsequent years, these choices were of course further conditioned by the flow of external events, by the changing cast of characters surrounding him in the Soviet leadership, and by the evolving condition of the Soviet economy. On the whole, however, none of these factors appears materially to have altered his original judgment about the political line of least resistance. Neither in times of external crisis nor in times of professed detente did this political equation change drastically. Seeking constantly to maximize his authority within a framework of consensus, Brezhnev found the dominant assumptions about Soviet military power, its uses, and its requirements constantly renewed over the years by a floating Politburo majority that—on this issue—was only modestly affected by changes in personnel. Shelepin went, Shelest went, Grechko went; the struggle over resources grew more and more fierce; but the Politburo's consensus regarding the role of its military instrument changed very little. Like the chicken heart tissue that Alexis Carrel kept alive for decades, the dominant Politburo orthodoxy lived on magically in its successor cells.

Brezhnev possessed the political prerequisites to profit from the shift away from Khrushchev's priorities. Since the early years of his career he had been acquainted with a large circle of military leaders whom Khrushchev's policies had estranged, most notably Marshal Grechko and Admiral Sergey Gorshkov. In addition to his politically enriching contacts with such leaders during World War II, he had served as political superviser of the navy in one period after Stalin's death, and as party secretary for military industry in another period.[47]

In the years that followed his betrayal of Khrushchev, Brezhnev appears to have set out quite consciously to show a public demeanor toward the military establishment which would contrast vividly with that of his predecessor. While in power, Khrushchev had not hesitated to complain publicly and repeatedly about military demands, and after his retirement he characterized "the people who run the armed forces" as "greedy and self-seeking." [48] Brezhnev took care never to talk this way. At a Kremlin reception in the first weeks of the new regime, he advertised his inclinations by toasting the military and inviting Defense Minister Malinovskiy to join the circle of Presidium toasters, to Kosygin's obvious irritation.

This posture was elaborated over the next two decades, and was supplemented, from late 1966 on, by the practice of awarding himself military medals, awards, and other such symbols. Late 1966 also witnessed the first steps in the promotion of the mythology of Brezhnev's military experience, which eventually grew to dimensions that far outdistanced Khrushchev's military cult. [49] In the second half of the 1970s, Brezhnev sought to legitimize his pretensions to military stature by advancing himself first to the rank of army general and then to that of marshal of the Soviet Union. Finally, he was alluded to publicly—but only once—as supreme commander in chief; [50] this title's close association with Stalin's authority apparently rendered it politically sensitive within the leadership.

Standing at the top of the party machine and holding the chairmanship of the Defense Council, Brezhnev was able to throw his weight behind the resource requests of those key service officials who were personally close to him: for example, he was able to support Gorshkov's program to build larger naval surface ships, a program that culminated in the construction of true aircraft carriers. At the same time, he could now exert decisive influence over key military appointments, the most important such case being his insistence that Marshal Grechko be named minister of defense when Malinovsky died in 1967. In return, Brezhnev repeatedly relied upon Grechko to render him tacit political support in his dealings with the party oligarchy; that is, through his association with Brezhnev, Grechko was to imply a military testimonial to the correctness of the party leader's political conduct, choices, evasions, and compromises. This relationship was invoked long before the defense minister entered the Politburo in 1973, but became more important thereafter. As a corollary, Grechko's own policy prejudices, particularly after he was elevated to the political leadership, became an increasingly important factor in the balance of political forces to which Brezhnev responded.

Finally, Brezhnev was on reasonably good terms with the traditional managers of Soviet military industry, with whom he was familiar from his earlier work as a Central Committee secretary under Khrushchev in 1959–1960.[51] He quickly approved the new regime's prompt formal recentralization of the ministries involved in the production of military hardware.[52] It seems likely that not long thereafter he approved the unpublicized establishment of the Military-Industrial Commission, under Deputy Premier L. V. Smirnov, to supervise the work of these industries. At the same time, Brezhnev appears to have had, throughout his tenure as party leader, a good working relationship with Dmitry Ustinov, the man who had continuously exercised overall control of Soviet military industry since the World War II. Again, this relationship contrasted with the attitude shown by Khrushchev, who in one notable speech in 1963 had made clear his personal hostility to Ustinov and the allocation of Soviet resources he championed and symbolized.[53]

With Brezhnev's support, Ustinov was brought into the party Secretariat early in the Brezhnev regime to serve as the tsar for military-industrial work, a position that made him Smirnov's superior. Presumably, Ustinov also assumed a place on the newly refurbished Defense Council at this time.[54] When Defense Minister Malinovskiy died in 1967, Brezhnev appears to have disagreed with those of his colleagues who wished to appoint Ustinov to the vacant post, evidently preferring his old associate Marshal Grechko instead.[55] When Grechko died a decade later, however, Brezhnev appears willingly to have endorsed the consensus judgment to make the Ustinov transfer, and during the last five years of his life, the general secretary conspicuously sought and apparently relied upon the political support of the new defense minister, as he had previously relied upon the backing of Grechko.[56]

THE INTERNAL EFFECTS OF THE THREE CRISIS YEARS

Not long after the first version of Brezhnev's Defense Council was set up, three successive years of external and internal crises, in

1967, 1968, and 1969, strongly influenced the evolution of the political leadership's relationship with the military. Although each crisis was different from the others, each directly affected the role of the Soviet military establishment. Their cumulative effect strongly reinforced the alrady powerful internal political pressures to maintain both the broad "all-service" program of military expansion laid down in 1965, and the rate of growth in military spending associated with that program.

1967: THE LEGACY OF YEGORYCHEV

A brief political crisis erupted within the Soviet leadership in the aftermath of the international crisis that accompanied the Arab-Israeli Six-Day War. As will be discussed later, Soviet behavior in Syria played an important role in unleashing the chain of events that led to the war, and although the Soviet Union did not intervene in the fighting, it did make direct threats to Israel in the war's closing stages. The implementation of these threats would have risked escalation involving the United States.

Shortly after the war had ended, an untoward event occurred at the Central Committee plenum convened to provide the customary ritualistic endorsement of the way in which the Politburo had managed the crisis. During the plenum's discussion of Brezhnev's report, Nikolay Yegorychev, first secretary of the Moscow city party committee and a well-known advocate of greater ideological discipline who had long been considered an ally of Shelepin's,[57] delivered a speech that evoked a violent reaction. Brezhnev evidently responded in his concluding remarks to the plenum, and immediately thereafter Yegorychev was removed from his Moscow party post and sent off, his career at an end, to a series of insignificant positions.

Yegorychev's offending statements have never been published. Some Western commentators speculated that he had criticized the Soviet leadership's conduct during the war, arguing either that the USSR had not done enough to help the Arabs,[58] or, on the contrary, that the USSR had assumed excessive risks in threatening to take action.[59] Much more plausible, however, is a subsequent and apparently well-informed press report that gave a different assessment of Yegorychev's behavior at the plenum. According to this account, the Moscow party secretary had attacked Brezhnev's conduct of the war not directly but obliquely, by alleging that the state of Moscow's air defenses was unsatisfactory.[60] His remarks implied that the Brezhnev leadership, by neglecting Soviet defenses, had rendered the Soviet Union powerless to act decisively to assert its interests abroad in a time of crisis.

Brezhnev undoubtedly received strong support from the consensus in the Politburo and Secretariat to demonstrate the rigor of party discipline by taking immediate punitive action against Yegorychev, who had committed *lèse majesté* against the Politburo. Suslov, in particular, is likely to have endorsed vigorous action to enforce political decorum, that is, to make it clear to all the party barons that they could not with impunity criticize Politburo conduct— and particularly sensitive military policies—in a forum such as a Central Committee plenum. The majority of the oligarchs were determined to ensure that the plenum remained a transmission belt from above and did not become an actual participant in the decision-making process. Moreover, the majority obviously agreed with the widespread conjecture that Shelepin had been responsible for Yegorychev's temerity, and had thus "demagogically" mounted an attack on the Politburo majority from below. Brezhnev therefore received the leadership's backing for prompt reprisals against Shelepin himself. As already noted, Brezhnev was thus at last able to remove Shelepin from the Secretariat, securing Politburo approval to appoint him instead to the newly vacated chairmanship of the trade union organization. Suslov was present to oversee the ceremony at which Shelepin was installed in his new and less powerful position.[61]

The speed with which Brezhnev was able to dispose of Yegorychev and to downgrade his patron should not, however, be interpreted as evidence that the party leader was immune to the political effect of the charges made at the plenum. As in many other cases, the song was over but the melody lingered on. Under its new management the Moscow party committee convened a meeting that said it "well understood" the "complicated conditions of the continually changing circumstances" under which the Politburo had had to make its "very important decisions touching on the basic interests of our country and the fate of war and peace." [62] This highly defensive formula hinted at the leadership's sensitivity to the political effect of Yegorychev's insinuation that Brezhnev had done less than his duty to strengthen the country and to defend Soviet interests abroad. When the Ukrainian party organization discussed the June plenum, the last two speakers were V. G. Kulikov, the commander of the Kiev Military District (soon to be named chief of the General Staff) and the director of the Kiev Aviation Plant.[63] It may be conjectured that Kulikov offered testimony regarding the adequacy of Soviet military capabilities, and that the plant director made statements about the Ukraine's contribution to the improvement of Soviet air defense. Even in defeat, Yegorychev and Shelepin had shaped the framework of debate.

In subsequent years, each of the Politburo members who participated in Defense Council discussions probably recognized the need to maintain a posture and to compile a record that would protect him against such political attack.

1968: Overcoming Brezhnev's Prague Blunder

Hardly had Brezhnev emerged from this difficulty when a second crisis overtook him. In December 1967, six months after his encounter at the plenum with Yegorychev, Brezhnev traveled to Prague to deal with a restive Czechoslovak Central Committee that wished to depose its first secretary. His decision to wash his hands of the matter and to allow the Czechoslovaks to replace Antonin Novotný with the supposedly reliable Alexander Dubček began a chain of events that, over the next year, again made Brezhnev vulnerable in his relations with his colleagues.[64]

As the divided Soviet leaders watched events unfold in Prague in the spring and summer of 1968, there was an unspoken assumption that Brezhnev's mistake had endangered the Soviet patrimony. Ideologues could argue that he had opened the gates to Western pluralism, the dreaded infection that now threatened the remainder of Eastern Europe and even the Soviet Union itself.

Party bosses in the western borderlands of the Soviet Union—led by Shelest in the Ukraine—could contend that their provinces had been rendered particularly vulnerable to this disease. The KGB—and, indeed, the entire Politburo—had reason to be alarmed at threats to air allegations that Jan Masaryk had been murdered at Soviet behest, and at indications that other Stalinist crimes in Czechoslovakia would now be unearthed.

Potentially most troublesome for Brezhnev's dealings with the oligarchy was the disquiet that began to spread through sections of the Soviet military leadership over the possibility that a new fissure would gradually emerge in the Warsaw Pact, this time in the Northern Tier. This is the most important sector of the line of East European states that serves as both buffer against and potential launching platform toward the West.[65] This fear, partially irrational, was exacerbated by the critical comments about the Warsaw Pact made publicly by Czechoslovak General Vaclav Prchlik on July 15, and was not assuaged either by the dismissal of Prchlik or by Dubček's repeated protestations of loyalty to the Pact.* That these fears were neither wholly pretended nor wholly irrational was suggested by the fact that one state (Albania) lacking a Soviet military garrison had already formally left the Pact, while another (Romania) had long since ceased to be a reliable member.

Brezhnev's first reaction to this perceived personal vulnerability was characteristic: he strove to place himself at the center of a leadership consensus demanding greatly intensified ideological vigilance and domestic orthodoxy. In a ferocious speech to a Moscow city party conference on March 29, he announced a policy of tightening all the screws. In this all-azimuth attack, he simultaneously reaffirmed party supremacy in all respects, warned the Czechs and the Soviet intelligentsia to get into line, and proclaimed

---

* Jiri Valenta is undoubtedly correct in emphasizing that the Soviets used the question of Czechoslovak loyalty to the Pact in self-serving fashion, as an instrument of pressure on Dubček intended to emasculate Czech capabilities to resist (*Soviet Intervention in Czechoslovakia, 1968,* pp. 74–75). At the same time, there seems little reason to doubt that there were serious concerns in the Soviet Ministry of Defense that Czech loyalty could not be reliably and permanently guaranteed until a Soviet army of occupation was in place.

a message of demonstrative Soviet economic nationalism which rejected Kosygin's pleas for increased reliance on the West for advanced technology.[66] The resulting chill spread quickly through all sectors of Soviet life. Such pugnacious retreats to Stalinist ideological verities have been repeated in other periods of external stress.

This posture was, in effect, the protective political wall behind which Brezhnev maneuvered in the spring and summer as he and the leadership vacillated over the decision to invade Czechoslovakia. It appears that whereas Brezhnev was somewhat unenthusiastic about accepting the political costs of an invasion and was personally inclined to temporize and delay, he realized that it was critical for him was to be seen as the decisive leader of a Politburo consensus when it finally emerged from the fragmented Soviet leadership. This consensus was slow to form primarily because the most ideologically oriented segment of the Politburo was itself divided: Suslov apparently harbored serious reservations about the invasion while Shelest led the pack that was pressing for action. Superimposed on these substantive differences over policy was the fact that both Brezhnev and Suslov surely saw Shelest's outrageous personal conduct in pressing his views—particularly at the July joint conference of the Soviet and Czechoslovak Politburos at Cierna-nad-Tisou— as a political challenge and as unforgivable.[67]

The considerable disagreement among the oligarchs in 1968 should not obscure the measure of agreement that had existed in the Politburo from the beginning, however. Throughout the crisis there was a broad consensus on the need to put intense pressure on the Czechoslovaks, and Suslov (if not Kosygin) clearly agreed with both Brezhnev and Shelest that ideological discipline within the Soviet Union must be strengthened.*

---

* To repeat: the famous July 1968 expanded plenum of the Soviet Central Committee, held to dramatize to the Soviet Party the extent of the ideological danger from Prague, cannot have been organized by Shelest in Kiev, but only by the central party Secretariat in Moscow. The speakers allowed to address the plenum cannot have been chosen by Shelest, but only by the managers of the Secretariat: that is, by Brezhnev, Kirilenko, and Suslov. Although Suslov was apparently unwilling at this stage to commit himself to the invasion, and therefore abstained from speaking at the plenum, there is every reason to believe from his conduct before and after that he endorsed the concomitant effort to tighten discipline within the USSR.

In the end, the confluence of forces pressing for an invasion, assisted by Dubček's political ineptness, produced the required consensus for Brezhnev to lead. It should be noted that while Shelest's hectoring had made him the most visible figure in the coalition that produced this result, he did not profit in the long run. As already suggested, he undoubtedly stimulated animosity both among those Politburo members who had disagreed with him and among those, such as Brezhnev, who apparently acquiesced with some misgivings. A price was exacted for this behavior four years later, when a suitable pretext arose.

On balance, the Soviet military establishment was a long-term gainer from the crisis.* Whatever difficulties may have been involved behind the scenes, the military task seemed to proceed with efficiency and dispatch, in contrast to the political task. (The Soviet leaders, contrary to their expectations, were unable to evoke a Quisling majority in the Czechoslovak Politburo immediately after the invasion, and so were reluctantly forced to deal with the incarcerated Dubček again for the time being.) Another consequence of the invasion was the substantial and permanent reinforcement of the Soviet military presence in central Europe. Although this increment was initially drawn from Soviet reserves in European Russia, these reserves themselves were apparently replenished over the longer term.[68]

It thus seems likely that the Czechoslovak episode subsequently impressed members of the Defense Council as an additional argument for the continued expansion of the Soviet ground forces. As has frequently been the case with Soviet external behavior, an essentially defensive concern—the consolidation of the Soviet position in Czechoslovakia—in the end produced a forward deployment and a potential enhancement of Soviet offensive capabilities.

---

* There were, of course, also negative consequences from the Soviet military point of view. In addition to whatever morale problems the Soviet armed forces experienced during the invasion, the Ministry of Defense thereafter had to reckon with a demoralized Czechoslovak officer corps and the significantly diminished potential of the Czechoslovak armed forces as a Soviet military asset (Johnson, *East European Military Establishments*, pp. 134–136). These considerations were probably somewhat outweighed by the other factors cited.

A decade later, the Afghanistan episode had a somewhat analogous result.

Another effect was the emergence of the defense minister in a more overt role as external political agent and emissary of the Politburo. This heightened role was most clearly demonstrated in the April 1969 sequel to the invasion, when the Soviet leaders finally secured Dubček's removal and the reconstitution of the Czechoslovak leadership on terms satisfactory to them. They apparently decided that this could be accomplished promptly only if Marshal Grechko were empowered to carry their message to Prague and thus to give credibility to a drastic threat.[69] This calculation was, in their view, justified by the result.

1969: THE LEGACY OF THE CHINESE SCARE

The second crisis thus overlapped the third, for Grechko's April 1969 visit to Prague to threaten summary action against the Czech leaders occurred a month after the two initial firefights between Soviet and Chinese forces on Damanskiy Island (called Chenbao by the Chinese) in the Far East. This bloodshed, the result of a Chinese ambush of Soviet border guards and a larger Soviet counterambush, began a series of armed skirmishes that continued sporadically for six months, alternating between points in the eastern and western sectors of the Sino-Soviet frontier.

These violent clashes were the culmination of a long series of nonshooting encounters that had grown increasingly serious since 1967 (evolving from arguing to shoving to clubbing), as each side resorted to aggressive border patrolling to enforce its claim to disputed points. The escalation to shooting in March 1969 was probably influenced by Mao Zedong's determination to demonstrate that he was not intimidated by the implications of the Soviet invasion of Czechoslovakia seven months earlier, and that he was particularly ready to act to defend Chinese rights to Damanskiy/Chenbao, where the Chinese claim was particularly strong.[70]

The Soviet Politburo was preoccupied with this Chinese crisis throughout the spring and summer of 1969. For the Soviet leaders, the central concern was to find a way to intimidate the PRC into desisting from border patrols in areas claimed or held by the USSR. In the view of the Brezhnev leadership, Chinese behavior implied a Chinese conviction that the Soviets were unwilling to accept the consequences of a full-scale war with China, even though the Soviets had such a marked advantage in conventional and nuclear firepower.

This Chinese calculation had some merit, for the Brezhnev leadership was indeed reluctant to begin such a conflict. Throughout the crisis there was widespread talk in the West, much of it encouraged by the USSR, to the effect that the Soviets were contemplating a "surgical strike" against the PRC. But although this viewpoint may conceivably have had some adherents in the Ministry of Defense, it seems unlikely that it ever gained ascendancy in the ministry, let alone in the Defense Council or the Politburo, the bodies that had the decisive say.

Nevertheless, the Brezhnev leadership was increasingly concerned to convince Beijing that there was a real danger the USSR *would* attack if the PRC did not desist. In its long campaign to establish credibility for this threat of escalation, the Politburo relied heavily on thinly veiled public threats of conventional or nuclear attack— threats reinforced and given verisimilitude by suggestions to the same effect which were planted in the West. Soviet military leaders, particularly Colonel General V. F. Tolubko, the former deputy commander of the Rocket Troops, and Chief of the General Staff Marshal M. V. Zakharov, were given major roles in this campaign of intimidation. Thus, five months after Minister of Defense Grechko had delivered his ultimatum to the leaders of a small state on the Soviet west flank, his ranking deputy published a dire threat against the much larger neighbor to the east.

In the end, by the fall, the Chinese were in fact intimidated. They at last tacitly consented to desist from aggressive patrolling in Soviet-claimed areas and thereafter entered border negotiations with the USSR, which immediately became stalemated.[71]

In the aftermath, however, the crisis had several long-term effects in Moscow. In the General Staff, in the Defense Council, and in the Politburo these events reinforced the conviction that the Soviet Union must deploy an excess of force in the Far East for an indefinite period in order to overawe the Chinese. Moreover, the crisis had again underlined the policy benefits of assigning a demonstrative political role to military officers. Tolubko and Zakharov, like Grechko earlier, had helped supply credibility to Politburo threats, and the brandishing of their names had thus increased Soviet leverage. And for the third time in three years, the oligarchs had been reminded of the transcendent importance of the military priority in Soviet resource allocation. As the Brezhnev Politburo entered the new decade, the political force behind the broad program of military growth laid out in 1965 was stronger than ever, despite accumulating hints of the economic troubles that lay ahead.

4 / The Evolution of Soviet Behavior in the 1970s

When the notion of significantly expanding bilateral dealings with the United States emerged in the Brezhnev leadership early in the 1970s, it was thus superimposed on a number of political realities that were unlikely to change. First, Brezhnev had formed a political alliance with the Soviet military establishment and the overseers of military industry, and wanted his most important Politburo colleagues to perceive him as working to maintain that alliance. For the reasons recounted in Chapter 3, this posture had become even more important to Brezhnev as a result of events in the last three years of the 1960s. Second, the Soviet leadership was committed to the 1965 decision to carry out a long-term, all-service expansion of the Soviet armed forces, an expansion that was linked to a 3 to 4 percent annual increase in the Soviet military budget. Third, Brezhnev was dependent for information, advice, and policy support upon a varied group of political lieutenants, apparatus functionaries, and area experts, a few of whom held reformist views but most of whom were ideologically conservative if not reactionary. Finally, since 1965 it had been the policy of the Brezhnev regime vigorously to pursue activities in the Third World which were predicated on the assumption that Soviet and American interests were incompatible.

THE PRE-DETENTE MOMENTUM OF SOVIET POLICY

It would be an oversimplification to assume that the Brezhnev Politburo was ever oblivious to the impact its Third World policies might have upon its political relationship with the United States. On the contrary, concern about the consequences for the bilateral relationship—over and above the risk of military conflict with the United States—was often an important consideration as the Politburo weighed its choices in the Third World. At no stage, however, was that concern allowed to become the dominant consideration. Indeed, for a number of years before 1971, the Soviet stake in its bilateral relations with the United States remained a peripheral factor in the Brezhnev regime's evaluation of opportunities. As I have already suggested, throughout the latter half of the 1960s the Politburo's attitudes toward the United States were overwhelmingly conditioned by its sense that the negative worldwide reaction to the Vietnam War constituted a rich opportunity to promote the erosion of American influence with a multitude of audiences.

THE POSTURE TOWARD AMERICA

In view of the indignant Soviet reaction in 1980 when the United States curtailed bilateral dealings with Moscow in response to Soviet behavior, it is important to recall that during the Vietnam War the Soviet leaders evaded several overtures from the Johnson administration seeking to improve the atmosphere of bilateral relations. This Soviet stance was allegedly a consequence of Moscow's moral abhorrence of U.S. behavior—an abhorrence that mysteriously became less important when the balance of perceived profit and loss changed several years later. The leadership's behavior in the late 1960s suggested a belief that it would not be politically cost-effective to give even the appearance of welcoming a broad improvement in the bilateral relationship with Washington. Thus, Lyndon Johnson gives this account of the byplay that preceded his cold meeting with Kosygin at Glassboro in 1967:

> I invited Kosygin to the White House, which I felt was the courteous thing to do, though it might pose problems for him. In the charged atmosphere of mid-1967 we recognized that the Soviet leader might prefer not to be an official guest in the U.S. capital. The Arabs, the Chinese Communists, the North Vietnamese, and others might misinterpret it or misunderstand the circumstances. I therefore

suggested Camp David as an alternative. Kosygin replied that he did not wish to come to Washington or even the Washington area—what was wrong with meeting in New York? [1]

The Politburo's finely balanced calculus of Soviet interests did permit the Soviet premier to venture as far south toward detente as New Jersey, however. Thereupon, Johnson continues, "with the Middle East, Vietnam, and other problems in mind, I suggested . . . that we consider setting aside one week a year during which U.S. and Soviet leaders could meet and review all the major issues dividing us. Kosygin noted that we now had the 'hot line,' and could [instead] use that whenever necessary." [2]

The Soviets apparently at this point believed that to consent to such meetings would be to project an appearance of warmth which would jeopardize highly prized prospects for gain in various "problem areas" even as it exacerbated the danger of ideological contamination at home and in Eastern Europe. A year after Glassboro, in the midst of the Czechoslovak crisis, *Pravda* therefore responded to President Johnson's public appeals for broad Soviet–U.S. cooperation by saying that the USSR had no intention of developing such relations with the United States, which would be "to the detriment of the interests of socialism, the national liberation movement, and the security of the peoples." [3] The felt need to maintain this public posture was apparently reinforced rather than weakened by the simultaneous maturing of the Soviet decision that it was in the Soviet interest to enter strategic arms negotiations with the United States. Gromyko formally announced this decision to the Supreme Soviet only eight days after the *Pravda* editorial just cited.[4] Far from making arms negotiations the centerpiece of a broad detente with the United States, the Soviet Union as yet apparently desired to offset any impression that such negotiations implied a Soviet desire for detente.[5]

THE TWO PRIMARY CLIENTS

In the half-dozen years before the advent of detente, Soviet opportunities and endeavors overseas had focused Soviet attention on the support and cultivation of two sets of clients: the Vietnamese in their struggle against the United States, and the radical Arabs in their struggle against Israel. Concerned to implant and sustain a position of influence against the challenge of powerful local rivals (the PRC in Indochina, the United States in the Middle East), the Soviet Union mortgaged its freedom of maneuver in both arenas to a considerable degree. Although the Politburo indeed put forward its own preferences privately on many occasions, it was generally resigned to conform in the end to the intractable interests of its clients.

In neither of these arenas, either before or during the era of detente, was the Politburo ever willing to risk the political capital its military hardware deliveries and propaganda backing had bought by threatening to withdraw this support in order to compel a client to compromise with the United States or its clients.* From time to time, however, the Soviets were willing to put fairly crude pressure on certain of their Third World clients in order to serve their own broad competitive interests *against* those of the United States. For example, Moscow pressed the Iraqis to stop hanging local Communists, and it urged Sadat to cease dallying with the United States. Because even such pressures were often unsuccessful, the Soviet leadership was all the more reluctant to endanger its own interests with quixotic and probably futile efforts on behalf of the United States. Before the advent of detente, the Politburo saw no incentive at all to make such efforts, and during the period of detente, not nearly enough. In the zero-sum universe of the Soviet

---

* Former President Nixon asserts that at the Kissinger-Brezhnev meeting in Moscow in April 1972, Brezhnev initially responded to the U.S. demand for Soviet pressure on Hanoi by claiming that "the Soviets had refused to answer any new requests for military equipment from the North Vietnamese" (Richard Nixon, *The Memoirs of Richard Nixon* [New York: Grosset & Dunlap, 1978], p. 592). Kissinger, in the relevant passage in his memoirs (Henry Kissinger, *White House Years* [Boston: Little, Brown, 1979], pp. 1144–1148) does not speak to this point. This is the only known report of such an alleged Soviet response to U.S. complaints about Soviet arms shipments to a Soviet client. If Brezhnev did make such a claim, it almost certainly was untrue, in view of the unbroken stream of Soviet arms shipments from that moment to the climax in 1975. Moreover, Nixon reports that later in the same meeting "Brezhnev refused to promise to put any pressure on Hanoi to achieve either a deescalation or a final settlement" (Nixon, *Memoirs,* p. 592).

leadership, such favors to the United States were necessarily injurious to the Soviet Union.

Given these attitudes, Soviet leaders apparently felt that the frequent U.S. requests that the Soviet Union produce concessions from the Vietnamese, the Syrians, or the Eygptians were in fact naive demands for unilateral *Soviet* concessions to the United States. Before detente these requests were commonly met with disdain, and with ritualized reciprocal demands for major unilateral concessions from the United States and its clients. Thereafter, the Soviet Union supplied the United States with pacifiers in the form of vague and generally unfulfilled promises.

In particular, the Soviet leaders appear to have believed that the United States deliberately exaggerated Soviet leverage with the Vietnamese because it wanted to belittle the political price the USSR was being asked to pay and therefore, in effect, to minimize the magnitude of the U.S. bilateral concessions that the Politburo could demand in return. In the meantime, the Soviet leadership remained extremely defensive about any suggestion that it might sacrifice its clients' interests to those of a Soviet-U.S. relationship.*

LANDMARKS IN THE INITIAL
COMPETITIVE BREAKOUT

Initially, however, the Soviet leadership generally was able to accommodate the interests of its clients without much difficulty. In particular, throughout the last five years of Nasser's life (roughly the first five years of Brezhnev's regime), Soviet behavior suggested a firm, indeed growing conviction that Soviet interests—including the interest in reducing American influence in the Middle East—were being richly served by encouraging and flattering Nasser's

---

*The Soviets had reason for such concern. Despite their consistent refusal to pressure their clients on behalf of the United States, the mere fact of their own negotiations with the United States at the peak of detente in two instances embarrassed the Soviets in dealings with those clients. One occasion was when the Soviets allowed the May 1972 summit to proceed despite the mining of Haiphong, and the other was when Sadat became suspicious about Soviet-U.S. talks in 1972 and 1973.

enthusiams and ambitions and by attuning Soviet policy to the tortuous evolution of his perception of his political and security needs. Wladyslaw Gomulka's former interpreter has asserted, for example, that during an April 1967 meeting with Walter Ulbricht and Gomulka, Brezhnev expressed gratification that the USSR had succeeded in "partly pushing the Americans out of the Near East," largely as a result of the "consistent application of the Leninist principle of seeking temporary allies." Nasser, Brezhnev continued, "is highly confused on ideological questions but he has proved that one can rely on him. If we . . . want to achieve progress, then we must also accept sacrifices. One sacrifice we bear is the persecution of Egyptian Communists by Nasser. But, during this phase, Nasser is of inestimable value to us." [6]

This compliant Soviet attitude was variously reflected at different stages: in the belated and obviously reluctant Soviet endorsement of Nasser's closure of the Strait of Tiran before the June 1967 war;[7] in the rapid Soviet jettisoning, in 1969, of its initial indications of interest in the Rogers Plan once Nasser decided to reject it; in the unprecedentedly large-scale dispatch of air defense personnel to Egypt in the spring of 1970 in response to Nasser's urgent demand; and in the Soviet cooperation, later that year, in surreptitiously moving surface-to-air missile sites to the Suez Canal area, in violation of the Israeli-Egyptian cease-fire agreement, and again in response to Nasser's felt needs.[8]

All of these actions involved some modification of the Brezhnev regime's evaluation of the level of risk latent in certain kinds of behavior, particularly when the region involved was relatively close to the USSR. In Southeast Asia—beyond the range at which the Soviet Union could project its armed capability with ease—the Politburo showed great caution throughout the Vietnam War in the face of the local concentration of American military power, particularly during the periods of U.S. bombing. Such caution involved the regime in protracted private and public polemics with the Chinese, in which Beijing charged the Soviets with, among other things, a cowardly preference for shipping sensitive military hardware overland through China rather than by sea.[9]

In the Middle East, by contrast, although Brezhnev's Politburo continued to pull back when confronted with an immediate possibility of escalation involving the United States, it showed a heightened readiness to take both political and military initiatives in pursuit of potential advantage without regard for open-ended consequences. Thus the regime increasingly incorporated into its behavior elements of a style it had condemned in Khrushchev as adventuristic and harebrained.*

For example, the false allegations of an impending Israeli attack on Syria, initially disseminated by Soviet representatives in Damascus, set in motion the chain of events that produced the Six-Day War. President Podgornyy repeated these allegations to the Egyptian government in Moscow on May 11, 1967, and Nasser regarded these statements as confirmation of claims to the same effect already being received from Syria. It was on the basis of this information that Nasser dispatched his troops into the Sinai a week later and requested the withdrawal of UNEF forces.[10]

This Soviet conduct was supplemented by an ingratiating and calculated ambiguity in dealing with the Arabs before the outbreak of hostilities, behavior that may have led certain Arabs to expect that the Soviet Union would play an active combat role. Nasser's confidant Mohamed Heikal alleges that Marshal Grechko made encouraging statements of this kind to Egyptian Defense Minister Shamseddia Badran at the close of the latter's visit to Moscow in late May 1967.† He also credibly implies that Syrian Prime Minister Nureddia Atassi received similar encouragement from Soviet sources during a visit immediately thereafter.[11]

Given the presence in the eastern Mediterranean of the U.S. Sixth Fleet, however, the Soviet leadership had no intention of allowing itself to become involved in hostilities. Yet the ensuing disaster to the Arab armies was sufficiently threatening to Soviet interests that the Politburo in the end felt obliged to threaten intervention if Israel did not halt its advance on Damascus.[12] The

* Less than three years before the Soviet threat to intervene in the 1967 war, at the Central Committee plenum that followed Khrushchev's ouster, Suslov had condemned Khrushchev's threat to intervene in Suez in 1956 as dangerous and adventuristic (*New York Times,* October 30, 1964).

† Grechko at the time, it should be remembered, had just assumed office as minister of defense.

Brezhnev leadership was surely relieved that it did not have to attempt to make good on this threat.

As noted earlier, the leadership's conduct of events during this crisis evoked controversy within the oligarchy. The sharp conflict that ensued at the next Central Committee plenum, almost certainly over the state of Soviet military readiness to support such risk taking, may be regarded as a watershed, for its ultimate effect was not to inhibit the trend toward such political and military assertiveness but rather to give it impetus. For Brezhnev and his colleagues, the Yegorychev episode provided fresh justification for the Soviet strategic buildup, which was a conclusive answer to complaints that the USSR was not strong enough to pursue a desirable forward line with appropriate vigor and safety.

A few months after the Six-Day War, Soviet combat pilots and military advisers briefly became active in a Yemeni civil war.[13] This was the first such direct combat involvement outside the Soviet bloc since the use of Soviet pilots in the Korean War.*

Two and a half years later, thousands of Soviet air defense troops arrived in Egypt to defend Nasser against the consequences of his war of attrition. Before the conclusion of a new Egyptian-Israeli cease-fire in the early summer of 1970, Soviet fighter pilots flew patrols ever closer to the Suez Canal; in one well-known incident, the Israelis shot down five.[14] Finally alarmed at the escalatory possibilities, and aware that more and more Soviet combat inputs might be required to deal adequately with Israel, thereby increasing the chance of a compensatory U.S. reaction, the Soviets ceased such patrols and showed heightened interest in an early cease-fire.

Always in the background, alongside the positive inducements to such risk taking, was a fear of the consequences should the USSR waver. Nasser took care to reinforce this fear by periodically making gestures toward the United States. The Politburo's natural disinclination to allow itself to be manipulated was outweighed by the assumption that it was creating an Egyptian dependence on the

---

* Unless one counts the Soviet SAM crews that brought down an American U-2 in Cuba in October 1962, or the very brief Soviet SAM combat involvement in Vietnam in 1965. The Yemeni episode was in any case the first use of Soviet pilots in combat outside the bloc since the death of Stalin.

Soviet Union that might in the end give it decisive and lasting leverage on Egyptian policy. More important, the Politburo was convinced that it was in any case acquiring inestimable advantages in the competition with the United States.

THE CONDITIONING EFFECT OF EMERGING MILITARY BENEFITS

It was of great importance for the subsequent evolution of Soviet policy that these advantages were, above all, military. Over the next few years, the Politburo members appear to have shared an impression that the aftermath of the 1967 war, by providing the political pretext for a major expansion of the Soviet military presence in the Middle East, had opened new vistas for further such advances. In retrospect, the leadership is likely to have believed that the Soviet Union had been the greatest gainer from the Six-Day War, particularly because the war had facilitated the USSR's emergence as a naval power in the Mediterranean and done so in circumstances such that no Arab leader could object.

Although this enlarged Soviet naval presence could be profitably portrayed to the Arabs as the essential offset to the threat that the Sixth Fleet allegedly posed to Arab interests, its primary operational significance for Moscow lay in its potential for countering the American strategic threat to the Soviet Union from the Mediterranean. This new military advantage, in turn, whetted appetites for basing rights to support the emerging naval presence. After the 1967 war, the Soviets undertook a massive effort to resupply the combatant Arab states and dispatched thousands of Soviet combat and military advisory personnel to Syria and Egypt. On the basis of this effort the Soviets also acquired naval rights in Arab ports and bases for naval air reconnaissance and other functions—all of which served primarily Soviet, not Arab, purposes. The Soviets have never ceased the search for more military benefits of this kind.

Although part of this suddenly swollen Soviet presence in the Middle East eventually evaporated, the tendencies in Soviet thinking that had produced it became increasingly dominant. As already suggested, the perception that more venturesome behavior at greater distances was producing higher payoffs made Politburo members more reluctant to give their colleagues or the supporting institutions reason to conclude that they lacked resolution in the drive to maximize gains. Whenever the Politburo showed an inclination toward action, Brezhnev, like his colleagues, was probably concerned that the others not believe, in the words of the common Soviet locution, that his "hand was trembling." In such a Politburo atmosphere, any behavior by a member of the oligarchy that can be interpreted as excessive caution must be offset with a display of zeal.

Such defensiveness about being thought less assertive in advancing Soviet interests than the risk/benefit ratio justified clearly afffected the Politburo's continuing evaluation of emerging opportunities and needs. Within two or three months after the one-sided 1970 encounter with Israeli aircraft had brought an alarmed Marshal P. S. Kutakhov to Cairo to investigate*—and a withdrawal of the Soviet-manned fighter patrols—the Soviet Union began a new venture in another arena. In the fall of 1970, the USSR commenced work at the port of Cienfuegos in Cuba on facilities intended to support the operations of Soviet nuclear-powered submarines in the vicinity of the United States.[15] Although this effort to exploit one of the many ambiguities of the 1962 Soviet-U.S. understanding over Cuba had almost certainly been under preparation for some time,† it was significant that it was evidently unaffected by unpleasant surprises encountered in the Middle East. The broad momentum of Soviet policy and the compartmentalization of its executing agencies

---

* Although Kutakhov, commander in chief of Soviet Air Forces, probably came to Cairo to investigate the mechanics of this tactical disaster, a more important issue for the Soviets was their initial misreading of the dangerous consequences that might follow from permitting the Soviet overflights of the Suez Canal. By placing units of the Soviet armed forces in a position where combat with Israel was at least much more possible than previously, the Politburo had led the USSR to a choice between accepting tactical defeat at Israeli hands, should it materialize, or escalating against Israel, thereby increasing the chances of a clash with the United States.

† Probably since a visit to Cuba by Marshal Grechko in November 1969.

was such that the difficulties encountered as a result of the aggressive courting of advantage on one side of the world could not halt an enterprise of at least equal risk already in train on the other side.

Similarly, the eventual Soviet retreat over Cienfuegos, in response to sharp private warnings from the United States, was followed the next year by the signing of a treaty with India that paved the way for the Indian attack on East Pakistan which created Bangladesh, and that for a time seemed to tempt India to contemplate the dismemberment of West Pakistan as well. The Politburo intended this treaty to be seen as a powerful instrument of deterrence against both China and the United States, and sought to bolster this impression through ostentatious naval movements to shadow American deployments in the Indian Ocean.[16]

This line of Soviet conduct in 1971, so different from the role of neutral peacemaker assumed during the Indian-Pakistan hostilities of 1965, was to set the pattern for Soviet behavior in 1978, when the conclusion of another Soviet treaty provided the prerequisite for the Vietnamese blitzkrieg into Cambodia. In addition to the broad geopolitical benefits vis-à-vis the United States and China which the Politburo sought by underwriting of Indian behavior in 1971, it may have hoped for concrete military benefits that were not forthcoming. A similar mixture of motives informed Soviet policy toward Vietnam at the end of the decade, but this time some military benefits did materialize, at Cam Ranh Bay.

THE DOMINANT CURRENT OF BEHAVIOR

In sum, a common thread ran through the increasingly assertive conduct the Brezhnev Politburo displayed in more and more distant places from the late 1960s on. The leadership's competitive instincts, the so-called attacking compulsion discussed in Chapter 1, were fueled by the internal considerations discussed in Chapters 2 and 3 to form a dominant trend that gathered impetus in the 1970s.

As we have just seen, this central trend in Soviet behavior was reflected, at the turn of the new decade, in the Soviet effort to make use of the needs of the Soviet Union's Arab clients to promote the expansion of the Soviet military and naval presence in the

Middle East. The same dominant tendency then produced the flood of Soviet weapons supplied to North Vietnam during the early and mid-1970s, overlapping the period of U.S.-Soviet detente. These arms deliveries, to Soviet gratification, played a decisive role in precipitating the eventual American humiliation in Vietnam in 1975, at the close of the period of detente. That central tendency next emerged in the Soviet exploitation of the new opportunities and techniques—such as the large-scale use of Cuban proxy forces—that the Soviet Union discovered in Africa after 1975. And finally, the same pattern of behavior produced the Soviet adventures in Indochina and Afghanistan at the close of the decade.

This continuous current of behavior was driven on by the Politburo's incremental discovery of the growing capability of Soviet military power to enhance the Soviet geopolitical position relative to that of the United States. In using their power, the Soviet leaders reacted throughout the decade to the emergence of successive avenues of opportunity. Some of these Soviet windfalls resulted from autonomous local processes, such as the breakup of the Portuguese empire in Africa by 1975 and the Cambodian provocation of the Vietnamese before 1978. But all opportunities were enhanced by the widespread impression, after the American debacle in Vietnam in 1975, that the American role and capability as a global actor were diminishing.

Detente with the United States from 1971 through 1974 can thus be visualized as an island in this stream of continuous Soviet efforts from the 1960s to the 1980s to displace the United States in the world. Like an island, detente neither halted nor changed the surrounding process.

THE RISE AND FALL OF DETENTE

Ironically, in the same years that the Politburo discovered that it could obtain geopolitical benefits at U.S. expense by adopting a more venturesome military posture abroad, it gradually came to acknowledge that the USSR had an interest in expanding its bilateral dealings with the United States. The leadership's painful movement toward a consensus on the urgent need for wide-ranging U.S. bilaterals was influenced by a mixture of well-known factors, four of which were probably dominant. Although each of these factors retains a certain importance in Politburo deliberations to this day, each for its own reason has been less and less able to induce restraint in Politburo policies affecting American interests.

THE CHINESE IMPERATIVE

To begin with, the Politburo found reason to establish a calmer relationship with the West—eventually including the United States—because of its extraordinary anxiety about China at the start of the decade.

The United States was from the start very much on the minds of the Soviet leaders as they reacted to the firefights on the Chinese border in 1969. Alarmed at what they considered the irrationality and unpredictability of Chinese behavior, and concerned that they might have to make good on their threat of drastic action, they initiated contacts with the United States in the summer of 1969.[17] Besides testing the U.S. reaction to the possibility of Soviet preemptive action, the Soviets apparently hoped that an alarmed Washington would leak the threat to the world, thus providing the Chinese with independent testimony to the credibility of the threat, and giving Beijing new grounds for caution. This, indeed, is what happened.

Meanwhile, the Politburo wanted to avoid complications with the United States at a juncture where there was thought to be a real possibility of escalation in the military combat with China. To this end, as Henry Kissinger notes, Soviet representatives abroad were apparently instructed in the summer of 1969 to indicate a willingness to minimize friction with the United States.[18] This instruction was evidently operative only during the period of acute military tension with China and was probably lifted with the start of Sino-Soviet border talks in October 1969. As we have seen, concern over China did not prevent the Soviet Union from embarking on a new path of direct military involvement in Egypt after January 1970, a policy that had a serious potential for involving the Soviets in a conflict with the United States. Nor did it prevent the Defense Council and the Politburo from authorizing the Soviet military to proceed with the Cienfuegos nuclear submarine venture in the fall of 1970.

From the first the Soviet leadership was extremely concerned that the United States would seek to use Moscow's China problem to extract bargaining leverage in its bilateral dealings with the USSR. As President Nixon and Secretary Kissinger have since testified, the Soviets had good reason for such concern.[19] The Politburo therefore resorted to numerous maneuvers in an effort to convey the impression that Sino-Soviet relations might soon improve and that the United States had no grounds for expecting such leverage. For example, the Soviets insisted on rescheduling the start of the Soviet-U.S. SALT I talks until a month after Sino-Soviet border talks had begun—a pattern that was to be followed in other contexts in ensuing years.*

Before important Soviet-U.S. negotiating sessions, the Soviet Union habitually sent Leonid Ilichev, its chief border negotiator, back to Beijing to face Chinese intransigence, evidently hoping to suggest that the Soviet Union, too, had maneuvering room in the triangle. In the early years of the Sino-Soviet border talks, these tactics were sometimes supplemented by statements to Western journalists implying that the talks had made significant progress. On occasion, early in this process, the Soviets proved so anxious to misrepresent the nature of the triangle that they intimated the possibility of Chinese military counteraction against American operations in Indochina—a threat Beijing had no intention of raising itself.

The Soviets meanwhile perceived themselves to be in a race to "normalize" relations with China before the United States completed its own normalization. They sought to escape their dilemma by searching for devices that might enable them to settle the border

---

* The United States had previously delayed agreeing to the start of talks for several months and the Soviet Union itself now probably wanted to avoid appearing too eager. This consideration probably reinforced the Soviet desire to have the Sino-Soviet talks begin first, hoping that this would suggest to the United States the imminence of Sino-Soviet harmony and the futility of expecting that the China problem would lead to Soviet concessions in SALT.

issue without granting what they considered the unthinkable demands of the PRC.[20] To this end, the Soviets from time to time offered China various palliative substitutes, such as nonaggression pacts, which Beijing always rejected. The Politburo at the same time sought vigorously and repeatedly for Chinese consent to a new Sino-Soviet summit meeting, particularly after high-level contacts between China and the United States began to surface in 1971.[21] In this, too, Moscow was unsuccessful. At one point, when the U.S. incursion into Cambodia in May 1970 briefly revived Chinese doubts that the United States indeed intended to withdraw from Indochina, the PRC appears momentarily to have tantalized the Soviet leadership with the possibility of an improvement in Sino-Soviet relations. As the eager Soviets discovered to their chagrin, however, this prospect vanished as soon as American troops left Cambodia, an action that reaffirmed the Chinese in their conviction that the threat to their security from the United States was diminishing.

The Politburo's repeated and unsuccessful efforts to appeal to a Chinese interest in improving relations on the grounds of a shared hostility to the United States did not prevent it from authorizing analogous appeals to the United States. In July 1970, soon after the Chinese disappointed the Soviet hopes they had raised in May, the Soviet SALT delegation proposed a plan for Soviet-U.S. "joint retaliatory action" against any third nuclear power that undertook a "provocation" against the USSR or the United States. This proposal was repeated through the SALT back channel to Kissinger in Washington.[22] Transparently aimed at China, though also potentially harmful to the U.S. relationship with France and Britain, this plan was quickly rejected by the United States. It is a reasonable assumption that China became aware of this Soviet gambit long before it was made public in 1973.

When events of the following spring and summer confirmed Soviet forebodings about Sino-American dealings, the Soviet leaders seem temporarily to have been inclined to conciliate the United States, despite their reluctance to allow Washington to exploit the USSR's weak position in the triangle. Thus, the implications of April's "Ping-Pong diplomacy" may well have influenced the Soviets in their May 1971 decision to stop procrastinating over a commitment to negotiate limitations of offensive missiles and an ABM treaty simultaneously.[23] The evidence of movement in Sino-American relations may have heightened Politburo awareness of a need, in the new circumstances, to make progress on a central aspect of the Soviet-U.S. relationship—progress of a kind that the Chinese could not possibly match. It seems quite likely that the China factor played a role in accelerating the Soviet decision to moderate the terms of a Berlin Quadripartite Agreement in June and July 1971, again after months of stalling. The announcement of the Kissinger visit to China in mid-July—which confirmed long-standing suspicions about Sino-U.S. contacts—apparently stirred Politburo fears about the magnitude of the Sino-American understanding. By increasing fears of Soviet isolation, it furnished a fresh reason for hastening agreement to a document that was a key to consolidating the Soviet position in the West.

This initial period of intense Soviet concern about the direction of the U.S. relationship with China reached a climax between December 1971 (when the Soviets saw the United States hold urgent consultations with PRC representatives to counter Soviet policy during the India-Pakistan war)[24] and February 1972 (when President Nixon visited China and the Shanghai Communiqué was signed). Soviet fears receded somewhat, however, after the first Nixon-Brezhnev summit was held in May 1972, and as the outline and initial limits of the new Sino-American relationship became clearer. After the summer of 1971, the situation in the Moscow-Washington-Beijing triangle never again had a demonstrable effect upon the Soviet propensity to make tactical concessions.

Nevertheless, throughout the first half of the 1970s Brezhnev and Gromyko never ceased issuing gratuitous private warnings to Nixon and Kissinger not to enter into a "military alliance" with China.[25] Moreover, late in the detente era the Soviet leaders made one final try to formally align the United States with them against Beijing. Richard Nixon states that at his last summit with Brezhnev in Moscow in July 1974, Brezhnev privately proposed "a U.S.-Soviet treaty which others could join where each country would come to the defense of the other if either country or one of its allies were attacked." This proposal also died a natural death.[26] Thus, in both the opening and the closing stages of the detente relationship, Moscow floated security proposals to the United States which were aimed at isolating the PRC and either preempting or breaking the American connection with China.

It has been suggested that the spectacular growth of Soviet efforts to expand their presence and influence in the Third World after 1975 was prompted, in part, by Soviet chagrin over the failure of their efforts to prevent or break the new American relationship with China. In this view, disappointment with the U.S. unwillingness to forego its China connection joined with other factors to disillusion the Soviets with the results of detente and to impel Moscow to launch an offensive in the Third World.[27]

This view seems implausible on several grounds. First, it is anachronistic in that it overstates the degree of Soviet anxiety about the Sino-American relationship in the middle years of the 1970s. Although Washington would not accept a security relationship with the USSR directed against China, Brezhnev's warning against a U.S. "military alliance" with the PRC addressed a contingency that was not, in fact, a real possibility during Kissinger's tenure in office. Although extensive Sino-American information and opinion exchanges went on during the Nixon and Ford administrations, Kissinger makes it clear that such security measures as U.S. arms sales to the PRC and joint-contingency planning—let alone the creation of an "alliance" with the PRC*—were outside active consideration in this period.[28] American policy did not begin to move in this direction until the end of the decade, late in the Carter administration.

It is reasonable to suppose that despite the repeated and vehement expressions of concern about the Sino-American relationship which the Soviets made in private, the Soviet leaders were well aware of the evidence that the Kissinger-Nixon policy toward China was a limited one, and that it was amply balanced by American concern to reach agreements with the Soviet Union. Indeed, the bulk of

---

* In addition, of course, neither then nor at any point since has the PRC desired a full-fledged "military alliance" with the United States.

Soviet published comment between 1972 and 1975—particularly after the signing of the SALT I agreement in May 1972—suggested a growing inclination to assume that the United States would not wish to jeopardize the arms control process and other overriding American interests by entering a close security relationship with Beijing.[29] It should also be remembered that even as late as the end of the detente period, in November 1974, the Chinese leaders were themselves highly chagrined when the United States consented to hold a summit meeting with Brezhnev at Vladivostok, adjacent to China. The Soviets had chosen this site with precisely that effect in mind, and can only have been gratified and reassured by the Ford administration's acquiescence in this slight to Beijing.

It can be argued, to be sure, that the Politburo was disturbed in this period not by an expectation that the United States would line up with China against the Soviet Union, but rather by the repeated confirmation that Washington would not consent to an arrangement with Moscow directed against China. It would be far-fetched to conclude, however, that Kissinger's refusal to depart from a course he steered between the two powers was sufficient provocation to inflame the Soviet leadership and incite it to undertake more active measures in the Third World to counter American interests.

Furthermore, we should not underestimate the continuity that Soviet competitive behavior demonstrated throughout the decade. Even as the Soviet leaders sought in vain to entice the United States to side with them against the PRC, they continued to give a higher priority to their efforts to damage the American position abroad, most notably in their arms shipments to Vietnam. As I have suggested, this priority was an inherited one, sustained from the time of the Soviet breakout into the Third World in the late 1960s to the period when the USSR found new opportunities to exploit in the late 1970s.

This is not to deny that the Soviet leadership had indeed become disillusioned with the fruits they were obtaining from the Soviet-American relationship by the close of the detente era. The central cause of this disillusionment, however, was not American policy toward China but rather the evolution of American attitudes regarding trade, technology transfer, and the extension of investments and credit to the Soviet Union. We shall turn to this question shortly.

THE EUROPEAN SECURITY IMPERATIVE

Another factor that strongly influenced Politburo strategy from the outset of the new decade was the progress of *Westpolitik,* the Soviet normalization with West Germany, which closely preceded and prepared the way for the emergence of detente with the United States in 1971–1972.

The reorientation of the Soviet posture toward the FRG in 1969–1970 was accomplished over stubborn rear-guard resistance from Ukrainian party Secretary Shelest, who maintained an alliance with East Germany's Ulbricht in seeking to obstruct the Soviet normalization with Bonn. As Grey Hodnett has shown, Shelest was remarkably slow in joining the Politburo consensus on this matter, continuing to carp and snipe at the West German regime as Brezhnev welcomed the Social Democrats' rise to power in the fall of 1969 and entered negotiations with them in 1970.[30] Shelest did not bring his statements on Germany into line with the new policy of the leadership majority until after Ulbricht himself had been pushed into retirement by the Soviets in the spring of 1971. This behavior was undoubtedly regarded by many of his colleagues as another breach of discipline, to be added to the account already waiting to be paid.

It would be a mistake, however, to counterpose Shelest and Brezhnev as "hawk" and "dove," or as hard- versus soft-liner. The two men shared a common view on the priority of Soviet military spending, and there was nothing particularly soft about the steps Brezhnev took during this period in regard to the Middle East, Cuba, and the India-Pakistan conflict. Moreover, after the events of 1968 and 1969, certainly neither the Czechs nor the Chinese had cause to regard Brezhnev as especially dovish. It seems more appropriate to say that the two leaders differed as to the appropriate *mix* to be maintained among the diverse aspects of Soviet foreign policy. Shelest, like Shelepin before him, favored a more consistent, ideologically oriented posture across the whole range of issues.

Brezhnev, and the Politburo majority, on the contrary, were moving to adopt a new, nonpugnacious tone in bilateral dealings with the major capitalist states while continuing to press for Soviet advantages over those states in the Third World, and while maintaining the long-term quest for military advantage.

The unfolding of Soviet and East European political and economic dealings with the FRG created a model for the eventual opening to the United States, but a more direct consequence was that it at last made possible the European security conference the Soviet leadership had long desired. At a minimum, the Soviets expected this conference to ratify and legitimize Soviet territorial gains from World War II; at a maximum, they hoped it would allow them to insinuate themselves into the management of West European security affairs, and reduce the U.S. role correspondingly.

Characteristically, the Politburo persisted for a considerable time in probing the chances of securing a conference from which the United States would be excluded. When finally convinced that this was impossible, and when confronted with Western insistence that one prerequisite for this conference was a Berlin agreement—to which the United States would have to be a party—the leadership concluded that the European front, too, required a new emphasis on negotiations with the United States.

Although conceding the need for such negotiations, the Politburo never lost sight of its intention to use its detente relationship with Europe to attenuate American influence there. This possibility was to become increasingly important from the middle of the decade on—after the 1975 European Security Conference—as Soviet operations in the Third World multiplied and a gap opened between U.S. and European perceptions of the meaning those operations had for their interests.

THE TECHNOLOGY TRANSFER IMPERATIVE

A third, closely related factor that influenced the Soviet posture toward Washington was the gradual emergence of a Politburo consensus that the difficulties of the Soviet economy justified a much more vigorous effort to expand the importation of Western technology and capital. Such an effort seemed at first necessarily to imply more extensive dealings with the United States, the leader in both regards. The Soviet leaders reached this conclusion, however, only after considerable internal turmoil.

Premier Kosygin had been pressing for such a turn in Soviet policy since as early as 1966, but could make no headway as long as Brezhnev continued for political reasons to oppose such a change.[31] As already noted, these different views had been reflected in the contrasting speeches the two men delivered in February and March 1968.[32] Brezhnev had consistently contended that the Soviet economy had the capacity to solve its problems of technological lag and declining productivity without large-scale recourse to the West, that is, without exposing the country to those dangers of ideological contamination and dependence on the enemy which became bogeys to the most ideologically oriented sections of the Party after the Soviet experience with Dubček and Ota Sik. The eventual shift in Brezhnev's position on this matter was the result of a mixture of factors, the most important of which was the evolution of the situation in the Soviet economy and the parallel evolution of Brezhnev's efforts to increase his leverage over his colleagues.

The Worsening Economic Picture. Nineteen sixty-nine was, for the oligarchs, a most disappointing economic year, and a foretaste of the future. Poor weather and a mediocre harvest followed the good fortune of previous years, subsequently necessitating the resumption of grain imports. Significant shortfalls were also registered in iron and steel output and in most branches of energy production. Although 1970 brought considerable improvement in many respects, many of the ambitious initial targets of the Eighth Five-Year Plan could not be met. By the standards of the 1980s, industrial rates of growth were still high, but the Soviet leadership had received its first strong hint of the downward secular trend to come.

These difficulties inevitably affected the tugging and hauling within the leadership over resource allocation for the next (Ninth) five-year plan (1971–1975). In 1969, one Soviet journal had acknowledged that the "exacerbation of the international situation"—that is, the three crisis years, 1967, 1968, 1969—had "prevented us from making the full quota of appropriations intended for agricultural investment." [33] Brezhnev, who in 1970 stated that unplanned foreign policy problems had indeed caused additional expenditures,[34] was determined that agricultural allocations be insulated from such budgetary raids in the new plan. At the same time, he remained equally convinced that it was politically necessary to protect the military share of the budget. Nevertheless, it was now apparent that the economic pie from which these slices were to be taken was not going to grow as fast as the leaders had hoped. Moreover, most (but not all) [35] of the oligarchs were more and more aware that growth rates could not be maintained, let alone increased, without improved labor productivity, and that this improvement would not occur without the material incentive that could be supplied only by a greater emphasis on consumer goods.

Finally, the strains created within the leadership by the intensification of competing economic pressures evoked, in some quarters, a certain defensiveness about the economic consequences of the Politburo's assertive foreign policy. In early 1970, a few weeks before the leadership decided to send thousands of Soviet air defense troops to Egypt, an *Izvestiya* editorial explained: "The socialist countries are steadfastly fulfilling their revolutionary international duty. This is placing a definite and considerable material load on the socialist countries. But what would happen if the aggressive forces were not receiving a decisive rebuff? In such a case they would be proceeding further along the path of armed adventures and would be creating an even greater threat to universal peace."[36]

The 1970 Leadership Confrontation. By the turn of the decade, some of the oligarchs were convinced that Brezhnev was seeking to use these difficulties as a vehicle to enlarge his own position at the expense of his colleagues. Indeed, there is evidence to suggest that he had been conducting an offensive behind the scenes for over a year, exploiting different devices in an effort to wrest increased authority from a collective leadership that proved slow to yield. In particular, Brezhnev had been unable to change the makeup of the Politburo; there had been no subtractions and only one minor addition since 1966.*

As one aspect of this Brezhnev offensive against collectivity, he had instigated since late 1968 an acceleration of the buildup in his reputation as a military hero. As another, he had arranged for a two-volume edition of his reports and speeches to be published for the first time in Bulgaria toward the end of 1969; it soon received a glowing review in *Kommunist.* This peculiar "out-of-town tryout" was apparently intended to ease the way within the leadership for the publication of Brezhnev's works in the Soviet Union and for Brezhnev's emergence as a new Marxist-Leninist classic. This indeed happened in 1970, but evidently with a Politburo caveat: the works of other members of the leadership, beginning with Suslov, would be published, too.

Meanwhile, in the spring of 1969 Brezhnev had made a more pointed effort to use his cult to enlarge his advantage over his colleagues, when his follower D. A. Kunayev, party boss in Kazakhstan, for the first time described Brezhnev as "head" of the Politburo.[37] It was several years before Brezhnev was able to get this formula accepted by the Politburo and enforced on his colleagues—particularly the senior ones—as obligatory verbal obeisance. The initial resentment and resistance in the oligarchy was vividly reflected in an article published four months after Kunayev's statement. The author recalled that on one occasion Lenin had received from a party official a letter addressed "To the Chairman of the Politburo," but had "crossed out on the letter the word 'chairman,' wrote 'there's no such person,' and readdressed it."[38]

Against this background, Brezhnev delivered a speech to a Central Committee plenum in December 1969 which was a landmark in several respects. The first in what was to become a series of annual, year-end jeremiads by the party leader on the state of the economy, this speech was short on practical solutions for the multiple shortcomings it criticized (in particular, the slow growth of labor productivity).[39] The primary *political* import of the speech, however,

---

* Yuriy Andropov, the new KGB chairman, had attained candidate Politburo status in June 1967.

was the strong implicit attack on Kosygin's stewardship of the economy. This proved to be the opening salvo in a campaign by Brezhnev over the next several years to gain personal control over the work of the Council of Ministers. In February 1970, he was responsible for a Central Committee decree that constituted unusually direct interference in the workings of a ministry,[40] and in late May he made an unprecedented personal appearance and speech at a Council of Ministers session that was considering the next five-year plan. In effect, he took the gavel out of Kosygin's hand on this occasion.[41]

This offensive apparently provoked a political confrontation within the leadership which continued through the first half of 1970. Early in the year, the often well-informed authors of the Soviet dissident journal *Political Diary* wrote that Suslov, Shelepin, and K. T. Mazurov had signed a letter criticizing Brezhnev for his speech at the December 1969 plenum, saying that the speech did not contain an analysis of the causes of the difficulties Brezhnev had cited, and that without such an analysis "you only have hysterics." [42] In reaction, Brezhnev was said to have postponed a new Central Committee plenum scheduled for March, and to have departed alone to Belorussia to attend military maneuvers with Marshal Grechko, ostentatiously seeking the political support of the defense minister.[43] In an April address, Brezhnev made a pointed reference to Lenin's disapproval of "factionalism," apparently alluding to his own critics.[44]

The confrontation came to a head in July 1970, the only month since the October Revolution in which the Soviet Party held two plenums of the Central Committee. After an initial plenum on Soviet agriculture at the start of the month, the members of the Central Committee were apparently obliged to wait in Moscow for ten days while the Politburo thrashed out an agreement.[45] A new plenum then met and announced the postponement of the 24th Congress of the Soviet Communist party until March 1971, contradicting Brezhnev's recent public assertions that the congress would meet in 1970.[46]

Christian Duevel and some others have advanced a plausible explanation of these events. Their thesis holds that at some time during the spring Premier Kosygin had offered to resign and retire, and that the leadership had since been deadlocked over Brezhnev's desire to use the occasion to take control of the premiership, either personally or by proxy. This impasse was resolved only in mid-July, when it was decided to retain Kosygin.[47] By then, in the view of the Politburo majority, it was too late to hold the party congress in 1970.*

In the years to follow, this setback to Brezhnev was to prove only one incident in a struggle that did not cease. The general secretary's efforts to strengthen his position in the Politburo were to meet with some success in 1971 when several key supporters were promoted to full Politburo membership, but it was not until 1973 that he was finally able to begin to remove his adversaries.[48] His efforts to promote his personal cult as a means of increasing his leverage on his colleagues also made progress over time, until by 1974 even Kosygin had acknowledged publicly that Brezhnev was the "head" of the Politburo. Yet Brezhnev's ongoing attacks on Kosygin's position and his attempts to seize effective control of the ministerial empire, which continued in different guises throughout the decade, met with little success until close to the end of Kosygin's life.[49] Blocked from seizing the premiership by a rigidly enforced Politburo convention,† Brezhnev was eventually forced to settle for the presidency, an inadequate compensation.

In 1970, the frustration Brezhnev experienced in his first effort to take personal control of the premier's economic domain is likely to have lent impetus to his immediately subsequent and more successful efforts to usurp Kosygin's role as the leading public spokesman in foreign affairs. Brezhnev's public speeches in 1970—particularly one delivered in June[50]—marked the transition in this process, and the enunciation of Brezhnev's "Peace Program" at the

---

* The issue of the premier's identity was linked to the formal announcement of the date of the congress because this statement traditionally designated him to deliver one of the two main reports to the congress.

† The October 1964 plenum that removed Khrushchev is reported to have resolved that henceforth the party leader could not simultaneously hold the premiership, as Khrushchev had done (T. H. Rigby, "The Soviet Leadership: Towards A Self-Stabilizing Oligarchy?" *Soviet Studies* 22 (October 1970), 175.

24th CPSU Congress in March 1971 signaled its culmination. By seizing the initiative in this matter, and by formalizing the opening to the West and the United States as party policy, Brezhnev was also legitimizing his new, primary role in dealing with the Western powers. The formal shift to the detente line thus permanently raised Brezhnev's public stature, and therefore assisted him in his long-term struggle to enlarge his elbow room within the Politburo.*

Brezhnev was able to gain such pesonal political benefits, of course, as a result of the new economic expectations which made detente seem attractive to his colleagues. It seems likely that the turn to the West, and to the United States in particular, served for Brezhnev as a tacit response to the charge that his strident complaints about the trends in the Soviet economy had not been accompanied by proposals that could remedy these difficulties. He had now furnished one such major proposal. It is thus probable that Brezhnev's conversion to Kosygin's position favoring the large-scale acquisition of American technology and capital was accompanied by high—and probably unrealistic—expectations about the long-term effects this policy would have on the economy. The Politburo was apparently "sold" on the thesis that this change, over time, would go a long way toward solving the economic problems to which Brezhnev had pointed at the December 1969 plenum, helping to raise productivity and preventing a continued decline in the growth rate of the Soviet economy. At the same time, the Politburo was undoubtedly convinced that the change would produce ancillary benefits for Soviet military technology.

From the outset, however, some of the Politburo members who agreed to the policy shift appeared to retain certain reservations. These reservations were reflected in the precautionary steps, discussed below, which were taken to guard against the political infections anticipated from expanded contact with the West. They were also reflected in the attitude the Politburo took toward Soviet military spending in the era of detente. Such reservations were to

---

* Moreover, as an added political benefit, this shift toward the detente line had the inadvertent side effect of finally enabling Brezhnev to find sufficient political support to remove Shelest, when the Ukrainian party leader for the last time dissented from the Politburo consensus. This incident is discussed below.

become much more important when the United States later sought to establish political preconditions for the expansion of trade.

THE SALT PROCESS

Finally, the shift to detente was influenced by the leadership's growing conviction that the U.S.S.R. had an interest in concluding a SALT I agreement with the United States, provided that it could be negotiated within certain severe constraints. These negotiating attitudes, and the assumptions with which the Politburo began, should be clearly visualized because they proved critical to the subsequent evolution of American and Soviet political attitudes toward the SALT process, and toward detente as a whole.

Soviet Assumptions. The Soviets approached SALT against the backdrop of a massive Soviet missile program, in train for the better part of a decade. They intended through this program to eliminate for all time the position of strategic inferiority that had allowed the United States to humiliate the Soviet Union in the Cuban missile crisis. Beyond this aim, they apparently sought to secure such advantages as fortune might decree. They knew that the United States was alarmed at the rapid pace of Soviet ICBM and SLBM deployment, which threatened soon to surpass a U.S. launcher total that had been frozen for several years, initially by conscious choice and thereafter by the paralyzing political and economic realities created by the Vietnam War.

The Soviets knew from statements in the American press that the United States was preoccupied with the counterforce potential of the SS-9, the largest deployed Soviet third-generation missile. In addition, U.S. conduct had probably convinced them that the United States did not yet know the Soviet Union intended to replace the SS-9 and other third-generation ICBMs with a new, fourth generation of missiles which the United States would eventually find even more threatening. They also knew, from American publications, that the United States was deploying multiple warheads (MIRVs) on its missiles as a less expensive substitute for the politically impossible enlargement of its missile force. They probably assumed that the United States did not yet know that the Soviet Union was planning to more than match this development by installing more and larger MIRVs on what were to prove the bigger missiles of its fourth generation.

The Soviets knew that the United States possessed a larger bomber force, superior submarine and antisubmarine warfare technology, and certain qualitative missile advantages that the Soviet Union was working to overcome. Finally, they knew that the superiority of the U.S. antiballistic missile (ABM) gave the United States one major strategic technological advantage. At the same time, however, they knew it was highly uncertain that the U.S. Congress and public would pay for the extensive deployment of the ABM, and realized that the United States might therefore be eager to trade an ABM ban off to the USSR rather cheaply. The Soviet leaders were of course aware of the public controversy in the United States in 1969 and 1970 about the weaknesses of the proposed American ABM system. But this system was sufficiently superior to the technology the Soviets then had available so that Moscow made the constraining of U.S. ABM deployment its primary objective in SALT I.[51]

In the USSR, in sharp contrast with the United States, all this information was probably shared only by the very small group of men who both planned and authorized Soviet weapons programs and formulated the strategy of SALT negotiations which would best protect those programs. These men included, first of all, the members of the Defense Council, and more broadly, the Politburo as a whole.

SALT and Military Costs. In the light of both previous and subsequent Soviet spending behavior, it seems probable that these Soviet leaders entered the SALT talks neither expecting nor desiring that the SALT process would reduce the share of Soviet GNP devoted to the military budget.* This does not necessarily mean that Soviet

---

*We must bear in mind that throughout the SALT process, a large majority of the funds in the Soviet military budget were devoted to a variety of nonstrategic purposes—such as procurement of conventional weapons—which were completely outside the SALT framework. See the CIA National Foreign Assessment Center papers, *Estimated Soviet Defense Spending: Trends and Prospects,* SR-78-10121, June 1978, and *Soviet and U.S. Defense Activities, 1971–1980: A Dollar Cost Comparison,* SR-81-10005, January 1981.

military costs were excluded from their calculations, but it does suggest that their role was a restricted one. Although writers such as Arbatov alluded to the prospect of a "peace dividend" in the budget,[52] the Defense Council and the Politburo probably visualized this dividend in terms of prospective additional costs that might be avoided, rather than of programmed costs that might be trimmed.

It is evident that the possible additional cost of greatest concern to the Kremlin was the expenditure that would be required for a full-scale deployment of a Soviet ABM system in the event that the United States eventually deployed its own system on a large scale. If, as might well have happened, these sums were simply added to the already designated military share of expenditures, the difficulties in economic resource allocation—already pressing on the Brezhnev leadership more strongly than before—would be aggravated. On the other hand, if a massive ABM deployment had to be absorbed within the current military share, existing defense programs would suffer accordingly. The increase in allocations to the National Air Defense Forces (PVO Strany) required for extensive ABM deployment would then necessarily have disturbed the delicate balance worked out within the Ministry of Defense to accomplish the broad military buildup begun in 1965. Most Soviet military and political leaders would have found it particularly unfortunate to constrict other programs for the sake of a weapons system they probably then considered marginal if not inadequate to its task and distinctly inferior to the counterpart possessed by the United States.

On the whole, whatever reservations some of the marshals may have had about the SALT process, they were almost certainly assuaged, long before the SALT I negotiations ended, by leadership assurances that the more essential strategic programs would be protected at all costs. Brezhnev furnished public notice to this effect, and this promise was kept.[53] As Edward Warner, Thomas Wolfe, and others have observed, there are good reasons to believe that most Soviet military leaders were satisfied with the results of the negotiation process in both SALT I and SALT II.[54]

By the conclusion of the SALT I negotiations, the Soviet leaders had indeed agreed at last to a halt in the growth in the number of ICBM launchers deployed, a stipulation that may possibly have required them to reduce somewhat the total of new fourth-generation heavy ICBM launchers they had initially planned to build. They further agreed to begin dismantling some older SLBM or ICBM launchers once their SLBM total reached a specified point.

The Soviets adamantly refused, however, to tolerate meaningful constraints on their plans to "modernize" the existing set of Soviet third-generation ICBMs by replacing them with fourth-generation launchers whose greater size and other capabilities would permit the USSR to outmatch the United States in multiple warhead throw-weight. They disguised their intention during the negotiation of SALT I, agreeing to qualitative language in the Interim Agreement signed at the 1972 Summit which implied that they would indeed be so constrained (language that U.S. negotiators later advertised as denoting just such a constraint). But the Soviet leaders insisted on sufficient ambiguity in the agreed text so that they were later able, without violating the letter of the agreement, to retrofit their old launchers with new ones of a size and capability the United States hoped to have prevented. The Soviets would have proceeded with these deployment plans in any case, with or without an agreement. But many in the United States later bitterly resented the misleading expectations aroused by the Interim Agreement, particularly since the implied but illusory Soviet concession had meanwhile served as tacit justification for certain concessions on the U.S. side.

The most important of these concessions was the U.S. agreement to an antiballistic missile treaty, which, as we have already seen, had been the most important Soviet objective in the SALT I negotiations. In addition, the scope of the constraints apparently accepted by the Politburo, but in fact rejected, served to justify a continuing freeze of American launcher totals at a level below those of the USSR. The language of the Interim Agreement legitimized this unpleasant reality pending the negotiation of a broader and more equitable SALT II framework.

On the Soviet side, these agreements were seen as the centerpiece of a bilateral relationship from which the Politburo expected to extract the much broader economic benefits already mentioned. Beyond this, they were viewed as having bought time for the Soviet

Union to complete the process of overhauling, and in some respects surpassing, the United States in strategic capability, after which a new and necessarily more difficult understanding would be necessary to constrain U.S. programs and maintain the relative position achieved.

On the American side, the real nature of the bargain struck in SALT I, which gradually became apparent as a result of Soviet post-agreement "modernization," served greatly to increase mistrust of the SALT process and of detente as a whole. The "modernized" Soviet heavy ICBMs whose advent the Soviets protected in SALT I both perpetuated and extended an asymmetry in the capabilities of the land-based missile forces of the two sides—an asymmetry that important sections of the American elite found threatening and, over the long term, unacceptable. In political terms, it was the discovery that this modernization had been slipped through the SALT I agreement that began the growth of opposition to what was, in my view, a somewhat more equitable SALT II agreement. That opposition in turn eventually eroded the benefit the Soviets themselves perceived in the strategic arms negotiation process.

THE SOVIET INTERACTION WITH AMERICAN PLURALISM

As the Soviet leaders pursued these four sets of benefits from bilateral intercourse with the United States, they were initially greatly impressed by the manipulative advantages offered them by American reality. In time, however, the Politburo became increasingly soured by the associated disadvantages.

SOVIET PROJECTIVE MISCONCEPTIONS

Themselves profoundly contemptuous of the ignorance and ephemeral passions of the masses, determined to allow no opening for the exertion of pressure from below upon party policy, and fearful of any tendency toward drift or passivity at the top which might give vent to inchoate popular spontaneity *(stikhiynost')*, the

Soviet leaders were alternately incredulous, gratified, and appalled at the extent to which U.S. leadership and the flow of U.S. policy were buffeted and conditioned by elite pluralism and mercurial popular pressures.

The Politburo members were incredulous because they were reluctant to come to grips with the implications of their discovery of a central class enemy not symmetrically shaped in their own image—that is, not in command of its forces, united by class interests in fundamental hostility to themselves, and projecting a single will abroad. The asymmetrical multiplication of diverse tendencies and unpredictable variables in the camp of the enemy opens the door uncomfortably wide to such banned phenomena as chance *(sluchaynost')* and coincidence *(kon'yunkturnost'),* and disorients the Manichaean world view.

The Soviet leaders therefore persistently tended to project rationalizing interpretations drawn from their own experience upon the chaos they saw in American life. Despite repeated lessons from American behavior and some warnings from their own Americanologists, they were slow to understand the dispersion of authority in the United States or to accept as real the fragmentation of causes of American political events. Of the many examples of this mindset, two may be cited as characteristic.

In 1973 and 1974, the Soviets were reluctant to accept the prospect that an American president could be overthrown simply because of Watergate, which seemed to them a politically irrelevant triviality. They instead preferred to believe, until very late in the day, that the campaign against President Nixon had been prompted primarily by more fundamental, hidden causes that were pertinent to their own interests—in particular, by the opposition in the United States to detente.[55]

In the winter of 1978–1979, a visiting congressional delegation was startled when a member of the Soviet leadership said he was sure that President Carter and the national Democratic party leadership had decisive influence over the SALT votes of Democratic senators because of their control of party campaign funds.

MANIPULATIVE EXPLOITATION OF ASYMMETRICAL VULNERABILITIES

But despite this recurrent tendency to try to rationalize the American kaleidoscope into accustomed patterns, most Politburo members—and the foreign policy apparatus supporting them—were constantly reminded by day-to-day events that American pluralism was real and that it did affect the Soviet Union by shaping U.S. behavior as bilateral negotiator and global competitor. To the considerable degree that they perceived practical advantages for Soviet policy in these phenomena, the Soviet leaders were of course gratified. They took it for granted that the asymmetries between American and Soviet social structures, political practices, and alliance systems would in any circumstance make it less difficult for them to influence U.S. decision making—and thus to bargain successfully—than for any U.S. president to manipulate them.

Ambiguous Generalizations. Soviet efforts to exploit the asymmetries latent in the detente relationship frequently involved an attempt to draw the United States into ambiguous and generalized mutual pledges. The Politburo ardently sought a wide variety of such joint commitments in principle with America and its allies. As a rule, these broad mutual promises were phrased in such a way that they committed the Soviet Union to nothing specifically defined. At the same time, however, each of these pledges had the potential to exercise some constraining effect upon the American public—and hence, upon the American government—because of the different conditions that prevailed in the United States.[56]

We have alluded earlier to the fact that the SALT I Interim Agreement of May 1972 contained one notable such ambiguous passage. This was the pledge in Article II not to convert "light" ICBM launchers into "heavy" ones of the types deployed after 1964. In the absence of any quantitative definitions of "light" and "heavy" missiles, definitions that the Soviets tenaciously refused to accept, the Soviets were later able legally to make conversions of a kind that the United States had hoped the agreement had prevented (notably involving the SS-19). This fact eventually proved extremely damaging to U.S. interests. Although the most important U.S. goal in SALT I was thus not achieved, the atmosphere in which the Interim Agreement was signed left the American public with the impression for some time that this ambiguous language marked an important advance in arms control.

The text of a document on "basic principles" of Soviet-U.S. relations, also signed at the May 1972 summit, included a similarly unspecific pledge to refrain "from efforts to obtain unilateral advantage at the expense of the other, directly or indirectly." The context of this sweeping pledge strongly implied that the parties were referring not merely to strategic weapon programs but to geopolitical conduct generally. The unrealistic (not to say un-Leninist) nature of this statement was surely clear to the Politburo when it was signed, and the Soviet leaders undoubtedly believed the U.S. leadership felt similarly. But such statements, viewed in the context of the package of agreements signed in 1972 and 1973, fueled the American public's perception that the Soviets had adopted a more benign, less competitive attitude toward the United States. This perception proved useful to the Soviet Union until it was undermined by the revelations of Soviet conduct in the October 1973 war in the Middle East.

Similarly, in the Agreement on Prevention of Nuclear War signed at the summit of June 1973, the two parties pledged to act "in such a manner as to prevent the development of situations capable of causing a dangerous exacerbation of their relations." At the moment this statement was signed, as will be seen below, the Soviet Union had long since had information, not possessed by the United States, which led it to attach much higher credence than the United States did to the likelihood of an Egyptian attack on Israel. Furthermore, the Soviet Union was supplying weapons systems to Egypt that it knew to be prerequisites for such an attack. The parties also pledged "to refrain from the threat or use of force" against either "the other party" or "the allies of the other party." Three months later this pledge was to be violated by both sides during the October War: first by the Soviet Union (in its threat to intervene unilaterally against Israel), and then by the United States (in its consequent movement to a heightened state of strategic readiness against the

Soviet Union). At the time that these vague and open-ended pledges were made, however, they served to obscure from the American public the fact that the Politburo continued to consider certain of its national interests incompatible with those of the United States.

These paper pledges were accompanied by Soviet advocacy of a variety of similarly sweeping but unenforceable proposals that, had they ever been adopted, would have had an unequal effect upon East and West because of the military and societal asymmetries involved. Some of these Soviet proposals—such as those for pledges of nonaggression, the permanent banning of the use of nuclear weapons, and the renunciation and destruction of all nuclear weapons—were routinely put forward in multilateral forums purely for political effect; the Soviets did not seriously expect that they would ever be adopted by the antagonist. One—the Soviet promise in 1982 that they would not resort to the first use of nuclear weapons in Europe—was transparently intended to influence public debate on nuclear deployments in Europe at a time when the Soviets possessed an advantage there in both nuclear and conventional forces.

One proposal of this kind, however, was repeatedly advanced by the Soviets not only in propaganda arenas but also in direct negotiations; it was highly symptomatic of Politburo attitudes throughout the 1970s, both during and after the era of detente. This was the proposal for equal percentage reductions in announced Soviet and U.S. military budgets. Since U.S. budget figures are published and debated in considerable detail, while the Soviet military budget is announced publicly in a one-line item whose total is fictitious and does not indicate even the trend of Soviet military spending, this proposal was unusually egregious. The fact that it was repeated to the United States in private at an official level therefore suggested a certain thinly disguised contempt.

The Economic Sphere. From the start, the Soviet leaders, like Dr. Kissinger, hoped to obtain advantageous political side effects from the construction of a web of economic relationships with the competitor. In this contest in mutual envelopment, the Soviets are likely to have felt they enjoyed specific advantages. Thus, they believed they could benefit considerably from the great disparity between the position of Soviet agencies and institutions, which were fundamentally responsive to a single political will, and that of the multiplicity of self-propelled American commercial and economic interests with which they interacted. There is also evidence that, on a purely tactical level, the Soviets believed themselves at an advantage in dealing with American commercial and economic negotiators because of the American propensity to regard compromise as both desirable and inevitable, and to experience feelings of frustration and failure when agreement was not achieved promptly. The Soviets prided themselves on their ability to operate with great deliberation, believing that ultimately this formula was likely to induce major concessions.[57]

As detente developed, the disparity between Soviet and American attitudes was compounded by an increasing lack of consensus in the United States—both in society and government—as to whether and how closely U.S. economic relations with the Soviet Union should be linked to U.S. political aims. Without any consensus on this matter, Washington had no effective mechanisms to set priorities and enforce them throughout the economic sphere.

Meanwhile, the Soviets may on occasion have felt that certain of their ongoing contacts with American business interests furnished a means to pressure the U.S. government into making concessions on trade-related matters. Indeed, the Soviets may have hoped for broader leverage on U.S. policy toward the Soviet Union generally, leverage they could exercise not only by offering inducements to the American business community but also by making threats. After a representative of one American company was seized in Moscow in June 1978, apparently in reprisal for the United States' arrest of two Soviets accused of espionage, Western diplomats were quoted as suggesting that the Soviets hoped their action would induce American business leaders to "use their political influence to press the Administration for a more cooperative attitude toward Moscow." [58]

In practice, the Soviet leaders failed, for reasons discussed below, to obtain economic benefits from detente on the scale they had initially envisioned. Nonetheless, even after detente began to fade, they apparently continued to believe that most of those benefits they did receive would remain insulated from changes in the atmosphere of U.S.-Soviet relations. Until the end of the 1970s, they apparently tended to assume that the American business and farming communities had acquired a vested interest in the relationship with Moscow that was sufficient to constrain the U.S. government from taking drastic action at the expense of Soviet economic interests, even if the United States considered Soviet activities elsewhere to be inimical. One of the major Politburo disappointments resulting from the U.S. reaction to the invasion of Afghanistan was the discovery that this vested interest, while indeed substantial, was at least temporarily insufficient to enforce such constraint.

Nevertheless, the Soviets were undoubtedly gratified when the Reagan administration later lifted President Carter's ban on grain sales to the Soviet Union. It has thus become clear to the Soviet leaders that even the most conservative U.S. leadership is highly vulnerable to the political pressures brought by American farmers to maintain grain trade with the USSR under almost any circumstances. To this extent, the Politburo was ultimately confirmed in its hope that the U.S. government would find it impossible consistently to harness its economic policy toward the Soviet Union to its political policy.

The Diplomatic Sphere. Meanwhile, throughout the 1970s the Soviet leadership increasingly took for granted an even more striking asymmetry in the diplomatic practice of the two states. The Politburo found that the very mechanism of diplomacy could be used, with the consent of the antagonist, to enlarge those tactical advantages the Soviet Union already derived from certain of the notorious differences between the two societies—particularly in regard to secrecy and self-discipline.*

---

* This legitimized asymmetry was reflected, for example, in the fact that throughout most of the SALT negotiations, the data about both U.S. and Soviet weapons was provided by the United States, because the USSR refused to supply such information until the talks were close to completion. What was instructive and noteworthy was not the Soviet refusal to depart from their norms of secrecy for the sake of the negotiation, but the ready U.S. consent to this asymmetrical situation.

With the advent of detente, Ambassador Dobrynin and his staff became, to a much greater degree than before, the primary channel for day-to-day intercourse between the two governments. Equally significant, Dobrynin and the Soviet Embassy notably expanded their activity in contact with the highest circles of the American decision- and opinion-making elites, greatly enhancing their opportunities both to procure informed assessments of U.S. policy for the Politburo and to lobby for the Soviet viewpoint.

Simultaneously, the relative position of the U.S. Embassy in Moscow, always much more circumscribed than its counterpart in Washington, declined still further. Not only were successive U.S. ambassadors kept in ignorance of matters to which Dobrynin was privy, but the American reluctance throughout the 1970s to use the Moscow channel served to encourage, exacerbate, and even legitimize the preexisting Soviet tendency to isolate the embassy as much as possible from decision makers, senior policy aides, and advisers.

This condition was superimposed upon the nonreciprocal handicaps long accepted and taken for granted by the United States in the everyday operation of its Moscow embassy. Such handicaps included: the police routinely stationed at embassy gates to intercept Soviet citizens seeking to do business with the embassy, the Soviet radiation of the embassy building, the necessity (because of Soviet travel realities) to have Intourist (and therefore, presumably, KGB) representatives permanently present in the building, the need (because of congressional penuriousness) to employ Soviet (and therefore, presumably, KGB) drivers for embassy cars, and so on.*

In sum, with the coming of detente the already extensive Soviet ability to assess and interact officially with the American decision-making elite was further enriched, even as the United States' po-

---

* For a further view of this extraordinary working asymmetry, see Richard A. Baker, Letter to the Editor, *Washington Post,* October 8, 1980, who states: "How many Americans are aware that the U.S. Embassy in Moscow is chock-full of Soviet workers—answering phones, handling correspondence, interpreting, translating documents, driving Embassy cars? How many think they aren't debriefed by the KGB on a regular basis? The Soviet Embassy in Washington, on the contrary, employs no Americans whatever—they import all their own personnel, right down to the cleaning ladies."

tential to do the same with Soviet counterparts in Moscow, already meager, was further reduced. The Soviets probably believed that the U.S. leadership accepted this incongruity at least in part because of special vulnerabilities inherent in the American reality. Washington could minimize leaks and external policy opposition only by dealing privately with Dobrynin, and, moreover, internal U.S. policy differences were often such that uncoordinated contact with the Soviets in Washington seemed preferable to the formal coordination of a U.S. position that could be presented to the Soviets by the Moscow embassy.[59] Kissinger acknowledges that such calculations took place during the Nixon administration,[60] but it should be remembered that those habits were almost equally prevalent during the Carter administration, after the decay of detente.

The Soviets duly noted all these diplomatic asymmetries, and absorbed them into their assumptions about the changing "correlation of forces."

The Sphere of Unofficial Interaction. As asymmetrical American vulnerabilities became obvious in the course of unofficial bilateral dealings, the Soviet leadership evolved special institutions and mechanisms to cope with and exploit them. These structures were intended to supplement but not to supplant older mechanisms of contact such as the Pugwash meetings.

One of the first of these new institutions was the USA Institute, which was created at the start of the 1970s as an adjunct of the Soviet foreign policy community. As the most important offshoot of the broader Institute of World Economics and International Relations, the USA Institute was one of a family of regional institutes that emerged under the Brezhnev regime. It was intended, in part, to provide senior policy-support institutions such as the Central Committee apparatus and the Foreign Ministry with a body of auxiliary specialists who could fulfill anonymous requests for detailed information or assessments regarding specified aspects of American life and policy. A past practitioner has said that the institute's reports are automatically and rigorously constrained by the postulates of Soviet foreign policy.[61] In any case, as suggested in Chapter 2, they are generally far removed from the Politburo, at best furnishing part of the large mass of background material used by the busy operating functionaries in their work for the leadership.[62] Apparently, however, USA Institute director Arbatov himself and a very few individuals in comparable institutions provide assessments that enjoy more direct access to the leadership.

Perhaps the most important function of the USA Institute, however, has been to provide an authorized channel for collecting impressions from, and disseminating rationalizations of Soviet policies among, a wide spectrum of American diplomats, journalists, scholars, businessmen, and other opinion makers.* There is evidence that the latter function, often carried out with considerable sophistication in both the Soviet Union and the United States, has been given a high priority by the regime.[63]

Late in the decade, after the decay of detente was well advanced, the private propaganda functions of this institute were supplemented by creation of a Department of International Information within the Central Committee apparatus. This department was especially intended to strive to influence Western journalists resident in Moscow.

These new organizations, along with a number of other Soviet instrumentalities, were designed to substitute for those policy-advisory institutions and persons serving the Politburo whose work was regarded as too sensitive to permit frequent contact with Western diplomats and journalists. The individuals thus substituted for included all except two or three of the functionaries of the International Department and the Socialist Countries Department of the Central Committee, almost all military officials, and the personal aides of Politburo members, such as Brezhnev's chief

* A related function of the institute's personnel is internal propaganda, including lectures about the United States to Soviet audiences that reportedly include "representatives of regional Party committees." According to Galina Orionova, these briefings give the minor party aristocracy a "more or less intelligent picture of the United States," but one which "is still very biased" and which "reflects the official line" (Barbara L. Dash, *A Defector Reports: The Institute of the USA and Canada,* Delphic Associates, May 1982, p. 223). The world-view of the provincial party baronage, from which the party leadership is eventually replenished, is thus conditioned and reinforced in a manner that provides more authority and versimilitude than is found in the mass media.

foreign policy aide A. M. Aleksandrov-Agentov. Borrowing increasingly from the political and public relations techniques they encountered in the United States, these Soviet instrumentalities throughout the 1970s sought to justify Soviet policies by encouraging the American tendency to project aspects of American life onto Soviet reality.*

In the aftermath of the invasion of Afghanistan, all such instrumentalities were mobilized, both publicly and privately, to argue that Soviet actions were essentially defensive and that they were justified by the previous trend of U.S. policies. Particularly noteworthy were the "background interviews" on Afghanistan given by unidentified "informed Soviet sources" in Moscow in early January 1980, apparently in conscious imitation of U.S. backgrounders. More sophisticated than the public Soviet propaganda, which they partially contradicted, these interviews were apparently provided by the International Information Department and received extensive, fairly sympathetic coverage in the American press.[64]

The Sphere of Interaction Abroad. By the middle of the 1970s, in part as a result of the broadening of bilateral contacts, the Soviet leaders had acquired an increasingly vivid sense of the constraints upon American actions abroad and, indeed, upon Washington's ability to concert U.S. foreign policy in general. These constraints resulted from the decay of the foreign policy consensus both inside and outside the U.S. government and the weakening of the presidency at the hands of competing power centers.[65]

This process went on through the decade, from the beginning of Nixon's second term to the end of the Carter administration. It

---

* Characteristic, in this regard, was the effort made on one occasion to persuade a leading American journalist that certain Politburo policies were necessitated by the pressure of Soviet "public opinion," which was implied to be an autonomous phenomenon with a breadth and constraining influence closely comparable to the influence of public opinion on the U.S. government (*Washington Post,* June 7, 1977). As already suggested, Politburo members are indeed sensitive—very sensitive—to the opinions of their peers and, to a lesser extent, to what they sense to be the consensus among the most senior representatives of the most senior institutions around them. This oligarchic consensus represents an order of reality different from that of American public opinion, however.

affected Soviet behavior at critical junctures, when opportunities arose and quick decisions had to be made. From the airlift into Angola in 1975 to the airlift into Afghanistan in 1980, the expectation of an internally enfeebled U.S. reaction, in political as well as in military terms, was one of the important considerations in the Soviet calculation of prospective costs and risks.

Through the end of 1979, bilateral intercourse with the United States gradually and cumulatively reinforced this Soviet perception of a paralyzing U.S. absence of consensus. The Carter administration brought a multiplication of public and private U.S. statements warning Soviet leaders to desist or refrain from a multitude of specific actions—from intervention in Angola and Ethiopia to punishment of the dissident Anatoly Shcharansky to naval entry into Cam Ranh Bay. These warnings were regularly brushed aside by the Soviets without incurring immediate and specific political consequences of any kind. It is therefore hardly surprising that their repetition encouraged the Soviets to adopt an attitude of familiar contempt toward such demarches.

This conditioning of Soviet expectations apparently led to a Soviet sense of grievance when one more such warning (over Afghanistan) was finally and unpredictably matched by major political consequences.[66] A senior State Department official concerned with Soviet affairs later told Congress that the United States had "expressed concern" to the USSR about the possibility of such military action "at least four or five times" beginning in late November 1979, but that for some reason the Soviet Union had "grossly miscalculated" the American reaction. He did not speculate as to why these repeated "expressions of concern" had been so ineffectual; this was, apparently, deeply puzzling.[67]

THE EROSION OF THE VALUE OF DETENTE

Meanwhile, however, all the advantages the Politburo could extract from American pluralism in the practice of detente could not disguise the fact that this pluralism also had effects that were harmful to the Soviet Union. The Soviet leaders became increasingly appalled at the extent to which the diffusion of influence over American foreign policy adversely affected their own interests. As the decade went on, the Soviets discovered that the weakening of the presidency, so convenient in other respects, was making it difficult if not impossible to carry out the advantageous bilateral agreements already reached with the United States. In general, the Soviets found it more and more difficult to cash in the benefits for the sake of which they had initiated detente in the first place.

Jewish Emigration. The Soviet leadership first began to question the value of detente in connection with Jewish emigration, an issue that an influential section of American opinion increasingly insisted should condition other aspects of the bilateral relationship. The Politburo had authorized the expansion of such emigration early in the decade for reasons that were never publicly articulated but that probably included, among other things, a decision to provide a safety valve for a disaffected but homogeneous section of the Soviet population.* The Soviets may also have calculated that this emigration could serve as a tacit *quid pro quo* in dealings with the United States, one that might be modulated at Soviet discretion. From the Politburo's perspective, toleration of any emigration was an act of extraordinary condescension, and, moreover, one that was not entirely without risk, in view of the unwholesome example it set for other disaffected segments of the Soviet population. This attitude was confirmed in the 1980s, after the death of detente, when the door was effectively closed against such emigration.

In the first half of the 1970s, the Soviet leadership was dismayed to discover that in practice it obtained little credit or leverage in the United States from the emigration it permitted but much blame for the emigration it did not allow.† The Soviet leaders found this issue transmuted by degrees into an instrument of broad American

---

*This is a pattern followed by Cuba in the early 1960s and again in 1980, by Poland after 1956 and after 1967, by China briefly in 1962, and by Vietnam since 1978.

† This was in contrast to the reaction in Israel, whose posture toward the USSR was influenced somewhat in the early 1970s by this emigration; and even more so to that of the FRG, where the repatriation of Germans from the Soviet Union proved to be an important instrument of Soviet leverage.

attack upon their internal security practices, beginning with the question of who would be allowed to leave their country and then embracing the matter of Soviet persecution of those who were not allowed to emigrate. As time went on, the Politburo oligarchs found this American challenge to their domestic prerogatives increasingly disturbing, particularly since they simultaneously felt obliged to sharpen rather than relax controls over dissident elements as a precaution against the ideological contamination expected from detente. Meanwhile, the emigration question became one of several major obstacles to the Politburo's hopes of obtaining capital and technology transfers from the United States on the scale originally envisioned. Finally, it eventually became one of the many complications contributing to the deteriorating prospects for the ratification of SALT II.

The December 1974 Watershed. Of all these accumulating disappointments, probably the most important was the decisive defeat in December 1974 of the Politburo's hopes for very large economic benefits from the bilateral relationship. This defeat occurred when the U.S. Congress passed the Stevenson amendment to the Export-Import Bank bill, thereby limiting to $300 million the total the bank could lend the Soviet Union over the next four years without seeking further congressional approval, and banning the use of any of this money for development and energy production.

During 1974, the Export-Import Bank bill, renewing the Bank's authorization to extend foreign credits for the next four years, had made its way slowly through the congressional process in parallel with the Trade Reform Act of 1974, which received far more attention from all concerned. Senator Henry Jackson, supported by many in Congress, had attached an amendment to the trade bill prohibiting the granting of most-favored-nation (MFN) status to any Communist state that curtailed the right of its citizens to emigrate or that demanded large exit fees from émigrés, as the Soviet Union had done in the recent past. Jackson's amendment also prohibited the granting of any U.S. government credits to such states. Meanwhile, Senator Adlai Stevenson III, also with broad support, had sought throughout the summer and fall to attach an amendment to the Export-Import Bank bill sharply limiting the amount of such credits that the bank could extend to the Soviet Union. Jackson's amendment became the focus of intense domestic bargaining and international negotiation; meanwhile, this was not the case with Stevenson's amendment, which in the end was allowed to win by default.

In the fall of 1974, Secretary Kissinger, on behalf of the new Ford administration, negotiated with the Soviets and the Senate supporters of the Jackson amendment a complex three-cornered understanding. Under this arrangement, the Soviets made a series of vague oral promises to Kissinger to the effect that they would cease to hinder emigration, that emigration would in fact increase, that there would be no punitive measures taken against would-be émigrés, and that Moscow would not impose special "exit fees" on them. Kissinger relayed these assurances to Senator Jackson in a letter which the senator published, and Jackson replied with a letter, also published, specifying criteria to judge Soviet compliance with the understanding. At the same time, Jackson in return agreed to revise his amendment so that President Ford would be empowered to declare the emigration requirements satisfied and give MFN status to the Soviets for an eighteen-month trial period.

This October compromise was rendered moot in December by the passage of the Stevenson amendment to the Export-Import Bank bill. The amendment's success resulted from a confluence of factors: congressional unease over Soviet behavior during the October 1973 war; concern over the pace of technological transfer to the USSR; concern that once very large credits were transferred to the Soviet Union, the Soviet debtor could exercise political leverage upon the American creditor by threatening to delay repayment; determination that henceforth all large credits be contingent upon Soviet behavior in all arenas; and resolve to assert the congressional will over the preferences of a weakened presidency, which wished instead to make large credits available promptly to the USSR as an inducement to *subsequent* good behavior.[68]

At issue, in particular, was the prospect of extremely large incremental U.S. loans to the Soviet Union over the next few years for the Yakutsk/North Star Siberian energy development projects.

These capital transfers and the associated technology inputs were the biggest single dividend the Politburo anticipated from the detente relationship. But many in Congress were uneasy about the low-interest loans the Export-Import Bank had already furnished the Soviet Union, and they found the prospect of massive, subsidized funding of Siberian energy development by an arm of the American presidency increasingly unacceptable.[69]

In the shadow of Watergate, the harassed and enfeebled executive branch was no longer able to defend these loans. In the final months of the collapsing Nixon presidency and the initial months of the Ford administration, Secretary Kissinger, preoccupied with negotiations with the Soviets and with Congress over the Jackson amendment to the trade act, gave inadequate attention to the potential consequences of the Stevenson amendment to the Export-Import Bank bill, which reached a decisive stage at the same time. There is good evidence to confirm that the latter legislation— halting American funding for Soviet energy production—and not the former, was decisive for the Soviets.[70] It can thus be said that just as the British acquired an empire in a spirit of absent-mindedness, so did the Americans relinquish detente.[71]

In mid-December 1974, at the same moment that a Central Committee plenum was meeting in Moscow, House-Senate conferees, desperate to get the Export-Import bill approved before Congress adjourned, agreed to the ban on loans or guarantees for Soviet fossil fuel production.[72] Three days after the withdrawal of this long-awaited reward, the Politburo took steps publicly to disavow and deny the existence of those tacit commitments Brezhnev had made with the United States in negotiations over the Jackson amendment regarding the scope and conditions of future Jewish emigration from the Soviet Union.[73]

Two weeks later, the Soviets dropped the other shoe. Focusing on the symbolic emigration issue and not mentioning the fact that the long-desired credits had just been cut to what they considered a pittance, the Soviet leaders abrogated the October 1972 Trade Agreement with the United States.[74] The Politburo now indignantly proclaimed that it could never be bribed to permit interference in Soviet internal affairs; in fact, the problem was that henceforth the bribe would be too small.

As I have argued earlier, even in the best of circumstances, even if this legislation had not been passed, it is very much open to question whether the economic benefits at stake would have induced Soviet leaders to follow a different course in the Third World during the next few years. In any case, however, the issue was never put to the test. The events in Washington and Moscow in December 1974 became a landmark in the refueling of Soviet pugnacity, and set the stage for the seizure of the opportunity that surfaced in Angola ten months later. The Soviets seemed characteristically unaware, however, of the extent to which their own competitive behavior in 1973 and 1974, discussed below, had contributed to congressional reluctance to grant them the economic benefits they had anticipated.

The Carter Presidency. Henceforth, Soviet encounters with American pluralism took place in an atmosphere of increasing bilateral acrimony, and against a background of revived and expanded Soviet pressure abroad. In the last years of the decade, during the Carter administration, the Soviet struggle against unwelcome American internal realities centered increasingly on the fate of the SALT II treaty. The Politburo now came to regard this treaty as the last major benefit it might derive from detente.

In these years, the Soviet leaders became increasingly impatient with the drawbacks of the weakened presidency. When the president's negotiators claimed that the Soviets must not only bargain with the administration on the matters at hand but also propitiate the supplementary concerns of Congress and public opinion, the Soviets became indignant at what they saw as an attempt to use the very weakness of the presidency as leverage to extract concessions from the Soviet Union.

In dealings with the gullible, the Soviets were themselves accustomed to buttressing their rhetorical position by claiming that constraints were placed on their flexibility by a Soviet public opinion that they of course knew to be mythical. Consequently, they were aggrieved at what they perceived as an American effort to elevate a mere propaganda expedient into a principal element of negotiation. Henceforth, they were inevitably suspicious that the Carter administration was intentionally exaggerating the difficulty of securing congressional and public consent to a given Soviet-U.S. agreement. To the extent that the Soviets accepted the reality of such difficulties, they became increasingly insistent, as the Soviet payoff from detente dwindled, that the U.S. leadership must bear the political costs of coping with them.*

When this proved impossible—as began to happen across a broad front of issues by the late 1970s—the Politburo increasingly focused on exploiting the foreign policy advantages that American pluralism was creating for the USSR. Its interest in struggling with the bilateral frustrations imposed by that same pluralism dwindled accordingly.

GALVANIZING DISAPPOINTMENTS AND BECKONING OPPORTUNITIES

THE INTERACTION WITH EGYPT AND THE FATE OF DETENTE

From the very outset of detente, a strong tension had existed between the Soviet interest in bilateral dealings with the United States and the Politburo's determination to preserve those political and military advantages vis-à-vis the United States which it had achieved in Egypt and the Arab world as a result of the Arab-Israeli confrontation. This Soviet task was further complicated by the death of Nasser and his replacement by an Egyptian leadership that the Politburo soon found to be more conservative, less inclined to Pan-Arab romanticism, more Egypt-centered, and consequently less easily harnessed to Soviet geopolitical interests. Soviet forebodings about Sadat had already been confirmed in 1971, first by his actions to suppress the Soviet-oriented left in Egypt, and second by his support of the Sudan's Jaafar al-Numeiry, whose relations with the USSR worsened drastically after an attempted Communist coup that the Soviet Union had applauded enthusiastically.

---

* To quote the aforementioned anonymous Soviet diplomat in Washington: "Should we rely on a worm-eaten American constitutional system? What business of ours is it if the President fails to get his treaties through the Senate? Should we wait and keep still? " (*Die Welt,* January 14, 1980).

In 1971, the Politburo had therefore sought to counteract these adverse trends and to erect artificial underpinnings for the relationship with Egypt by inducing Sadat to sign a treaty of friendship with the Soviet Union. From the Soviet perspective, this treaty furnished a legalistic justification for the continuation of the Soviet military presence in Egypt and for the USSR's efforts to expand its extraterritorial rights. From the Egyptian perspective, it was a document on which to base Sadat's insatiable demand for Soviet arms.

From 1971 through 1973, simultaneous with the expansion of Soviet dealings with the United States, the Soviet leaders were thus under continuous pressure from Sadat to supply what he regarded as the military hardware necessary to renew the offensive against Israel.[75] In responding to this pressure, the Politburo was influenced by a mixture of motives: anxiety to preserve the military advantages they had obtained in Egypt, skepticism that any amount of weaponry would enable Sadat to succeed, concern that the USSR might be forced to take undesirable risks to rescue him after the expected defeat, and desire to use the military-supply relationship as leverage upon Sadat both to improve the position of the Egyptian left and to head off any opening by Sadat toward the United States.

The Politburo therefore equivocated. Some weapon systems the Soviets refused to furnish, many others they promised and indeed promptly supplied, still others they promised and then repeatedly delayed delivering, yet others they promised and repromised and then reneged upon.[76] But the Soviets found Sadat extremely resistant to pressures exerted in this fashion. The important types and large quantities of weapons they did supply earned them little credit in Egypt, either then or subsequently, whereas the weapons they withheld evoked threats and punitive action. In the summer of 1972, Sadat ordered the bulk of the Soviet military presence withdrawn from Egypt, implying that Soviet delays in weapons delivery had been influenced by Soviet dealings with the United States. It is noteworthy that this drastic step evidently did improve Soviet delivery performance over the ensuing year.[77]

Despite Sadat's subsequent tendency to belittle what the Soviets did supply, the Soviets knew by 1973 that the scope of their deliveries was radically changing Egyptian capabilities. They also knew, from ongoing contacts with Egypt and Syria, that the Arab intention eventually to attack was far more serious than the United States or Israel believed. The Politburo did not communicate this information to the United States, because that would have undermined the Soviet position with their clients. Instead, Brezhnev made a vigorous effort at his June 1973 summit meeting with President Nixon to induce the United States to compel Israel to satisfy the Arab demands.[78] When this effort failed, the Soviet leadership in effect washed its hands of responsibility and allowed matters to drift toward war.

When the Soviets became aware in early October that hostilities were imminent, they withdrew their dependents from Cairo and Damascus while continuing to maintain contact with the United States, apparently to make sure that the United States had not become aware of impending events and was not about to warn Israel. According to both Sadat and Heikal, Brezhnev made some efforts to induce Egypt and Syria to agree to a cease-fire soon after the war began. After these initiatives failed, however, the Soviets blocked any UN effort to halt the fighting and concentrated their efforts on stimulating other Arab states to support the war effort. After the Soviets began to resupply their clients, they disseminated false reports that the United States had already done the same for Israel—clearly attempting to precipitate a hostile Arab reaction. After the United States did finally begin to resupply Israel, the Arab oil suppliers responded by imposing a petroleum embargo on the United States, and the USSR, which had previously encouraged such a step, now applauded.* Once the Arab battle position became grave, the Soviet leaders cooperated with Washington to procure a cease-fire; but when Israeli violations of the agreement rendered Sadat desperate, the USSR first proposed joint intervention with the United States to police the cease-fire and then threatened unilateral intervention, at last inducing the United States to compel Israel to comply.[79]

---

* This is not, of course, to imply that Soviet encouragement had significant weight with OPEC; it did, however, again indicate Soviet priorities in the era of detente.

This line of conduct over a three-year period testified to the relative weight of Soviet priorities. Though always sensitive to the possible consequences of particular actions for its relationship with the United States, the Politburo maintained a frame of reference in which Soviet competitive needs remained paramount at all times. Throughout this period, Brezhnev on a number of occasions publicly reiterated his view that "hotbeds of war" in the Third World must be eliminated before they led to clashes between the superpowers. His conduct suggested that this was indeed one consideration in his behavior toward Sadat. But it is also clear that this consideration was secondary to the Soviet conception of its overriding competitive interests, and thus could not induce the Soviet leaders to accept the political consequences of the drastic action that would have been required to head off a war they knew was coming and had helped to prepare.

Instead, as events drifted toward war and the USSR became more anxious to do what was required to avoid a complete break with Egypt, the anti-U.S. aspects of Soviet behavior in the Middle East grew increasingly important. More and more attracted by the prospect of the damage a war might do to the United States in the eyes of both radical and conservative Arab opinion, the Soviet leadership was increasingly concerned to do its modest best to render that damage permanent. As already noted, the Soviets appear to have awaited with some eagerness the Arab use of the "oil weapon" against the United States, and loudly welcomed the decision when it materialized. And as we have also noted, these Soviet attitudes in turn interacted with U.S. congressional opinion a year later to help produce the critical downturn in prospects that massive American credits and capital investments would be made to the Soviet Union.

Nevertheless, in the immediate aftermath of the October War, the Politburo members believed they had serious grievances against the United States. In the first place, they were aggrieved because the United States had declared a higher state of military readiness at the moment of impasse over the cease-fire, thereby superimposing a global and strategic dimension upon a regional crisis. Second, and even more important, the Soviet leadership strongly resented

President Nixon's public suggestion, made at a press conference immediately thereafter, that his action had faced the Soviets down.[80] They did not believe Nixon's claims, because in their view the United States had in effect done what the USSR had requested by compelling Israel to comply with the cease-fire. In addition, the Soviets resented Nixon's implication that the Soviet achievement of strategic parity had not removed the stigma of inferiority implanted by the Cuban missile crisis.

These initial postwar grievances against the United States were subsequently reinforced when American initiatives and what the Soviets saw as Egyptian ingratitude combined to undermine the Soviet position in Egypt. These developments could only strengthen the long-established Soviet tendency to pursue an assertive line in the Third World.

THE GROWING INTERNAL PREDISPOSITION TO ACT

Brezhnev's continuing need to display a militant fact to the Party was also a factor in the Soviet behavior just described.

We have seen that in the face of a challenge from within the leadership Brezhnev had earlier felt called upon to demonstrate that the growth of Soviet military strength had not been neglected and was in fact fully commensurate with the degree of risk taking indulged in during the Six-Day War. In subsequent years, through 1971, he may have felt defensive over, and tacitly obliged to compensate for, even minor retreats from the generally more venturesome line of Soviet foreign policy. And now, in the era of detente, Brezhnev seems to have perceived an obligation to demonstrate to his peers and their institutional subordinates that the substitution of vague and flowery language for the ideologically charged rhetoric earlier used in his dealings with the main antagonist did not signify a willingness to sacrifice the Party's fighting qualities *(boyevost')*.

This felt need to justify himself was enlarged rather than diminished by a new personal victory in the inner-party struggle over the acceptability of the detente strategy.

THE FALL OF SHELEST

It has been widely and credibly alleged that Ukrainian party leader Shelest had objected to his colleagues' decision to proceed with the May 1972 summit despite the American mining of Haiphong.[81] At the Central Committee plenum following the apparently prolonged and heated Politburo session that made this decision,[82] the oligarchs at last removed Shelest from his stronghold as party boss of the Ukraine, thus preparing the way for his expulsion from the Politburo in 1973.

The motives for this climactic leadership action were complex. After his fall all the explicit and public criticisms of Shelest centered on his encouragement and protection of Ukrainian nationalism, and there is little doubt that this aspect of his behavior had contradicted the russifying line favored by the Politburo majority.[83] The evidence suggests, however, that this had probably been the case since as early as 1965,[84] and it is surely more than coincidence that decisive action against Shelest was finally taken at a Politburo meeting called seven years later to render a delicate and controversial decision about dealings with the United States.

As I have suggested, the context thus implies that Shelest's colleagues had a long-standing internal policy grievance against him—his permissive attitude toward Ukrainian nationalism—which gradually had been reinforced by an accumulation of resentments over his behavior on foreign policy issues. In May 1972 this mixture of grievances at last became sufficient to precipitate his downfall.[85] In the broadest terms, therefore, Shelest was found guilty not of Ukrainian nationalism and not of opposition to detente, but rather of systematic disrespect for the policy supremacy of the Politburo consensus.

However, Brezhnev's victory over Shelest on this occasion did not eliminate the political force of the foreign policy issue the Ukrainian boss had raised—the ideological acceptability of detente with America. Rather, like Yegorychev five years earlier, the fallen Shelest left Brezhnev with a heightened need for self-justification on an issue about which Brezhnev already felt defensive.

From the opening stages of the movement toward detente, the defensive reaction of the Brezhnev leadership had taken two forms.

One was an effort to tighten ideological discipline within the Soviet Union, to strengthen controls in order to withstand the subversive effects anticipated from greater contacts with the West. The other was a sporadic effort to demonstrate—to one's peers and retainers— that Soviet opportunities to advance abroad were not being sacrificed to detente.

THE INOCULATION AGAINST DETENTE

The first trend—the effort to batten down the hatches for the intensified "ideological struggle" expected to accompany detente— had gone on since 1971. Despite the moderate line Brezhnev took at the 24th Party Congress in March 1971, a strong campaign for vigilance and ideological discipline unfolded after a Central Committee plenum in November of that year.[86] In May 1972—almost simultaneous with the fall of Shelest and the Soviet-American summit—a conservative ideologue was appointed to head the Institute for Concrete Social Research,[87] replacing the liberal *apparatchik* A. M. Rumyantsev.* In June, Yuriy Arbatov, a strong partisan of detente, felt obliged to observe at a party meeting that the normalization of Soviet-American relations would require "the greatest vigilance," adding that "we all know that not even the most successful talks and the best agreements change the unpleasant fact that a tense class struggle will continue to be waged between the world of socialism and the world of capitalism." [88] In July, formal steps were taken to tighten controls over institutions of higher education, to intensify the indoctrination of students, and to punish scientists and scholars found guilty of "amoral, antipatriotic, and other acts incompatible with the title of scholar." [89]

A year later, in June 1973, a samizdat document reported that Moscow city party secretary Vladimir Yagodkin had privately re-

---

* This was a symbolic event of some importance. It will be recalled from Chapter 3 that Rumyantsev, a Central Committee member, had been dramatically fired from his job as editor of *Pravda* in September 1965, an event that was an early watershed victory for conservative, ideologically inclined forces in the Soviet leadership. Now, at the outset of detente, Rumyantsev was removed from his new sociological institute, apparently for probing too frankly into Soviet reality. He now went down for the last time.

minded a group of scholars that a recent Central Committee conference had warned of "the increasing danger of bourgeois ideology in direct connection with the broadening of contacts with the imperialist world." [90] Yagodkin claimed that the Central Committee leadership had been exercised by the "mendacious" idea of a mutual ideological liberalization in the two opposing camps. Warning his audience against "opportunist illusions" arising out of foreign policy developments, Yagodkin insisted that there was no detente "in the struggle between the two systems," and called for unceasing vigilance against "ideological diversion" by the American imperialists.[91]

At the same time, Yagodkin pointed out that the opposite extreme was also mistaken (although not, he said, as dangerous). This was the view of the "dogmatic negativists"—read Shelest—who "believe it is no good sitting down at the conference table with the imperialists." But here, said the Moscow party secretary, "it is appropriate to recall the words of Marx in one of his letters, that in politics you may conclude alliances with the Devil himself if you are certain you can cheat the Devil." [92]

These remarks were allegedly made shortly before Brezhnev's June 1973 journey to the United States for his second summit meeting with President Nixon. Whatever their value as evidence of Soviet negotiating attitudes, they provide a background against which we can understand Brezhnev's already mentioned statement to a group of militant followers in April 1973.[93] In claiming that detente would prove to be an expedient, an interlude for strengthening after which (by 1985) the Party would be in a position to assert itself against the "imperialist" powers more vigorously, Brezhnev was projecting, from complex variables, future consequences that he certainly could not anticipate with great confidence. Moreover, this was in any case an outcome that he must have suspected he would not live to see. Nevertheless, he evidently felt that the private enunciation of this rationalization supplied him with a measure of political insurance.[94]

In the same sense, the policy the Soviet Union pursued in the Middle East between 1971 and 1973, in contradistinction to the public professions of detente, protected Brezhnev's own interests by protecting what the consensus of his colleagues perceived as the interests of the Party.

THE SHIFTING POLITICAL BALANCE

The fall of Shelest had another long-term political effect. As part of Brezhnev's reaction to the foreign policy challenge Shelest had raised in 1972, he sought to shore up his consensus against any future such challenge by elevating the heads of the leading national security bureaucracies—the foreign minister, the defense minister, and the chairman of the KGB—to full membership in the Politburo in 1973. Over the long term the most important single consequence of this change was the legitimization of a policy-making role for the defense establishment in areas of foreign policy from which it had hitherto been nominally excluded.[95]

This formal change in Grechko's role became more and more important as the atmosphere in the Politburo gradually shifted after the October 1973 war, especially as the Soviets saw their position in Egypt slipping away to the United States. Harsher notes now began to be sprinkled among the leaders' statements. In November, Kirilenko gratuitously observed that Soviet foreign policy was devoid of "any illusions whatever" regarding imperialism; and on New Year's Day, Brezhnev made several equally gratuitous tributes to the Soviet military, pledging to "take care of the strengthening of the defense of our homeland." [96]

In May 1974, Brezhnev's old associate Admiral Gorshkov went so far as to declare that imperialism had "regrouped its forces" and had "now launched preparations for a new world war under the guidance of the monopolies across the ocean." [97] That same month, Defense Minister Grechko celebrated his first anniversary in the Politburo with an unusually unrestrained appeal for an interventionist policy of distant force projection:

> At the present stage the historic function of the Soviet Armed Forces is not restricted merely to their function in defending our Motherland and other socialist countries. In its foreign policy activity, the Soviet state actively, purposefully opposes the export of counterrevolution and the policy of oppression, supports the national liberation struggle, and resolutely resists imperialist aggression in whatever distant region of our planet it may appear.[98]

This was not at the time an accurate description of Soviet use of their armed forces; it was, in effect, a prediction, which began to be borne out when the Soviets started to project their forces into Africa a year and a half later.

The next month Suslov observed that the "lessons of the past" proved that the Soviet Union must do everything to strengthen its military capabilities, remarking that detente "is based precisely" on a change in the world correlation of forces in favor of socialism. Suslov went on to insist that Soviet diplomacy was opening "more favorable prospects for further pushing ahead by revolutionary forces." [99] In June 1974 Marshal Grechko reminded the leadership that strengthening peace and strengthening Soviet defense were "indivisible" goals.[100] Several days later his Politburo colleague Mazurov portrayed Soviet foreign policy as combining a "constructive" approach to the West with "a firm rebuff to imperialist aggression and uncompromising struggle with the class enemy." [101]

Taken as a whole, these statements were essentially transitional positions. Although many statements continued to support the notion of detente, the mix was changing, with a gradual growth in emphasis on what might be termed the military-revolutionary side. The climax of this transition came at the end of 1974. In November, the tentative SALT understanding reached at Vladivostok confirmed that the Soviets had failed to ensure that SALT II would accommodate their demands for compensation for the West's so-called Forward Based Systems (FBS).* This failure, in turn, probably confirmed Soviet determination to deploy the SS-20 IRBM as unilateral compensation for FBS, with the consequences we know today.

In December, a Brezhnev visit to Egypt was widely heralded and then cancelled, reflecting the Soviet recognition that its influence in Cairo had been reduced since the October 1973 war. During the same period the aforementioned Central Committee plenum was held and the U.S. Congress rushed through the last-minute maneuvers that culminated in the passage of the Stevenson Amendment to the Export-Import Bank Bill. Some Western observers have speculated that Brezhnev was given a difficult time in leadership meetings in this period, perhaps by Shelepin, and perhaps centering

---

* That is, the French and British nuclear delivery systems and the U.S. land- and carrier-based nuclear weapons in Europe.

on the charge that Brezhnev had encouraged illusions about what might be expected from the United States. Although this view has not been confirmed, it is noteworthy that Shelepin, after being tolerated as a vestige for several years, was finally dropped from the leadership the next spring. This suggests that Brezhnev had discovered a new motive to make a special effort to get rid of him.

In any case, it seems likely that the general secretary, with his strong instinct to remain within the consensus, did not resist what was apparently a strong tide among his colleagues in December. Brezhnev probably readily acquiesced in—perhaps even proposed— the two Politburo decisions taken at this time which had humiliating implications regarding his past dealings with the United States. The first of these decisions was to deny publicly, and thus to repudiate, the private assurances on Jewish emigration which Brezhnev had confirmed to Kissinger as recently as November 1974.[102] The second was to repudiate formally the trade agreement he had signed with the Americans, amid much fanfare, in October 1972.[103]

THE CHANGE IN 1975

Nineteen seventy-five saw the decisive crossover in Politburo attitudes toward the United States, away from the expectations of grandiose benefits from the bilateral relationship toward a more forthright flaunting of the pursuit of competitive advantage. In this new Politburo mind-set, the SALT process retained importance, but it was less and less regarded as the centerpiece of a broad and expanding bilateral relationship. Meanwhile, the Helsinki Agreement was at last signed in 1975, the ceremonial culmination of years of Soviet effort to secure a European security conference and document. But whereas for West Europe this event became a way station in an ongoing detente process, for America it proved a terminal irony in a dying relationship.

Over the long term, it was not the signing of the Helsinki Final Act but three other developments in 1975 which had the greatest effect on the future evolution of Soviet behavior.

One event that had a major impact on the political atmosphere within the Soviet oligarchy was the Communist effort to take control in Portugal in the spring and summer of 1975. Alvaro Cunhal, the leader of the Portuguese Communist party, tried to seize on the favorable opportunity created by the failure of an attempted rightist coup in order to eliminate the Party's major political competitors and ride to power in Lisbon. These events created a dilemma for the Brezhnev leadership. The general secretary had long been skeptical that any Western Communist party would come to power for many years,[104] and he was keenly aware that a Cunhal triumph would have an adverse effect on Soviet relations with the bourgeois West. Nevertheless, Brezhnev was also highly sensitive to any intimation within the leadership that he was unenthusiastic about this prospect for introducing the "dictatorship of the proletariat" into Western Europe, and unready to accept a windfall.* The dilemma was complicated by Cunhal's aggressive tactics in "slicing the salami"—that is, in pressing the Portuguese leftist military junta to carry out an incremental purge of his party's rivals and former allies, and in seeking to avoid allowing free elections to settle the issue. This behavior created considerable alarm in the West, and was criticized by the Italian Communist Party.

The Soviet leadership resolved this dilemma with a compromise. Throughout 1974 and 1975 the Soviet regime funneled large sums into Portugal through different channels in order to help Cunhal.[105] At the same time, the Soviet leaders and most Soviet press commentary showed public restraint until Cunhal's offensive began to run into difficulties in August 1975. Finally, an authoritative ideologue was twice authorized to publish a thinly-disguised rebuke to the Italian Communists, which was an implicit defense of Cunhal's conduct.

This ideologue was Konstantin Zarodov, editor of the Soviet-run international communist journal *Problems of Peace and Socialism*. In April 1975, on the eve of Portuguese elections, Zarodov published in this journal a strong attack on those who would simply rely on a "mathematical" majority, assailing those (meaning the

---

* Suslov, it will be recalled, had asserted in June 1974 that the times were propitious for "further pushing ahead by revolutionary forces." This statement was made two months after a coup in Portugal had toppled the Caetano dictatorship and opened the way for the subsequent "pushing ahead" by the Portuguese Communist Party.

Italian Communists) who relied only on "declarations or votes" and were willing to "wait interminably" to take power, and demanding "the ability to consolidate one's revolutionary gains and raise them to a new plane." [106]

In August, with Cunhal now on the embattled defensive, Zarodov was given space in *Pravda* for an article that restated this message more prominently and created a public stir. He quoted Lenin as stating that "the proletariat must stage *a socialist coup,* winning semi-proletarian elements of the population to its side, in order to smash the bourgeoisie's resistance *by force* and paralyze the irresolution of the peasantry and petty bourgeoisie" (emphasis added). Zarodov gratuitously added that this instruction "reads today as if it referred to developments before our very eyes." [107] This statement in the central organ of the CPSU evoked considerable reaction in the West, including recriminations by the Italian and some other Western Communists.

The political denouement of this drama came on September 17, after Cunhal had suffered a major setback, when *Pravda* announced that Brezhnev had met with Zarodov and had "highly appraised" the work of the journal he edited. It is virtually certain that the general secretary intended this as symbolic confirmation–to his colleagues and to foreign Communists—that he endorsed Zarodov's position. It also seems plausible that Suslov had supported and encouraged Zarodov's line, and that Brezhnev now intended, by making this public obeisance to militant orthodoxy, to shore up his position within the oligarchy. Once again he had reasserted the Party's revolutionary legitimacy in order to offset the rhetoric of detente.

Even as this controversy unfolded, there occurred the second major event of 1975 that conditioned Soviet policy for years to come. This was the American defeat in Vietnam. In 1974 and 1975, the Soviet leadership's increasingly resolute determination not to forego any opportunities to advance had been reflected in continued and expanded military shipments to North Vietnam. Those deliveries greatly assisted Hanoi in its determination not to abide by the terms of the 1973 peace agreement, and were indispensable to the events that led to the sudden South Vietnamese collapse and the American humiliation in Saigon in the spring of 1975.

Events in Vietnam in turn furnished one of the preconditions for the third fundamental development of 1975: the new stage in Soviet behavior that began late in the year when new opportunities opened up in Africa.

THE ADVENTURES IN AFRICA AND SOUTHEAST ASIA

SOVIET CALCULATIONS IN AFRICA

The Soviet involvement in Africa after 1975 was both a new departure and the extension of an already well-established process. The continuity was provided by the increasing military contribution to Soviet policy since the later 1960s and by an evolving propensity, which had grown unimpeded throughout the era of detente, to seek geopolitical profit at U.S. expense through involvement in the security concerns of Third World clients. What was new came as a result of a fortuitous juxtaposition of five favorable historical factors: (1) Salazar's death and the Portuguese revolution, which precipitated the dissolution of the remnants of the Portuguese Empire and thus led to a showdown between rival Angolan factions; (2) the overthrow of Haile Selassie by a radical but ineffectual regime, whose hold on part of the inherited Ethiopian Empire was presently menaced by a traditional irredentism from Somalia; (3) the culmination of the American disaster in Vietnam, whose effect on American public opinion insured the paralysis of U.S. opposition to Soviet overseas ventures for years to come; (4) the growth of Soviet airlift and other logistical capabilities, which provided Soviet power-projection efforts with a new reach; and (5) the discovery that Cuba had the potential to furnish, for intervention under Soviet aegis, a corps of combat soldiers that would be both quantitatively and qualitatively significant under African conditions, yet far less offensive to African opinion than a Soviet expeditionary force of comparable size.

The Soviet Union gradually explored these possibilities as they emerged between 1975 and 1977. One notable aspect of Soviet behavior was the care the USSR took to minimize local political risks. Thus, the Cuban intervention on the side of the MPLA in Angola caused only modest disturbance among African observers; the much larger Soviet-Cuban effort on behalf of Haile-Mariam Mengistu was actually regarded with more sympathy than not, in view of the general distaste for Somalia's effort to alter African boundaries by force; and the scope of the subsequent Soviet-Cuban advisory role in support of ZAPU operations against Rhodesia was constrained within the framework set by the leaders of the Black African states that supported the Patriotic Front. The Soviets observed that this seizure of the dominant political heights rendered U.S. opposition to their efforts not only toothless but politically counterproductive. That is, the circumstances in the Horn of Africa and in south-central Africa, if not in Angola, were such that even if U.S. efforts to oppose the Soviets and Cubans by force had not been ruled out by American public opinion, they would have been deterred by their negative political consequences for American interests in Africa.*

Because the United States was thus doubly deterred on political grounds, and because there was consequently very little risk of military confrontation with the United States in any case, the Soviet achievement of strategic parity had only peripheral relevance for Soviet efforts in Africa. It was significant only to the extent that it continued to fuel Soviet confidence overall, and thus generally to encourage the broad outward thrust of Soviet policy. But despite the limited effect of the changing world military balance upon African events, many observers sensed a linkage. The repeated spectacle of vigorous Soviet action and U.S. inaction in a region where Western influence had formerly enjoyed an unchallenged predominance could only feed that general impression of a shifting balance of power already fostered by American misfortunes elsewhere. The Soviet leadership was cognizant of this impression and increasingly sought to play upon it.

* In the late 1970s, the strongly pro-American Kenyans, for example, were also fearful of Somali irredentist claims on Kenyan territory, and consequently wanted no active U.S. military support given to Somalia.

INDOCHINA

Soviet calculations were quite different in Indochina, the other significant arena that saw major Soviet security involvement before the invasion of Afghanistan. Here Soviet combat involvement was virtually nil, the major Soviet role was one of deterrence, and the implicit military risks were considerable. The net result was a further expansion of Soviet presence and influence at the expense of both the PRC and the United States.

Later, when the Sino-Vietnamese-Soviet military crisis of December 1978–March 1979 had subsided, the Soviets surely regarded the military benefits they had obtained from their new relationship with Vietnam as a useful offset to the adverse developments that had occurred in the Far East during 1978. Since Zbigniew Brzezinski's visit to Beijing in May, the Soviets had observed gradual and unwelcome changes in the U.S. position on Western arms sales to the PRC. In August, Japan had finally consented to sign a Sino-Japanese friendship treaty, long bitterly opposed by the Soviet Union, essentially on Chinese terms.

It is unlikely, however, that these developments *prompted* the drawing together of Vietnam and the Soviet Union, as some observers have suggested. It should not be forgotten that the decisive shift occurred in the position of Hanoi, and not in that of the USSR, which had long coveted military facilities in Vietnam and courted Hanoi for an alignment in opposition to China. The Vietnamese drift toward the USSR and away from China had been going on for several years before 1978, for reasons that had little to do with Chinese policy toward Japan and the United States. This process reached its culmination in November 1978, when a sudden jelling of Vietnamese intentions toward Cambodia made it much more urgent to secure a deterrent against China. Vietnam was now willing to accept the dependence on the USSR which Moscow had long desired and which Hanoi had long avoided.

Thus, the Politburo probably had an accurate sense of Vietnamese intentions when the USSR signed a friendship and security treaty with Vietnam in November 1978. The Soviet leaders surely knew that in at last agreeing to this formal act of alignment, the Vietnamese were consciously purchasing insurance against whatever military reaction the Chinese might mount when Vietnam acted to solve its problems with Pol Pot by overrunning Cambodia. This Hanoi then proceeded to do in the next two months.

Neither Moscow nor Hanoi appears to have foreseen, however, either the persistence of Pol Pot's resistance or the likelihood that the Chinese would in fact attack Vietnam in response. It is likely that the Soviet leadership was somewhat misled by its experience during the India-Pakistan war of late 1971. On that occasion, they had found that the military threat they posed on China's northern frontiers, together with the internal disarray created in Beijing by the Lin Biao crisis,[108] had prevented the PRC from coming to Pakistan's aid against an opponent bolstered by a new treaty relationship with the Soviet Union.[109] The U.S. government, according to Kissinger, had been gravely concerned that the PRC would march against India, thus precipitating a Sino-Soviet conflict with dangerous consequences for the United States.[110] Since this expectation had proved mistaken, the Soviet leaders apparently concluded, when they signed their November 1978 treaty with Hanoi, that the Chinese reaction to the anticipated Vietnamese blitzkrieg would again be totally paralyzed.*

In retrospect, the Soviets were quite fortunate that the Chinese military effort to teach Hanoi "a lesson," which unfolded in February and March 1979, was restricted in both scope and time and that the PRC thus made no attempt to penetrate to the Red River delta and threaten Hanoi. Despite the Soviets' large firepower advantage on the Sino-Soviet border, the Politburo's response during this episode demonstrated its great reluctance to become involved in a land war with China or to take any initiative that might seriously risk precipitating such a war.[111] Had the Chinese proceeded

---

* The Soviet calculations of November are likely to have been seriously complicated, however, by the sudden culmination of Sino-American normalization in December and the Deng Xiaoping visit to Washington the next month. Observing the extensive Sino-American consultations, the Brezhnev leadership probably remained uncertain as to the nature and extent of U.S. commitments, regardless of any private or public American disavowals. By the time that Sino-Vietnamese fighting began in February 1979, the Soviet leaders were probably somewhat less confident that a crisis with China would not lead to U.S. involvement.

to menace the viability of the Vietnamese regime or its capital, the Soviet leadership would have found the political costs extremely high had it not responded with some actions against China. But such actions would greatly have increased the possibility of a Sino-Soviet war, with incalculable possibilities for U.S. involvement. Once again, in order to score a quick gain for Soviet geopolitical interests, the Politburo had accepted an open-ended commitment whose implications had not been envisioned clearly.

In exchange for accepting these undefined risks, for supplying the Vietnamese war economy, and for providing certain logistical support to Hanoi, the Soviets at last found the Vietnamese, after years of equivocation during the struggle against the United States, totally aligned with them and isolated in dependence on them. Although the Vietnamese regime was still not subject to Soviet political control, it was now far more vulnerable to Soviet leverage than it had ever been. Moreover, by following in the footsteps of the Vietnamese as they consolidated their dominance over the Indochinese peninsula, the USSR was able to strengthen its political presence in Laos and to reestablish its presence in Cambodia. Finally, the Soviet military establishment was able to secure benefits it had long coveted: the right to conduct naval visits to Vietnamese ports, to use and develop large naval support facilities in those ports, to build and operate electronic facilities at the former U.S. base at Cam Ranh Bay, and to use Vietnamese airfields to stage long-range naval reconnaissance flights from the Soviet Far East.[112]

These benefits offered some conveniences to the Soviet Union in its gradually increasing effort to compete with the American naval presence in the Indian Ocean. More broadly, they provided a new increment in the slow but continuous process of supplanting the United States in those parts of the world where its presence had previously predominated.

THE INTERVENTION INTO AFGHANISTAN

Seen against this background, the question whether Soviet motives in invading Afghanistan in December 1979 were primarily defensive or essentially offensive is an illusory one.

Although there is little doubt that the Politburo regarded its immediate purpose in dispatching large forces to depose Hafizullah Amin, install Babrak Karmal, and take over the counterinsurgency struggle as primarily defensive, this is so only in the peculiar sense generally characteristic of Soviet assertive behavior. That is, the Soviet leadership saw itself as thereby defending *gains* that the Soviet Union had already won but not yet consolidated. In the process, the Politburo was also seeking to eliminate the possibility of an outright setback, which had arisen as a result of the very effort to advance: the unprecedented possibility that anti-Soviet rebels might take power in Kabul.

The Soviet Union was thus intervening militarily to defend a tentative and precarious advantage under challenge, just as it was simultaneously asserting itself politically in Europe to defend the advantageous balance of forces it had achieved there against NATO's effort to respond with nuclear deployments. In both cases, there was an offensive essence to a defensive concern.

At the same time, there is little doubt that the Politburo saw the advantage it wished to consolidate in Afghanistan not as an isolated circumstance, but as another in a progression of favorable changes that had taken place in different parts of the world in recent years. This sense of continuity had consequences. In allowing itself to be incrementally enticed into guaranteeing a Communist regime against the wishes of the Afghan population, the Politburo was almost certainly influenced by the trends of the past decade reviewed in this chapter. If the Soviet invasion was largely foreordained by the growing Soviet involvement in the defense of the Afghan regime since April 1978, that involvement was itself powerfully conditioned by the Politburo's perception of the trend in the world correlation of forces and by its vivid awareness that Soviet boldness in seizing opportunities had repeatedly been rewarded since 1967.

Given this context, the Politburo could never again be satisfied with the old Soviet relationship with Afghanistan. Although previous "neutral" Afghan regimes had been respectful of Soviet interests, the April 1978 Kabul coup had promised something more, the December 1978 Soviet-Afghan treaty had formalized this Soviet expectation, and neither the wishes of the Afghan majority nor the peculiarities of Amin could now be allowed to prevent its realization. Moreover, in 1978 and 1979 the Soviet Union had made increasingly heavy investments in men, weapons, and military prestige in an unsuccessful advisory effort to halt the Afghan insurgency. These investments had become additional reasons why the Soviets would pay almost any price to make the Afghan revolution "irreversible."

Finally, even as the difficulties of pacification multiplied, the lure of the strategic benefits waiting at the end of this process seems to have become more important. After the signing of the treaty of December 1978, buffer status was increasingly seen as insufficient for Afghanistan. More and more, this country appears to have become predestined, in Politburo thinking, to help to project Soviet geopolitical influence to the south.

Indeed, the Politburo probably believes that this has already begun to happen. Although the Soviet troop presence in Afghanistan has intensified animosity toward the USSR in neighboring Iran and Pakistan, it has also increased their fear of the Soviet Union. In the case of Pakistan, this movement of Soviet power southward has enhanced Soviet geopolitical leverage. The Soviet leaders may believe that over the long term this intimidating presence may enable the Soviet Union—even if it does not cross any additional boundaries—to inhibit Pakistan's military association with the United States and eventually to promote Pakistan's neutralization. The Politburo probably assumes that the American public is unlikely to endorse U.S. military guarantees to Pakistan strong enough to offset the demoralizing effects of Soviet military proximity.

The Politburo is likely to become accustomed to this new, risk-free geopolitical benefit, and this will probably become a supplementary reason for retaining a permanent Soviet military presence in Afghanistan, even in the unlikely event that the security situation there should ever, itself, permit a Soviet withdrawal. Over the long term, therefore, it is highly probable that the Soviets will remain in Afghanistan, although they may continue to drop hints about the possibility of withdrawal in an effort to reduce the adverse political consequences of their conduct. As in the case of the Soviet forces stationed in Czechoslovakia, the strategic advantage of forward deployment outside the USSR will increasingly reinforce the security motives that originally led them to intervene.

To be sure, this is by no means the whole story. The Soviets are acutely aware of the negative consequences of their intervention into Afghanistan, including their ongoing, long-term problem in pacifying a traditionally ferocious and defiant population. I shall defer to Chapter 5 a discussion of how the Soviet leaders are likely to balance what they see as the positive and negative aspects of their occupation of Afghanistan, and what effects this experience may have on their behavior in the 1980s.

In this chapter we have examined the panorama of Soviet behavior in the last decade from several perspectives, seeking to show the dynamic interaction over time of various internal and external factors. One such factor was the complex Soviet heritage from the 1960s, which throughout the 1970s imposed a certain pattern of relationships on the Soviet oligarchy and imported a certain momentum to Soviet behavior in the Third World.

A second factor was the evolution of the Soviet economy, which had consequences both for relationships within the Politburo and for the Politburo's behavior toward the West in general and the United States in particular.

A third factor was the intersection of Soviet external policy and internal politics with autonomous, unexpected external events, each of which nudged Soviet behavior on along a somewhat altered path. Such events included: the Chinese behavior on the Sino-Soviet border in 1969, the election of the Brandt government in West Germany in 1969, the evolution of hostilities between India and Pakistan in 1971, the emergence of the Portuguese Communist opportunity in 1974–1975, the Portuguese decision to pull out of Angola in 1975, the Somali invasion of the Ethiopian Ogaden region in 1977, the emergence of a Communist opportunity to stage a coup in Kabul in April 1978, and the ultimately disastrous pugnacity that Cambodia showed toward Vietnam before 1978. The Soviet leaders reacted to each of these developments sometimes by modifying previous policy but more commonly by deciding to accelerate it. In each case, as I have suggested, the Soviet reaction was conditioned by an underlying conviction that most Soviet and American interests are fundamentally incompatible.

Finally, perhaps the most profound influence on the whole Soviet experience with detente was the complex intertwining of Soviet and American domestic political realities. By resorting instinctively to preemptive repression in response to the domestic threat it felt detente posed, the Soviet leadership in the end undercut its ability to exploit the many asymmetrical vulnerabilities that detente simultaneously exposed in American society. Meanwhile, Brezhnev's own political needs in his various dealings with his colleagues led him first toward detente and then away from it, and this change was strongly influenced by the consequences of the secular decline in the American presidency during the Nixon, Ford, and Carter administrations, as the coherence of American policy was increasingly beset by a rampaging pluralism.

This tale of two cities did not end in the 1970s. In Chapter 5, we shall review the most recent developments in the Soviet and American leaderships, and examine their effects on the worldwide interaction between the United States and the Soviet Union.

5 / Brezhnev's Legacy to His Successors

In conclusion, we will now consider the salient events of the last few years within the Soviet regime, as well as their implications for future Soviet behavior in the world arena. I will first comment on the political and economic circumstances surrounding Brezhnev's final struggle, and then review Andropov's behavior in his first year in power. Against this background, I will draw conclusions about the prospects for the leadership's attitude toward America in the light of the policy heritage from Brezhnev and the trends at work in the United States.

THE GRINDING DOWN OF THE BREZHNEV REGIME

Toward the end of the 1970s, many of the terms of the domestic political equation set forth in this book had begun to change. Within the leadership, gradual subterranean shifts in personal relationships, proceeding in barely perceptible fashion throughout the second half of the decade, inched the oligarchy toward the factional eruption and radical realignments that took place in 1982.

THE TWO PROCESSES OF DETERIORATION

The oligarchs were affected, above all, by two long-term parallel processes: the continuous, apparently insoluble deterioration of the

174

economic situation, and the progressive decline in Brezhnev's phys- ical capabilities. The political effects of the two trends intertwined with and reinforced each other.

The flattening of the economy's growth curves, the dislocations in key economic sectors, and the increasingly severe dilemma of resource allocation appear to have promoted a growing sense of malaise and exasperation among certain of the oligarchs. This sense of unease was heightened by the impression that the country was beset by deteriorating social morale and ever-widening corruption. In retrospect it is clear that those oligarchs who felt this way—like many persons outside the leadership—tended to identify this creep- ing economic and social paralysis with the perpetuation of Brezh- nev's power as his health declined. Meanwhile, as we shall see, the radical and painful choices that were made in resource allocation in the latter half of the 1970s further weakened Brezhnev's political consensus.

The consequences became plainly visible, however, only in Brezh- nev's last year, when his political control was gravely damaged by the disappearance of Suslov, the quickening of his own physical decline, and the widespread perception that his end was near. He then suffered—for the first time since he had replaced Khrushchev— decisive defections by former supporters as well as a major defeat that had long been in the making. This set the stage for the new coalition that took power upon his death, led by Yuriy Andropov.

In retrospect, the events of the late 1970s appear to have created three areas of potential vulnerability for Brezhnev, though the general secretary proved strong enough to avoid the consequences until circumstances produced the moment of truth in 1982.

THE SUPPLANTING OF KIRILENKO BY CHERNENKO

First, Brezhnev had created a latent vulnerability in the Secre- tariat, where his potential strength was considerably diminished as a result of the gradual decline and eventual eclipse of his erstwhile lieutenant Andrey Kirilenko and the substitution of a new favorite, Konstantin Chernenko. As an experienced and respected party administrator with great seniority, Kirilenko until the middle 1970s had buttressed Brezhnev's position in the Secretariat and increased the general secretary's leverage in dealing with colleagues who were not Secretariat members. Chernenko, a staff official with no "line" experience, had never enjoyed comparable respect. Indeed, several of Brezhnev's leading colleagues evidently regarded him as an upstart and usurper, a humble retainer whom Brezhnev had catapulted into the Politburo against the will of the leadership consensus.

Brezhnev's insistence that Chernenko be elevated to the oligarchy—and subsequently that he be promoted as a major contender for the succession—thus violated a tacit Politburo understanding in the post-Stalin era that experience in the administration of major party committees or large government bureaucracies is a prerequisite for admission to the leadership. Chernenko's advent may well have reminded some of the oligarchs of Khrushchev's plan in 1964— forestalled by his ouster—to place his son-in-law, A. I. Adzhubey, on the party Secretariat.[1] Because of its implications for the succession, this unilateral elevation of Chernenko may have been the most serious offense Brezhnev ever committed against the oligarchic consensus. Brezhnev was presumably well aware of his colleagues' reactions.

Why did Brezhnev take the political risks involved in jettisoning Kirilenko and advancing Chernenko? Any judgment about the causes of Brezhnev's estrangement from Kirilenko in the late 1970s must be speculative, but two interrelated explanations seem plausible. One hypothesis concerns the effects of the growing differences over resource allocation; the other involves Brezhnev's perception of the new political needs created by his advancing age and deteriorating health.

It is probably not coincidental that Kirilenko's political decline, which began very gradually in the second half of the 1970s but accelerated at the turn of the decade,[2] proceeded in parallel with the leadership's drastic and far-reaching decision to reduce the planned growth rate of capital investment. This annual rate was halved in the Tenth Five-Year Plan, which went into effect in 1976, and sharply cut again in the Eleventh Five-Year Plan, which began in 1981. These radical and unprecedented decisions were taken in reaction to the progressive slowdown in the growth rate of the economy, and reflected Brezhnev's determination to preserve a stable share of the resource pie for agriculture and the military while cushioning the impact of the slowdown upon consumption. In the absence of compensating advances in productivity, which Brezhnev kept demanding in vain, this capital starvation had an increasingly negative effect on most of Soviet industrial production.

It is therefore quite possible, as Myron Rush has suggested, that Kirilenko, overseer and ardent defender of the machine-building industry, objected strenuously to these decisions.[3] If this was indeed the case, then the rift between Kirilenko and Brezhnev probably grew as—and because—Brezhnev continued to pursue this policy, which culminated in the adoption of the final version of the Eleventh Five-Year Plan.

Kirilenko may well have been willing to oppose Brezhnev on this issue because his own hopes of succeeding Brezhnev were now in any case rapidly dwindling. Ever since Kirilenko joined the central Secretariat in 1966, he had been the logical if unannointed heir apparent to the party leader. As Brezhnev's chief lieutenant, he played a role somewhat analogous to that which Brezhnev had played for Khrushchev after 1963. But the hopes evoked by this precedent had virtually disappeared by the time the general secretary entered his eighth decade, clinging to power more tenaciously than ever despite his worsening health. Kirilenko was several months older than Brezhnev.

Meanwhile, Brezhnev, for his part, also recalled the role he had played for Khrushchev—particularly in October 1964. After the mid-1970s this memory apparently helped to change his mind about the qualities he now required in a first lieutenant. As his physical capabilities deteriorated, Brezhnev evidently became increasingly convinced that his chief agent should not be a powerful ally with views and interests of his own—interests that would inevitably include an eventual desire to supplant his faltering patron. Rather, Brezhnev now needed an obedient and trustworthy figure who was completely dependent upon him, who could be trusted precisely because of his lack of independent political strength. Elevated to the Politburo, this agent would move at Brezhnev's side when

Brezhnev could function and maintain vigilance during the increasingly frequent periods when he could not. It seems probable, therefore, that Brezhnev's primary motive in engineering Chernenko's scandalously rapid rise was not concern for the succession but rather the desire to safeguard his own power as long as possible against the hazards created by his physical decline.*

It should also be noted that Brezhnev had other alternatives; he could have taken steps to move a more credible alternative than Chernenko into Kirilenko's place in the Secretariat. One leading option of this kind was surely to promote Vladimir Shcherbitskiy, who had succeeded Shelest as first secretary of the Ukrainian party and who was, like Chernenko, a longtime personal associate of Brezhnev's. The general secretary's failure to implement this option evidently reflected his determination not to introduce into the Secretariat any new figure whose political stature might enable him to display independent views—or to dislodge the leader.† The result was that Shcherbitskiy, a full Politburo member since 1971, remained marooned in Kiev, deprived by his patron of the Moscow platform from which he could play a leading role in the increasingly imminent succession struggle. It is not surprising, then, that Shcherbitskiy is reported to have joined those who deserted Brezhnev at the turning point of Brezhnev's last year, the showdown that occurred in May 1982.[4]

THE ESTRANGEMENT OF THE ANDROPOV-USTINOV-GROMYKO PHALANX

Even as Brezhnev's latent strength in the Secretariat was being eroded, the potential was growing for future difficulties with three senior Politburo members who were not members of the Secretariat:

---

* This conduct of course had major consequences for the succession, but these consequences surely were not Brezhnev's primary concern. To the last day of his life he fought to maximize his own power, not to ensure Chernenko's role after he was gone. He did not stand in the cold on Lenin's mausoleum for two hours on November 7—the event that probably precipitated his death—in order to enhance Chernenko's position in his funeral cortege.

† One may also speculate that Shcherbitskiy too had reservations about the drastic new cuts in investment, and that this was known or surmised by Brezhnev.

KGB Chairman Andropov, Defense Minister Ustinov, and Foreign Minister Gromyko.

As we observed in Chapter 2, Brezhnev had evidently intended the admission of the heads of these three "national security" bureaucracies to the Politburo in 1973 to create a new source of political support, supplementing and extending the advantage he derived from his control of the Secretariat and the central party apparatus. The leaders of these three organizations, nominally subordinate to the Council of Ministers but in fact responsible only to the Politburo and the general secretary, formed a prestigious phalanx within the oligarchy which Brezhnev for a time was indeed able to employ in support of his interests. After the start of the new decade, however, he paid a price for his action in 1973. As Brezhnev's strength ebbed and the succession grew closer, this phalanx turned away from him to prepare for the future. One of these three men, Andropov, then set out to position himself to succeed Brezhnev by seeking to undermine the general secretary's power; and the other two supported this effort.

The Military Withdraws Its Blessings

Even as these changes were gradually eroding both the personal loyalty of the national security triumvirate and Brezhnev's ability to use the Secretariat to dominate the Politburo, Brezhnev's long cultivation of the military establishment was also beginning to produce diminishing returns.

As already suggested, there is reason to suspect that military leaders had ample cause for unhappiness with the continuing slowdown in Soviet economic growth. Despite Brezhnev's efforts to protect the military priority, this slowdown was reducing the expansion of the economic base—particularly in machine building—on which future military-industrial needs would depend.

Beyond this, there is now some reason to suspect that at long last, the extent of the military priority itself may have begun to appear seriously insufficient to the military leadership. In 1983, Western press accounts and congressional studies increasingly suggested that the growth in spending on Soviet defense may have slowed down since the late 1970s, largely because of a leveling off of weapons procurement. In this view, "the share of the economy devoted to defense—the military burden—did not change" over this period, because the growth in military spending was, in effect, held down by circumstances to the slowing rate of growth of the economy as a whole.[5] One explanation offered for this phenomenon was that "problems in the economy, such as transportation bottlenecks, inadequate supplies of steel and energy, and inability to assimilate new technology, had harmful effects on defense production." [6]

If these suggestions are accurate, it would seem plausible to suppose that some Soviet military leaders became increasingly discontented with this trend, particularly in view of the inauguration of the new U.S. military buildup during the Carter administration and its acceleration thereafter. Under these circumstances, the point at issue may have been the desire of professional military leaders to make even greater demands on the already strained resources of the civilian economy that feed military production, in order to compensate for a declining ability to extract the quantities of hardware they desired from the sums allocated. There is some fragmentary evidence, considered below, to suggest that the frustration of this desire had led important elements in the Soviet military hierarchy to become somewhat disillusioned with Brezhnev by the start of the new decade. Despite the breadth of Soviet military programs, the enormous results achieved, the very large proportion of GNP that continued to be devoted to military purposes, and the sacrifices this continued to mean for civilian consumption, some military leaders now seemed unhappy with the man who had cultivated their support since 1965.

In the year before Brezhnev's death, this disillusionment became publicly visible. Particularly in a notable article in the July 1981 *Kommunist,* Chief of the General Staff Nikolay Ogarkov began stridently to insist that there existed a real danger of war; clearly, his extravagant terms were intended to imply the need to increase military spending. What was especially noteworthy was that Ogarkov went so far as to criticize "party propaganda" explicitly, claiming it had not done enough to inculcate awareness of this danger among the population.[7] This was, on the face of it, an apparent violation of protocol: ordinarily no Soviet military man is ever authorized publicly to criticize the operations of the centralized party propaganda machine. Almost inevitably, many readers of the leading party journal must have interpreted the words of the country's leading professional soldier as implicit criticism of Brezhnev, who was ultimately responsible for the management of the party machine and the line it was following.

That some tension existed between Brezhnev and sections of the military establishment in the last years of Brezhnev's life was also suggested by certain passages in the speech Brezhnev delivered before the assembled military leadership a month before his death. While assuring the marshals that the party leadership "adopts measures to meet all your needs," he implied that the military leadership must make more vigorous efforts to translate the resources given them into greater military capabilities. At the same time, he went to extravagant lengths in his praise of Defense Minister Ustinov, whom he termed a "loyal son of the Leninist party" and his "comrade-in-arms." [8] It seems likely that the general secretary was appealing for Ustinov's support on two fronts: on the one hand, to help contain the dissatisfaction of the marshals,[9] and on the other hand, to help Brezhnev withstand the political challenge being mounted by Andropov. The second appeal, however, was by then a forlorn cause.

The Final Year

Brezhnev thus began the last year of his life amid contradictory portents. On the surface, his power still seemed quite impressive. In the last few years he had been able to railroad his colleagues into accepting a number of changes that many of them certainly did not like. As already noted, he had used personal fiat to push Chernenko up three rungs of the ladder of Soviet leadership in indecent haste, making him a secretary of the Central Committee by 1976, a candidate member of the Politburo in 1977, and a full member in 1978. As Brezhnev turned against Kirilenko, he in 1979 demoted Kirilenko's associate Yakov Ryabov from his position as party secretary for military industry after only three years on the job. When Premier Kosygin resigned in ill health shortly before his death in 1980, Brezhnev without difficulty inserted one old crony (Nikolay Tikhonov) in his place and appointed another crony (Ivan Arkhipov) as Tikhonov's first deputy.[10] Simultaneously, he forced through a series of controversial resource allocation decisions beginning with the drastic cuts in investment and concluding with the enormously expensive Food Program. And finally, his growing cult, to which all his colleagues were compelled to defer, reached a peak at the 26th Party Congress in February 1981.*

But like the wonderful one-horse shay, Brezhnev's structure of power had decayed on the inside without giving any overt sign, and in 1982 it broke down all at once. The decisive change, which cleared the way for all the others, was the death of Suslov in January. As was generally recognized in the West, the passing of the Kingmaker removed the key element of balance and stability in the oligarchy. In particular, it immediately made Brezhnev vulnerable in two respects.

First, by removing the primary guardian of Politburo political decorum, it exposed Brezhnev to multiple indirect attacks that focused on the general secretary's toleration and protection of corruption in the Soviet aristocracy. These attacks appear to have been engineered primarily by Andropov. Suslov had evidently opposed the airing of the corruption issue within the oligarchy, for he was aware that the phenomenon was so widespread that an offensive against it could, like destalinization, easily be employed as an instrument of factional combat. Unfortunately for Brezhnev,

---

* Similarly, Khrushchev's cult had reached a peak at his birthday celebrations in April 1964, six months before his overthrow. It would appear that Western observers have somewhat overestimated the operational significance of a cult of the leader in the present Soviet oligarchy. The ability to compel colleagues to defer in this manner cannot necessarily be translated into an ability to compel loyalty at critical turning points. Rather, the use of the cult by both Khrushchev and Brezhnev appears to have increased resentments that strengthened the tendency toward treachery by erstwhile supporters. The use of the cult in the post-Stalin leadership has thus resembled the Chinese practice of beating cymbals to frighten away demons. Although the accompanying noise is intended to intimidate, it has often served to distract attention from underlying weaknesses.

Suslov's death came soon after the first such oblique attack on Brezhnev's position, an attack that involved his daughter Galina Churbanov.[11]

Even more important, Suslov's passing inevitably posed the issue of who would replace Suslov as the ranking Central Committee secretary under Brezhnev, and thus brought the question of succession to the fore. Since Kirilenko was in disfavor, on his way out of the leadership and in any case in poor health, Chernenko was now the most senior candidate in the Secretariat. Should he be confirmed as Suslov's successor, and should there be no other serious contender in place in the Secretariat when Brezhnev died, Chernenko would have a considerable advantage in the succession struggle. When after Suslov's funeral Chernenko in fact began to receive protocol treatment as the second-ranking Soviet leader—obviously at Brezhnev's direction—many of the oligarchs evidently became alarmed.

The issue was made more pressing when Brezhnev was disabled for several weeks in April by what was rumored to be a mild stroke, reminding all concerned that the succession crisis could occur at any moment. Soon after his apparent recovery, the political turning point of the year occurred, at a Politburo session that approved the transfer of Yuriy Andropov to the party Secretariat from the chairmanship of the KGB. This decision was duly announced to a May plenum of the Central Committee, and then to the world.

Andropov's return to the Secretariat allowed him to escape from a post in which it would be very awkward and difficult to aspire for the General Secretaryship. He now held a position that made him the logical alternative to Chernenko. For Brezhnev, Andropov now represented an alien and hostile force in the body that controlled the party machinery. It is most unlikely that Brezhnev welcomed this change. Some reports have alleged that the Politburo was sharply divided on this occasion, with Brezhnev and a few of his closest adherents losing to a coalition made up of the three heads of the national security bureaucracies, three independent party figures, and one apostate, Shcherbitskiy.[12] It is by no means certain, however, that the issue was in fact brought to a formal Politburo vote; such formal confrontations are infrequent in Soviet practice. But it is probable that Brezhnev in any case yielded reluctantly to what he recognized as an extraordinary combination of Politburo opinion against him.

Brezhnev's remaining months were apparently taken up with the sparring that resulted from the new situation, as Chernenko lobbied for support with regional party organizations and Andropov bided his time. It would appear, however, that Brezhnev's setback in the May decision to transfer Andropov had diminished his power to intimidate, thereby weakening his political position considerably. The changed situation was demonstrated by Brezhnev's continuing inability to halt the steady flow of rumors hostile to him and Chernenko and favorable to Andropov which Andropov supporters disseminated to the Western press throughout the year. As we have seen, Shelepin's supporters had conducted a similar campaign of calculated anti-Brezhnev leaks in 1965, but this effort proved counterproductive to Shelepin's interests because it intensified anxiety about Shelepin within the oligarchy and united a leadership coalition intent on constraining him. In contrast, by the spring of 1982 a majority hostile to the Chernenko succession and favorable to that of Andropov appears already to have coalesced in the leadership, and the new campaign of leaks tacitly reflected the views of this majority. By demonstrating the invulnerability of those who planted the leaks—their identity was presumably well known to the KGB—Andropov was also demonstrating Brezhnev's inability, in his physically weakened and politically damaged condition, to grasp the levers of power firmly enough to exact reprisals.[13]

Nevertheless, so long as Brezhnev occupied the general secretary's office, his powers of initiative were formidable, and if he had lived another year it is not out of the question that he might have reversed the political tide. His address in October to the assembled military leaders was, among other things, a vigorous attempt to convey the impression to all concerned that he was still in charge. It was probably because the Andropov camp feared the consequences of a prolonged stalemate that another leak—claiming Brezhnev would step down at the end of the year—was disseminated to the West in the fall of 1982 and then officially denied.[14] Since

Brezhnev evidently would not have retired voluntarily, it is conceivable that an attempt to force him to do so might eventually have materialized within the leadership.

In any event, no such action was necessary; Brezhnev passed away in November, and the Politburo thereafter ratified the choice that had been forecast by the decision in May. Several accounts agree that the most vigorous voice heard in support of the Andropov candidacy was that of Defense Minister Ustinov.[15]

Thus, fourteen months after General Wojciech Jaruzelski had taken control of the Polish party, and eleven months after he had imposed martial law and "discipline" on Poland, the man who had headed the KGB longer than anyone else in Soviet history became head of the Soviet party. He enjoyed particular support from the minister of defense, and he held aloft the banner of "discipline" for the Soviet Union. It is by no means impossible that the Polish example had contributed to the Soviet result.

PROSPECTS: THE DOMESTIC INHERITANCE

Thus supported, Andropov was propelled into power in November 1982 amid general expectations that he would impart new vigor, adroitness, and flexibility to Soviet policy, both foreign and domestic. In general, however, the events of his first year in office did not bear out these predictions. Both at home and abroad, the new general secretary seemed constrained by the intractable forces of Soviet inertia, and by an evident reluctance to assume the personal political risks involved in striving vigorously for policy changes. And as the year went on, once again the prospects for meaningful change in the Soviet Union became further encumbered by a Soviet party leader's worsening health.

In the realm of leadership politics, Andropov made some progress in strengthening his personal position, but this progress was uneven and inconsistent, and by the end of the first year there was still a large gap between his growing titular status and his power over his colleagues. Within eight months he succeeded in gathering to himself the two auxiliary offices that Brezhnev had required much longer to conquer: the chairmanship of the Defense Council, and the post of chairman of the Presidium of the Supreme Soviet (the Soviet "Presidency"). Andropov's assumption of the Defense Council position, publicly revealed by Ustinov in the spring of 1983, was probably not difficult. As suggested earlier, there was ample precedent regarding this organization and its precursors upon which to build a consensus that the Defense Council must be headed by the general secretary. The conquest of the presidency proved a more complex task, however. There were strong hints of a leadership impasse on this question from the outset, and it was only at a June 1983 plenum of the Central Committee—or rather, at the Politburo meeting that preceded this plenum and may be presumed to have determined its decisions—that the issue was decided in Andropov's favor. Simultaneously, the new general secretary was able to secure a plenum resolution that for the first time asserted that the Politburo was "headed by Andropov."

Andropov had more difficulty, however, in translating this heightened status into the ability to begin to pack the leadership with trusted supporters. To be sure, some important changes at secondary levels proved possible.* There is no doubt that the general secretary obtained some advantage from these lower-level shifts in his ongoing contention with his Brezhnevite opponents, Secretary Chernenko and Premier Tikhonov.[16] But in striving to alter the balance of forces in the Politburo and Secretariat, Andropov was forced to work through indirection, making advances on the margin, seeking alliances. During his first year the inner circle of full Politburo members shrank; there were three subtractions—produced by the death of Brezhnev, the removal of the ailing Kirilenko, and the death of Suslov's old ally, Control Commission chairman Arvid

---

* The heads of some organs of the Central Committee apparatus were purged (as in the case of the Propaganda Department's Tyazhelnikov) or else shifted laterally to other responsibilities (as in the case of I. V. Kapitonov, head of the Organizational Party Work Department). Charges of corruption furnished a pretext to replace a few of the most vulnerable Brezhnev cronies in the government (such as Interior Minister N. A. Shchelokov) and in the regional party apparatus. Promotions or death also gave Andropov opportunities to place new men at the head of the party machines in Leningrad, Belorussia, and Azerbaydzhan.

Pelshe—but only one addition, not very helpful to Andropov.* It was obvious that at least during the first year, the coalition that had placed Andropov in office was unwilling or unable to help him reshape the Politburo to his liking.† It also appears probable that this coalition was in any case loose and potentially unstable.

Meanwhile, it was also evident from the beginning that to consolidate his position, Andropov had a strong need to build a personal power base in the Secretariat, traditionally the most important lever of power in the regime, to complement the strength he derived from his "national security" constituency outside the Secretariat (that is, from his influence in the KGB and the military and from the personal backing of Gromyko). At the outset, Andropov apparently not only lacked the power to advance his own protégés to senior positions in the Secretariat, but also lacked suitable protégés—that is, an appropriate coterie of loyal party functionaries from which to select. Having come to the top from outside the regional party ladder, Andropov lacked the network of regional party clients traditionally accumulated by an *apparatchik* on the rise, and his past associates in the KGB and the party foreign policy apparatus were implausible candidates to propose to the Politburo for senior Secretariat status. In this respect, Andropov began with a handicap that had not faced Brezhnev in 1964.‡

Andropov was therefore forced to seek allies among those full Politburo members who were either already on the Secretariat or who could readily be transferred to that body. In the first category he found Mikhail Gorbachev, the youngest member of the Politburo

---

* This was the Azerbaydzhani leader Geydar Aliyev, apparently on good terms with both Andropov and Chernenko, who was soon advanced to be first deputy premier and a full Politburo member. This consensus appointment was later followed by the designation of Foreign Minister Gromyko, one of Andropov's firmest allies, to be another first deputy premier, strengthening somewhat Andropov's leverage in the Council of Ministers.

† Subsequently, however, Andropov at last began to make some progress; in December 1983 Vitaliy Vorotnikov and Mikhail Solomentsev were promoted to full Politburo status and KGB Chairman Viktor Chebrikov became a candidate Politburo member.

‡ Andropov did manage to find protégés to introduce into the Secretariat in a junior capacity: the technocrat Nikolay Ryzhkov in November 1982, and the new head of the Organizational Party Work Department, Yegor Ligachev, in December 1983.

and the secretary in charge of agriculture, who evidently found it to his advantage to conclude a working alliance with a sixty-nine year old general secretary who was already in uncertain health. As this alliance progressed, Gorbachev was evidently rewarded with additional scope in the Secretariat, including some responsibilities for overseeing personnel changes.

In the second category Andropov settled for the transfer of Grigoriy Romanov, the Leningrad first secretary who throughout Brezhnev's tenure had competed with Shcherbitskiy of the Ukraine for elevation to Moscow. Both men seem likely to have sided with Andropov during his 1982 struggle for the succession against Chernenko; the choice of Romanov in 1983 may have reflected some subsequent cooling of relations between Shcherbitskiy and the new general secretary. Romanov now joined Gorbachev as the ranking members of the central Secretariat after Andropov and Chernenko, and barring further changes, these two relatively young Andropov allies thus became the best-positioned early possibilities for the eventual succession to Andropov. Romanov's transfer, however, bore the signs of a consensus Politburo decision; he appeared to be a compromise choice, and was thus a highly uncertain addition to Andropov's strength. His rather tough views also seemed an ominous portent for the post-Andropov future.*

In sum, by the end of his first year in office, Andropov had achieved some changes in the balance of forces within the Secretariat, but the ultimate effects of these changes remained ambiguous. At the age of sixty-nine, his serious health problems raised increasing doubt whether he would be given sufficient time to build his personal position. As many Western observers noted, he had both a pressing need and the obvious desire to act much more quickly than Brezhnev had at a comparable stage in building his personal power and

---

* Andropov apparently found Romanov the best he could get from his colleagues to resolve the problem of how to bolster the depleted Secretariat. But it seemed by no means certain that Romanov, a forceful and independent figure who had acquired a reputation as an ideologically conservative version of Khrushchev, would in future see eye to eye with the general secretary on contentious policy matters. In particular, it seemed possible that the Romanov appointment might complicate Andropov's future dealings with the military establishment on resource allocation issues. As party leader in Leningrad, a major center of Soviet military industry, Romanov had been an exceptionally outspoken partisan of defense industry.

pushing through his program—processes that were mutually dependent. Yet it remained an open question whether the evolving constellation of forces in the Politburo would allow him to do so in the limited time available. Much would depend upon his skill in building ad hoc coalitions within the oligarchy to force through specific controversial changes. Much would also depend upon the sequence in which his aged senior colleagues left the scene, and upon Andropov's ability to coordinate within the Politburo advantageous replacements.*

In domestic policy, the new leadership's first months were dominated by the expansion of the campaign against corruption which had helped to bring Andropov to power and by an associated and widely publicized drive to tighten discipline in all fields. The avowed central purpose of both campaigns was to extract from the Soviet working population the increase in productivity that had eluded Brezhnev. These campaigns had some utility, both for the Soviet Union and for Andropov. Nevertheless, this usefulness appeared limited on both counts.

So far as the efforts to enforce worker discipline were concerned, although the novel and stringent measures initially adopted against shirkers and absentees probably had a shock value that gave a temporary boost to productivity, a point of diminishing returns was soon reached. The draconian steps originally taken were presently found to be so depressing to morale as to be counterproductive to material incentives, and they were gradually relaxed.

So far as the anticorruption campaign was concerned, Andropov faced two inherent difficulties, one economic and the other political.

---

* In this connection one potentially contentious appointment issue looming for the Politburo was the question of what to do when Defense Minister Ustinov (seventy-five by the end of Andropov's first year) passed away. The leaders would then face the dual decision of whether to appoint a military professional (such as Ogarkov) to replace Ustinov as defense minister, and whether to elevate the new defense minister to Ustinov's place on the Politburo. These two decisions, taken together, were likely to have an effect on the political status of the military establishment. It is noteworthy that the pattern set in 1973, when the heads of the three national security bureaucracies were placed on the Politburo, has now been reaffirmed by Brezhnev's heirs, since Andropov's replacement as KGB chief—Viktor Chebrikov—was named a candidate Politburo member in December 1983. This could become a precedent. (See the discussion in Dimitri K. Simes, "National Security under Andropov," *Problems of Communism,* January-February 1983, pp. 32–39.)

On the one hand, efforts to wipe out illegal economic activity soon raised the question of where the line was to be drawn, since the functioning of the legal Soviet economy overseen by Gosplan had become to a considerable extent dependent on the supplementary effects of widespread, technically illegal but long-tolerated activities outside official supervision that were made possible and furthered by official corruption.[17] Thus, corruption in the Soviet Union is the necessary result of winking at the "second economy" while declaring it illegal. The more sweeping the attack on corruption, therefore, the more this offensive impinged on the "second economy," and the more likely it was to produce dislocations in the Soviet economy as a whole, particularly in the supply of services. Moreover, as earlier noted, because corruption had become so endemic in the Soviet system, efforts to combat it were necessarily to some extent arbitrary and selective, and the process of selection inevitably had political overtones, affecting the relative status of functionaries throughout the feudal party apparatus, including those in the Politburo. Anticorruption actions were therefore innately political ventures, offering both potential advantages and disadvantages to Andropov. Since the resentment they fostered in some quarters within the leadership could sometimes be counterproductive to his interests, it is likely that here, too, the general secretary was aware of a need for some discretion.

On the whole, these campaigns gave the impression of being inadequate substitutes for meaningful change—evasions and improvisations that masked the new leadership's inability to come to grips with the underlying difficulties of the Soviet economy. It is likely that the post-Brezhnev leadership's propensity to put off addressing these fundamental issues was accentuated by the improved economic results of 1983. The discipline campaign evidently helped produce a considerable spurt in industrial production early in the year, although the rate of increase fell off rapidly thereafter. Thanks largely to much better weather, crops also improved in Andropov's first year over the previous year's bad performance, and the rate of growth of the economy as a whole, which had declined to 2 percent in previous years, also seemed likely to be somewhat better. But fulfillment of the Eleventh Five-Year Plan remained unlikely, and Brezhnev's heirs continued to face the adverse secular trends that had bedeviled the economy under Brezhnev, notably the stagnation of productivity and the long-term decline in new labor imputs. The burden of defense upon the civilian economy remained enormous, and a systematic attack on this problem remained incompatible with the Politburo's view of the Soviet Union's position in the world. As before, Soviet leaders faced almost equally great political difficulties should they wish to turn to either of the two major remedies for the economy's problems generally discussed in the West: a large-scale reallocation of resources away from the military sector, or a fundamental economic reform involving far-reaching devolution of control from the hands of the central industrial managers. While Andropov—and still more, some of his advisers—seemed attracted by the notion of economic reform,[18] Andropov's behavior appeared highly inhibited by the entrenched resistance throughout the regime to such reform.

Less inhibited was the evident inclination of Brezhnev's heirs to tighten the ideological screws in the Soviet Union, to clamp down on lack of conformity among the intelligentsia, and to try to impose greater controls and increased uniformity on the East European regimes. This tendency was apparently regarded within the Politburo as a necessary response to the worsening international atmosphere and the increased danger of ideological subversion. The harsher ideological trend furnished an ironical commentary to the effort Andropov's unofficial representatives in Moscow had made at the outset of his regime to portray him as a closet liberal.[19]

As Archie Brown has observed, Andropov had originally appealed both to those around him who craved the imposition of greater discipline and to those who saw an urgent need for reform.[20] It would appear from his first year in power that he found it much easier—at least at the outset—to build personal support within the Party by pleasing the first audience than by relying upon the second. By the close of that initial year, the deferred agenda of reform seemed likely to be further deferred by the growing uncertainty whether Andropov would long survive, and by the commencement of jockeying in the Soviet leadership for another succession to an ailing leader. Within the unchanging oligarchic framework, a new cycle in the struggle for power had commenced. Meanwhile, the Soviet socioeconomic difficulties inherited from Brezhnev continued to accumulate, and impinged increasingly on the leadership's foreign policy choices.

PROSPECTS: THE FOREIGN POLICY INHERITANCE

After Brezhnev's death, the internal landscape of Soviet politics and Soviet economic policy seemed, for the first time in many years, to raise the possibility of historic change but provided little assurance that this promise would be fulfilled. What of the external dimension? What is the likelihood that Brezhnev's successors will significantly modify the foreign policy assumptions of his regime, particularly in shaping Soviet behavior toward the United States in the world arena? Any attempt to answer these questions must seriously consider the extent to which the momentum of Soviet policy and the weight of existing attitudes and interests will determine future behavior. In the world beyond Soviet borders, Andropov inherited a complex set of achievements, obligations, dangers and possibilities. The behavior of Brezhnev's heirs has inevitably been affected by the continuity of perceived Soviet interests.

FOUR MAJOR ACHIEVEMENTS UNDER CHALLENGE

As suggested in Chapter 1, Andropov came to power during a period when the Soviets were digesting earlier gains, that is, when the Soviet leaders were struggling to consolidate advantages that had been seized during the previous decade but that opponents of the USSR had not yet legitimized as irreversible realities. Among many other things, Andropov assumed responsibility for defending four particularly important military and geopolitical gains made in the 1970s but still challenged by Moscow's adversaries.

Soviet Military Gains Relative to America. A long-established Politburo consensus evidently believed that the most important of these gains was the Soviet attainment of a robust equality with the

United States across the many dimensions of military power. This achievement was the heritage of the all-service military buildup Brezhnev had initiated in 1965, a process carried out while America was preoccupied with successive waves of self-torment. Moreover, the Soviet buildup had long held out the prospect that the USSR would achieve something better than equality, and in a few respects this was not the case. The Politburo was well aware that had the trends visible on both sides in the mid-1970s continued for another decade, the Soviet Union would have surpassed the United States in many more of the indexes of military strength.

Since the late 1970s, however, the Soviet leadership had seen this agreeable prospect threatened by the American reaction against it—that is, by the rearmament effort begun in the Carter administration and enlarged thereafter. Moreover, this American response had begun when the Soviet leadership confronted a secular decline in the growth of the Soviet economy, and had therefore placed pressure on already traumatic leadership choices in resource allocation. We have seen that in the last years of the Brezhnev regime, at the same time that the new American military programs were commencing, the Soviets were apparently discovering that they could not avoid allowing their own procurement rates for some military items to grow more slowly than before. Some members of the Soviet military leadership were evidently disturbed at what they considered insufficient growth in funding. In the last year of Brezhnev's life, as we have seen in Chapter 2, the Defense Council was apparently reconstituted, perhaps because of this tension, to bring a larger portion of the Politburo membership into dealings with the marshals. It was against this background that Brezhnev died and Andropov assumed his leadership responsibilities, including the chairmanship of the Defense Council.

There seems little doubt that the new Soviet general secretary will operate as party leader in a Politburo that places highest priority upon Soviet retention of the gains in military power which were achieved during the Brezhnev era. Although the Soviet leadership will have strong reasons to find a way to transfer significant military resources to the distressed economy during the 1980s, the felt need to maintain the USSR's relative position vis-à-vis the United States—

and if possible to improve it further—will be one of several factors that will operate powerfully in the other direction. In this connection, Andropov must be affected by the fact that Defense Minister Ustinov—with his personal background as the paramount supervisor of Soviet military industry since the Second World War—played such a key role in placing him in office. Should illness cut short Andropov's tenure prematurely, a need for the political support of the defense minister is similarly likely to impinge heavily on the policy options of his successor.

During the Brezhnev era both Soviet weapons programs and Moscow's strategy in arms control negotiation seemed to assume that assured deterrence depended on a significant military advantage, perhaps even a decisive advantage, which of course could not possibly be enjoyed simultaneously by both sides. It is in this sense that the Soviets apparently believed Soviet and Western security interests to be fundamentally incompatible. Unfortunately and rather ironically, this Soviet attitude toward the requirements of deterrence appears to have won converts in the United States in the last decade. The implied rationale behind Soviet weapons-building behavior has thus evoked a reciprocal response among some Americans, reflected in the explicit demand of important groups in the United States that America restore military "superiority" over the Soviet Union. However unlikely it is that this goal will be achieved by the United States, its mere evocation is likely to reinforce pressures on the leaders to defend the strategic postulates of the Brezhnev era.

Complicating the general secretary's task as he assesses the prospects for the 1980s, however, is the fact that the extent of the challenge that will actually materialize from the United States remains somewhat ambiguous. Despite the very large spending programs launched by the Reagan administration in 1981 and 1982, and despite the obvious intention of that administration to delay any new strategic arms agreement with the Soviet Union until certain of the existing Soviet force advantages were overcome, considerable uncertainty had evolved about the size of the U.S. force structure that would emerge during the decade.

In the early 1980s, Andropov and his colleagues had evidence that the scope and pace of American weapons programs had also been placed under some pressure: on the one hand because of economic difficulties the Americans, too, were experiencing, and on the other hand because of the implicit political challenge to those programs created by the American nuclear freeze movement. Unfortunately, from the Politburo's perspective, the ultimate cumulative effect of these countervailing factors on the American side would probably not be fully visible for several years. There were probably therefore strong pressures in the Soviet Union to plan on the basis of "worst-case" assumptions about the U.S. programs.

The Nuclear Advantage in Europe and Asia. Andropov was also charged with defending those military advantages that the Soviet Union had achieved during the last decade in both Europe and Asia through the unilateral deployment of the SS-20 and the Backfire bomber. He thus inherited a strenuous ongoing Soviet effort evidently intended to protect the bulk of the SS-20 deployments in Europe while heading off the threatened Western response. Simultaneously, he inherited the task of combating Japan's growing tendency to increase its military cooperation with the United States in response to Soviet nuclear deployments in the Far East.

In both cases, Andropov's options appeared to be constrained politically by the momentum Soviet policy had acquired since the decision to deploy the SS-20 had been taken, and by the apparent existence of a long-established Politburo conviction that the advantages unilaterally achieved were now a vested Soviet right.[21]

The Domination of Afghanistan. Andropov also inherited the new satrapy of Afghanistan, along with an ongoing punitive war in which little progress had been made against Afghan resistance in the three years since the Soviet military occupied the country in December 1979. There is little doubt that Andropov found this war inconvenient, to some extent because of the negative political attitude toward it in quarters important to the Soviet Union (such as India), but more particularly because the Soviets to some degree are pinned down by it, constrained somewhat in their reactions elsewhere because of its existence.

Nevertheless, as noted in Chapter 4, Soviet leadership attitudes have been profoundly conditioned both by the accumulated Soviet investment in blood and by the new expectations for the future evoked by the seizure of Afghanistan. These factors have apparently created a lasting assumption in the oligarchy that any attempt to put an end to this war on terms that did not guarantee continued Soviet hegemony would be treasonous.

Consequently, although vague hints have continued to be dropped in Moscow—for tactical reasons—to the effect that Andropov would find a way to close out the conflict, there seems very little likelihood of this. The Soviet leaders appear resigned to carrying on the war for as many years as may be required to crush the insurgency, and there is a substantial chance that Andropov or his successor may remain shackled to this responsibility throughout the 1980s.

The New Advantage in Indochina. A fourth burden of achievement which the new general secretary had to assume was the geopolitical gain the Soviet Union had registered in Indochina at the end of the 1970s. It is likely that this advance, remote from Soviet borders, has never been regarded by the Soviet leadership as nearly as important for Soviet national interests as the three gains just considered. Nevertheless, it would be difficult indeed for the Soviet leaders to abandon the long-sought advantage over both China and the United States they achieved in 1978 when they enticed Hanoi into its de facto alliance with Moscow. Any Soviet leadership would find it painful to relinquish the pleasure offered by the sight of Soviet naval vessels in the former American base of Cam Ranh Bay, the leverage on China created by the new Soviet position in Indochina, and the advantages obtained for Soviet naval operations in the South China Sea and the Indian Ocean.[22] Moreover, the Vietnamese conquest of Cambodia, like the Soviet conquest of Afghanistan, has been proclaimed to be "irreversible," and any Soviet display of softness in one case would have adverse implications regarding Soviet resoluteness in the other.

Consequently, as in Afghanistan, the Soviet leadership has appeared to be locked into indefinite support of the stalemated Vietnamese war in Cambodia. This issue thus promised to remain, as it was under Brezhnev, a focus of some ongoing Soviet friction with both China and the United States.

The Inherited Battle Line in the Third World. In addition to these four particularly important and intractable vested interests, Andropov and his colleagues inherited a network of Soviet positions staked out in the 1970s throughout the Third World—some stable, some vulnerable, and some still advancing.

As suggested in the initial overview conducted in Chapter 1, the Soviets are now essentially marking time in the Middle East, Africa, and South Asia, awaiting the next swing of fortune that will again open avenues of opportunity for advance. In these areas they have, in effect, fallen back upon certain geopolitical bastions attained in the 1970s—Syria and South Yemen in the Middle East, Ethiopia and Angola in Africa. In each of these places their position is fortified by a sense of mutual need shared with their client and by a concrete security relationship, anchored in each instance by some military presence of the Soviets or their allies.

Beyond these core interests, the Soviets retain a wide assortment of more ambiguous connections with regimes and organizations of differing hues, ranging from a frayed tie to Iraq to their long-standing arms-supply relationship and political understanding with Libya's wealthy patron of terrorists, Mu'ammar Qadhafi; their enduring if somewhat cooler arms-supply relationship with India; their new arms-supply relationships with Nicaragua and North Yemen; their ideological ties with Mozambique and Congo Brazzaville; and the relationship they have sought to build with Namibia's nationalist organization, SWAPO.

From Andropov's perspective, overall trends in the ebb and flow of Soviet influence around the world at the time of Brezhnev's passing were least satisfactory in East Asia. There, the significant increase in Soviet geopolitical weight accomplished by the Brezhnev military buildup and the gratifying advance of the Soviet military presence into Indochina and Afghanistan had been accompanied by a cooling of Soviet relationships with some Asian states as a result of those very advances. This was the case with Japan, whose drift toward closer military cooperation with the United States was being impelled rather than retarded by the threatening Soviet nuclear deployments in Asia and the Soviet fortification of the southern Kurils. The Soviet relationship with the ASEAN states of Southeast

Asia also remained very cool, partly because of the Soviet Union's support of Vietnam's conduct in Cambodia, and partly because of concern over the Soviet bases in Vietnam and the growing Soviet naval and air presence in the South China Sea. Even in India, where the arms-supply relationship remained a cornerstone of Soviet policy in Asia, concern over the Soviet advance into Afghanistan and the ongoing war there had led New Delhi to mend its fences with the United States and to seek to diversify its foreign sources of weapons supply. The important advantages the Soviet Union derived from the gains it had made in East Asia in the 1970s thus coexist with the adverse consequences of those same gains.

In contrast, in Latin America the post-Brezhnev leadership undoubtedly sees the situation as still actively moving in the direction of Soviet interests. In this remote and difficult terrain in the vicinity of the United States, the Soviets continue to follow a policy of cautious incrementalism and minimal visibility, slipstreaming quietly behind the advance of Cuban revolutionary influence. Although they have no large new options for bold action here, the Soviet leaders are probably now more optimistic about their long-term prospects in this area than they have ever been before. They see the situation in parts of Latin America—particularly in the Caribbean basin—as steadily evolving, with some help from them and much more from the Cubans, in a direction which is gradually eroding U.S. influence. They see the United States as unable to arrest these trends, and they probably judge many of Washington's recent efforts to turn the tide to be counterproductive.

The Soviets are likely to regard the American-sponsored armed harassment of the Nicaraguan regime as unlikely to succeed either in overthrowing that regime or in deflecting it from its evolution toward Marxist dictatorship and ever-closer alignment with Cuba and the Soviet Union. At the same time, the Soviet leaders are undoubtedly gratified at the prospect that these U.S. measures will further erode the American foreign policy consensus and aggravate the split between the United States and important sectors of public opinion in Latin America and Europe. The Soviets also probably expect to reap some net political profit from the U.S. participation in a joint intervention into Grenada in October 1983. In return for their loss of a client Marxist regime on a small Caribbean island, the Soviets can anticipate that this American action will significantly strengthen the influence of those Europeans who tend to portray the two superpowers as moral equivalents, add to differences between Beijing and Washington, reinforce anti-Washington sentiment in many Latin American countries, and encourage the long-term growth of American foreign policy divisions.

In regard to El Salvador, meanwhile, the Soviets probably believe that no matter how the future course of battle develops—and whether or not the Marxist insurgents triumph—the United States cannot fail to lose. There they see the United States as indefinitely trapped, bearing the onus of identification with a regime whose legitimacy is challenged by its inability either to put an end to the Marxist insurgency or to halt the endemic and anarchic terrorism of its own right wing.[23]

Overall, the Soviet leaders see Cuba's role in the regional process as immensely profitable to themselves, and as one which so far has entailed only manageable risks for the Soviet Union. Their geopolitical bastion in Cuba is therefore now their most productive strongpoint in the Third World, and one that Brezhnev's successor will certainly be obliged to continue to cherish and support.

The Reduced Dangers in Poland and China. Finally, the new general secretary could congratulate himself that in the year before he took office, two grave dangers, one on the western and one on the eastern flank of the Soviet empire, had each been effectively neutralized. One was the menace of Polish Solidarity, the threat of Polish nationalist defiance of the Soviet Union, and the prospect that the USSR would be forced to invade Poland to bring it to heel, with all the adverse consequences that such an action would have entailed. All these dangers had been averted, at least for the time being, by the imposition of martial law in December 1981 and the crushing of Solidarity by the Polish military regime. The other danger he did not have to face as head of the Soviet party was the threat of a Sino-American military alliance against the Soviet Union. Once feared by Moscow as an imminent prospect, this possibility had now, also since 1981, been rendered more remote by the emergence of a somewhat more reserved Chinese posture toward the United States and the concomitant Chinese turn toward limited improvement of relations with the Soviet Union. It was thus surely Andropov's duty to strive to preserve both of these fortunate trends.

THE POLITBURO'S PERSPECTIVE

In sum, considering the panorama of inherited interests just described, and considering the nature of the political backing with which Andropov arrived in office, the post-Brezhnev leadership seems more likely to introduce somewhat greater adroitness into Soviet behavior over the remainder of this decade than to change the thrust of that behavior. Despite the multiple problems and grave difficulties the Soviet regime faces, Andropov was likely to be fairly optimistic about Soviet prospects in its dealings with its adversaries. He almost certainly drew considerable comfort from his perception of *their* multiple weaknesses, to be discussed shortly.

In dealings with major actors other than the United States, it is possible that Moscow will eventually attempt—to the degree that the balance of opinion in the Soviet leadership and the consensus view of Soviet interests permits—to modify some of the rigidities in Soviet tactics that have in the past played into the hands of the United States. Although it is likely that the Soviet leaders will continue to place greater emphasis upon intimidation than upon inducements in dealings with the neighbors of the Soviet Union, some changes in this ratio are conceivable. In dealings with Japan, for example, it is not impossible that along with the customary threatening posture, some gestures will be made in Tokyo in the 1980s to attempt to thaw Soviet-Japanese relations and to head off the growth of Japanese-American military cooperation. It is clear that the Politburo will actively pursue the conciliation of China begun under Brezhnev, although it is also likely that the USSR will find it extremely difficult to make more than token gestures to Beijing in response to the Chinese demands for both huge reductions in the Soviet force structure opposite China and Soviet withdrawals from Afghanistan and Indochina.

The Soviet oligarchs probably assume that the recent slowdown in the Soviet advance in much of the Third World—the main battleground between East and West—is not likely to persist to the end of the 1980s. The new Soviet leadership is well aware that past Soviet advances have been predicated upon opportunities created by civil and international instability and violence, and that the Soviet Union is at a great disadvantage in competing with the West in economic dealings with the Third World states in the absence of such turmoil. But Brezhnev's successors have reason to be confident that more such instability and new such opportunities will be generated in Asia and Africa in the 1980s, as they are already being generated in Lebanon and Central America. In such countries as the Philippines and Pakistan, the Soviet leaders may already see the seeds of such future opportunities.

The Soviets are also likely to be acutely aware of the counterproductive effects of using Soviet military force for purposes of geopolitical advance in the crude and undisguised manner employed in Afghanistan. The emphasis here, however, is upon "crude and undisguised."

We have seen that during the 1970s the Soviets became increasingly active in dispatching Soviet and proxy forces at the invitation and in the service of sympathetic Third World regimes. Until the invasion of Afghanistan, the apeal for Soviet assistance and the services rendered to the Third World client were in every case genuine, as such varied clients as Le Duan, Nasser, Sadat, Asad, Neto, Mengistu, and Nkomo could testify.[24] Also until Afghanistan, acceptance of Soviet assistance in no case entailed transfer to the Soviet Union of effective political control over the client's regime. This was, to be sure, in many cases not for want of Soviet trying.[25] The face remains, however, that although several states (particularly Cuba and South Yemen) have an exceptionally close relationship with Moscow because of a perceived commonality of interests, there are still no noncontiguous Soviet puppets in the world today.[26] Soviet presence and influence has, on the whole, expanded considerably in the Third World since the late 1960s. Thus far, Soviet control has not.

The Politburo is well aware that its clients and prospective clients in the Third World are generally sensitive to this distinction and that the Soviet success in advancing the Soviet presence in the Third World during the 1970s was conditioned by a client assumption that the USSR would be unable to extract control as the price of its services. Soviet behavior in Afghanistan was a radical departure from this pattern and a challenge to this assumption. The Afghan invasion was a parody of previous Soviet ventures precisely because the alleged invitation to intervene was generally perceived, inside and outside the country, as a fictitious justification for the violent assertion of Soviet control. If Soviet clients such as the Syrians and Ethiopians are thus far not greatly disturbed by this precedent, it is largely because of their continuing and overriding need for Soviet services; but it is partly also because they see Soviet behavior in Afghanistan as an isolated and nonthreatening instance. Undisguised repetitions of the Afghanistan pattern elsewhere, however, would probably have some cumulative negative effect upon the Soviet relationship with clients whom they do not control.

These considerations give the Soviet leadership important additional reasons to prefer better political cover for any future military attempts to establish Soviet hegemony. This does not mean, of course, that the USSR will not vigorously pursue its efforts to expand its political and military presence in the Third World. On the contrary, the Soviet leadership will do this in any case on the pattern successfully practiced in Africa, when and if suitable new clients in need of Soviet security assistance emerge. But as a rule the Soviets are likely to consider their acceptance of a relationship of less than complete control, with a sympathetic regime heavily dependent on the USSR (as in Ethiopia, Syria, and South Yemen), to be on balance more advantageous than an effort to repeat what they did in Afghanistan. The profitability of their past and present joint operations with the Cubans, and the fact that the Cubans have up to now been widely perceived by clients as less threatening, also suggests that, other things being equal, the Soviet leadership will have reason to continue to emphasize the use of such proxies to the extent feasible.

Nevertheless, let us note a major caveat. Such preferences, even if now considered by the Politburo to represent the balance of Soviet interests in the abstract, may yet be sidetracked by the spontaneous evolution of short-lived opportunities in circumstances where the ultimate political costs are initially ambiguous. The Soviet leaders have established two sets of disquieting precedents in the last decade that could entice them to override the cautionary considerations discussed. First, they have three times assisted client regimes to conquer rivals across established boundaries (in India's attack on Pakistan in 1971, in Hanoi's attack across the 17th parallel beginning in 1972, and in Hanoi's onslaught against Cambodia in 1978). They could therefore be led to do this again and in some circumstances to play a larger and more independent military role. Second, the Soviets have been willing to accept thinly supported conspiratorial coups—in Aden and Kabul—as sufficient pretext to establish security relationships with the resulting regimes. Despite any present misgivings, they will be under temptation to do so again should such coups materialize in places that are both important to the Soviet Union and within the geographical range of Soviet effective power projection capabilities. Within this radius, the Soviets may therefore be more ready than heretofore to intervene in civil wars in which such regimes are involved. Indeed, on their immediate periphery they are now more likely than before to seize on any pretext offered by U.S. conduct to justify such Soviet intervention in a civil war as a response to a U.S. initiative. Finally, they could also be tempted, given the appropriate combination of circumstances, to seek to stimulate coups in nearby states in order to establish the political base for a subsequent military presence.

THE POST-BREZHNEV LEADERSHIP AND AMERICA

We may conclude by inquiring how the post-Brezhnev leaders—whose views have been conditioned by the course of the struggle with America since 1965—now view the United States as a long-term competitor. I will commence with their likely perception of U.S. leadership since 1980, and will then consider their probable judgments about the constraints placed on any U.S. leadership by certain characteristics of the American polity and the U.S. alliance system. In this connection, we may ask, more broadly, what conclusions they may draw about America in the light of the vicissitudes of the Johnson, Nixon, Ford, Carter, and Reagan administrations. What net judgments can any new Soviet leader extract from Soviet experience with the American public and the parade of American leaders during the Brezhnev era? And how is he likely to weigh these conclusions against his perception of Soviet domestic and external difficulties?

We may note to begin with that the Soviet leadership's perception of U.S. behavior during recent years is almost certainly more complex than Soviet comment has suggested. The vehemently avowed unhappiness with trends of the last few years in the United States is likely to have been largely or wholly offset by a deep— if less readily acknowledged—satisfaction with certain factors perceived to be at work in both America and the West generally.

On the one hand, the Soviet leaders have undoubtedly been somewhat surprised and chagrined at the strength of the adverse tide in American public opinion with respect to themselves that began after the invasion of Afghanistan, in the last year of the Carter administration, and helped to bring to power President Carter's successor. Although the Soviets vaguely sensed that their own past pattern of conduct might have had something to do with this phenomenon, they were far from concluding that anything they had done in the past decade might have been inappropriate.[27] Certainly they were not prepared to give up anything they had won to conciliate the United States. Rather, they considered the American public reaction inappropriate, a reflection of the unfortunate influence of misguided or intransigent forces in the American elite who were unable to accept with grace the historical inevitability of either the U.S. defeats of the 1970s or the Soviet advances, and unable to prepare with due equanimity for an endless train of more such defeats and advances.

The Soviet leaders were soon disappointed in their initial hopes that the Reagan administration might rise above such emotions to do business with them as the Nixon administration had done. They were then disturbed at the hostile rhetoric emanating from the president and his officials, although this was not so much because they were insulted by that rhetoric, and still less because anything that was said was untrue. Rather, they were aggrieved because they correctly surmised that the statements assailing the USSR were being employed to mobilize support in the American public for the administration's anti-Soviet program, the delays in arms negotiation, and most particularly, the accelerated weapons program. By the third year of the Reagan administration, Soviet spokesmen in informal remarks were frequently suggesting that the USSR had given up on the present American leadership, and was waiting for the next one.

At the same time, and despite all this, the Soviet leaders are likely to have sensed many factors at work in the United States, and more generally in the West, that were deeply encouraging.

THE COUNTERPRODUCTIVE EFFECTS OF ANTI-SOVIET RHETORIC

First, the capability of anti-Soviet statements, however accurate, to mobilize the American public soon reached a point of diminishing returns, and presently became counterproductive. Among an increasing segment of the population, this rhetoric appears to have stimulated more alarm about the possibility of war than anger at the Soviet Union. This result was greatly heightened, in the United States and even more in Europe, by the maladroit public statements some officials initially made about contingencies in the event of nuclear war and the possibility of Soviet nuclear attack. This was language that—in conjunction with the new U.S. arms program— helped to promote the notion that the U.S. administration was heading for a nuclear collision with the USSR.

It is unclear to what degree the Soviet leaders have themselves believed that the danger of war has increased in recent years. Despite the increase in hostile rhetoric, the general slowdown in progress in arms control, and the advance of Western programs for arms production and deployment, there does not appear to have been a comparable increase—in comparison with the supposedly more stable 1970s—in the number of flash points in the Third World where military confrontation between the United States and the Soviet Union might readily arise. This anomaly is no doubt partly the result of the slowing of the Soviet offensive in the Third World in the early 1980s. Nevertheless, the Soviet leaders have sought as best they could to exacerbate Western fears with strident rhetoric of their own, charging that the United States was seeking to "unleash the flames of nuclear war." The net effect of American official rhetoric and Soviet cynicism was thus to feed the growth of the nuclear freeze movement in the United States and of the "peace movement" in Western Europe.[28]

THE CHASM BETWEEN AMERICAN AND EUROPEAN PERCEPTIONS

Second, Andropov was likely to believe that the American leadership has been increasingly handicapped by the enormous gap that has opened between the United States and much of Western Europe in both the perception of the Soviet Union and the dominant assumptions Americans and Europeans hold about appropriate policy toward Moscow. These differences, which grew through the 1970s and early 1980s to embrace a wide range of issues, have emerged in large part out of a contrast in circumstances.

The inhabitants of the European peninsula, forced to live in intimate proximity to Soviet military power, have necessarily been preoccupied primarily with peninsular concerns. For them, the prospect of the demise of detente implied a much more immediate military danger and vulnerability than it did for the Americans. Consequently, most Europeans were determined to cling to the detente relationship as a talisman of calm, safety, and economic profit,* at the same time that Soviet behavior in the world at large rendered detente less and less acceptable to the American majority.

To a majority in the United States, the only nation that confronted Soviet power in all regions of the world, the succession of Soviet actions discussed in this book increasingly appeared to describe an alarming pattern; if there was no Soviet "master plan," as some

---

* To West Germans, of course, the preservation of European detente with the Soviet Union was also an essential prerequisite for the continuation of the West German "special relationship" with East Germany, which was increasingly seen as a vital FRG national interest.

contended, there was at least an open-ended process whose implications were profoundly hostile to the United States. But the European majority, much like a minority in America, discerned little pattern or process in Soviet behavior in the Third World, and even less did they see an intimate connection between that behavior and Soviet conduct in Europe. For many Europeans, especially intellectuals, the American contest with the Soviet Union in the world at large was merely a struggle between the ambitions of rival and equally ignoble superpowers, or, worse, simply a consequence of the ambitions of the United States alone. The insouciance with which Europeans accepted Soviet actions in Africa, Indochina, and Afghanistan—and the outright hostility with which some Europeans regarded the acute American dilemma in Central America—in turn reverberated in the United States to increase the disenchantment of many Americans with Western Europe. In short, the growth of the Soviet presence around the world in the Brezhnev era had the indirect effect of contracting the community of interest between the United States and Europe.

In parallel with this, there was a related and more subtle divergence of view between many Europeans and the United States over Eastern Europe. Although neither Europeans nor Americans would—or should—take any risks to succor East Europeans in their vain strivings to escape from Soviet hegemony, many in the United States were deeply offended by the hardly disguised display of relief with which some European leaders responded to the imposition of martial law in Poland. This contrast in reactions reflected a discrepancy of view over the legitimacy of Soviet hegemony in East Europe, which many in Western Europe openly regarded as a necessary—indeed, desirable—guarantee of European stability. American leaders could not share this view, in part because of the presence of large numbers of East European descendants in the United States, but more important, because of a fundamental asymmetry in the American relationship with the Soviet Union. As noted earlier, the Soviets continue to demonstrate that they do not recognize the legitimacy of any U.S. sphere of influence, anywhere in the world, and they indeed continue to press within the limits of prudence to help to contract American influence in areas close to

U.S. borders. The assumptions underlying this conduct make it impossible for many in the United States to share West European equanimity and satisfaction about the inviolability of the Soviet sphere of influence in Eastern Europe.

Given this polarization of perceptions, the attempts that began in the last year of the Carter administration and grew under the Reagan administration to impose a central focus upon Western policy toward the Soviet Union were fatally handicapped. The boycott of the Moscow Olympic Games, the American grain embargo, the attempt to block the consummation of the European gas pipeline deal with the Soviet Union, and the effort to impose joint, stricter constraints upon the supply of technology or credit to the USSR, were all partially or totally undermined by the perceived European self-interest in maintaining calm and profitable economic intercourse in their own relations with Moscow. Indeed, the abortive U.S. attempt to compel the Europeans to give up the gas pipeline arrangement evoked bitter resentment. This anger was intensified because the Europeans perceived the Reagan administration as simultaneously persisting in a hypocritical refusal to make the comparable economic and domestic political sacrifice that would be involved in the cessation of profitable grain sales to the Soviet Union.*

Finally, the prolonged political struggle over the Western response to the unilateral Soviet deployment of the SS-20 became another source of division within the Western community. It is true that despite the fierce opposition, a much larger segment of the European population sided with the United States on this issue than on the others mentioned, because many believed that European self-interest was involved. Nevertheless, the question of the new nuclear deployments in Europe—originally taken up by the United States in response to a European request—became another focal point for

---

* It is true that this European argument was to some extent self-serving, since other grain producers would not in any case have supported a continuation of the U.S. grain embargo even if the United States had chosen that path; nor, certainly, would the Europeans have abandoned the gas pipeline contracts. Nevertheless, the U.S. administration's disregard for the principle of equality of sacrifice gravely weakened the U.S. case.

the mobilization of neutralist and anti-American sentiment among a sizable fraction of the Europeans. For the Soviet Union, the most dramatic and important long-term consequence of this trend in the last few years has been the steady evolution of the German Social Democratic party to the left, away from the consensus in support of NATO, away from the connection with the United States, and toward increasing accommodation to Soviet power.

From Andropov's perspective, all these trends, while not necessarily decisive on matters of immediate primary concern to the Soviet Union (such as the issue of the Pershing II and cruise missile deployments), yet offered sizable immediate benefits and greater hopes for the future. On the one hand, Europe offered the Soviet Union a point of powerful leverage upon the United States, blunting U.S. efforts to curtail the flow of technology and credit which nourished the Soviet ability to maintain its military priorities. On the other hand, Washington was subject to European popular pressures for concessions in the INF negotiations, and the Soviets could hope—despite their failure in 1983—that these pressures might eventually prove sufficient to force from the United States an agreement that would preserve Soviet asymmetrical advantages. Finally, the Soviet leaders could also hope that, given enough time, the multiple divergences between Europe and America would grow sufficiently to produce a schism, leaving Europe alone with the Soviet Union.

SHIFTS IN THE EVALUATION OF POLITICAL RISK

A third factor from which Brezhnev's successors may derive encouragement is the Western reaction to a new foreign policy measure the Soviet leadership evidently authorized in the last years of the Brezhnev era, one that broke sharply with certain major political constraints long observed by the Soviet Union. This was the Soviet decision beginning in the late 1970s to manufacture and transfer to Vietnam, for use against opponents first in Laos and then in Cambodia, the chemicals of bacterial origin known as mycotoxins.[29] The Soviets will have observed that despite the efforts of the Reagan administration to indict the Soviet Union for this behavior, the reaction of many influential circles in the West was, first, to express skepticism when the initial American evidence was regarded as inadequate, and thereafter to fall silent as the accumulation of evidence grew stronger. Few in the West saw fit to draw practical conclusions from this Soviet behavior.

The operational significance for the West of the mycotoxin phenomenon lay not so much in the morality of Soviet conduct as in the implications for arms control. The manufacture and use of these weapons, unlike other chemical weapons, constitutes a violation of an arms control agreement signed by the Soviet Union: the 1972 Bacteriological Weapons Convention "prohibiting the development, production, and stockpiling of bacteriological and toxin weapons," which the USSR ratified in February 1975.[30] Although there have been persistent allegations in the United States of Soviet evasions of particular aspects of the SALT agreements, the violation of this biological-weapons convention was the most straightforward case to date of Soviet noncompliance with an arms control agreement. Normally, as noted in Chapter 4, the Soviet leaders take care when negotiating such treaties to imbue their provisions with an ambiguity and flexibility sufficient to protect Soviet interests, thereby obviating the need to resort to actual violation.

The practical significance of this precedent lies not so much in the Soviet action as in the Western reaction. In the event of a future Soviet decision that Soviet interests require the USSR to bypass unambiguous commitments made in another arms control treaty, the consequences would depend not merely upon Western ability to verify Soviet noncompliance, but also upon Western willingness to act upon such information. Indeed, the credibility of such Western willingness to react must be one of the major factors in Soviet calculations.

Unfortunately, this credibility—the likelihood that a major Soviet treaty violation would in fact bring about major consequences in the West—has almost certainly been diluted considerably in the Politburo's estimation by the general indifference Western elites have shown to the fate of the Bacteriological Weapons Convention. The West has, in effect, confirmed the optimistic Soviet estimate that must have preceded the decision to supply mycotoxins to Vietman.

In sum, in this case, the central issue the West must confront is not merely the acts of which the Soviet leadership is accused, grave as they are, but rather the questions about the future that emerge from the rather contemptuous evaluation of the West that seems to underlie Soviet behavior.

THE OSCILLATION OF AMERICAN PERSPECTIVE

Fourth, Moscow is probably encouraged by a sense that the United States is seriously handicapped by a lack of continuity to which it seems oblivious. In contrast to the methodical endeavors of the Brezhnev Politburo described in this book, the American Presidency has been characterized during the Brezhnev era by remarkable oscillations in perspective. The violent swings in attitude and strategy visible as power passed from Johnson to Nixon to Ford to Carter to Reagan have occasionally affected the Soviets adversely, and they have then deplored this "zig-zag behavior." But more commonly, the Soviet Union has derived considerable indirect benefits from this disease of the American body politic. The arrival in office of administration after administration, each convinced of the fatuity of the external behavior of its predecessor, has greatly complicated efforts to carry out consistent lines of policy across the four-year frontiers, and thus to think consecutively about how to deal with the Soviet Union in the world arena. The new Soviet leadership is well aware of the practical consequences, which have been most vivid in the case of the U.S. relationship with China.[31]

To be sure, the effects of this episodic, fluctuating aspect of American policy should not be exaggerated, since despite this handicap there remains a large measure of continuity, particularly in respect to the core American interests in Western Europe, Japan, and the Middle East. Nevertheless, the elements of disagreement in the American polity are so strong and the potential for periodic reversals in many areas of policy is sufficiently great that friends and adversaries of the United States alike have a continuous incentive to dread (or hope for, as the case may be) the fresh changes that may come with the advent of each four-year cycle.*

As a corollary, Andropov as a foreign policy expert was likely to believe that the United States often lacks expert leadership, and almost always has insufficient continuity in expertise. Since every fourth year brings, in effect, a new "amateur night" at the White House, the transmission across administrations of the painfully acquired experience that has over time tempered the original preconceptions of each incoming administration is rendered extraordinarily difficult. This behavior has been characteristic of both major American political parties, and of both left and right. The periodic infusion of arrogant ignorance at the top has been rendered still more serious, in the Carter and Reagan administrations alike, by the contemptuous attitude taken toward the permanent bureaucracy, which with all its grave faults is the only available repository of American institutional memory. Andropov was well aware that this practice lies at the polar extreme from the customs of his own regime, where Gromyko in the Foreign Ministry, Ponomarev in the International Department, and Ustinov in the military and weapons field have dominated their policy-making and policy-support realms for decades, accumulating honors and power in the process. The rigidities imparted to Soviet attitudes by this situation are well known, and I earlier alluded to them at some length. The Soviet Union receives a measure of compensation, however, in a steadiness of gaze at the world scene which the United States often lacks.

THE UNITED STATES STILL (AGAIN) LACKS FIRM CONSENSUS

Finally, surveying the panorama of American internal and external behavior during the Brezhnev regime, Andropov had reason

---

* The case of China has already been mentioned, and is sufficiently obvious. There are many other examples; one is the question of the durability of the U.S. commitment to maintain troops in South Korea to ensure the stability of peace in the Korean peninsula. The original Carter decision to withdraw U.S. forces, which was deferred late in the Carter administration and then formally reversed by President Reagan, has left a residue of anxiety both in Seoul and Tokyo that this reversal may itself eventually prove ephemeral.

to conclude that the succession of wounds inflicted on the United States by history has still not healed completely. Three consecutive catastrophes—the murder of President Kennedy, the Vietnam tragedy, and the Watergate melodrama—have left a residue of damage not only to the American self-image but also to the American policy consensus. Fresh external causes of internal division—under Carter, Iran, and under Reagan, El Salvador—have seemed to emerge periodically to tear at the scab.

Although the center of gravity of American opinion regarding the USSR has undoubtedly shifted considerably since the early 1970s, there is still no general agreement on the appropriate American posture toward the Soviet leadership. A large minority in the United States apparently continues to believe that much of the American position in the world against which the Soviet Union steadily presses is fundamentally illegitimate. This semipermanent estrangement of the left has sometimes been matched, in recent years, by an arrogant tendency toward self-isolation on the part of the right—a solipsistic assumption that when recalcitrant views on policy toward Moscow are encountered at home or in Europe, they can be overridden or simply ignored.

One practical consequence, for the Soviet leadership, is that despite America's great military strength and the scope of the American military buildup, the occasional pretensions of U.S. leaders to have the option to take military action at will in defense of announced American interests must appear questionable. As Seweryn Bialer has argued, former Secretary of State Alexander Haig's intimations in 1981 that the United States might take forceful action against Cuba in response to Castro's incendiary conduct in the Caribbean lost credibility as time went on, particularly in view of the administration's obvious domestic concern to convince the American public that the United States would never be drawn into such combat.[32] Soviet skepticism on this score has probably not been eliminated either by the anguished and precarious U.S. involvement in Beirut or by the U.S. participation in a multilateral intervention in Grenada in October 1983. Indeed, the net long-term effect of both these episodes may have been to reduce further any administration's political margin for future action of this kind.

Attempts to imply to the Soviet Union that the American public is willing to tolerate large-scale U.S. involvement in extended overseas fighting are apt to provoke disbelief and may only encourage the Soviet leaders to conclude that the American leadership is prone to bluff. Such a Soviet view, in turn, may have many unfortunate consequences, including the growth of the possibility of miscalculation.

MUST THE RIVALRY BE ZERO-SUM?

From the Politburo's perspective, all of these defects and weaknesses in the American and Western competitors of the Soviet Union are of course matched by countervailing factors: the innate strengths of the West and the grave problems of the Soviet Union. The Soviet leaders retain enduring respect for the American and Western technological advantage. Although they are encouraged by Western economic difficulties, they probably do not really believe that these troubles of a cyclical nature are comparable in scope or continuity to the problems raised by the secular decline in the growth of the Soviet economy. Despite a better harvest in 1983, they have not yet solved their agricultural problem, probably have little confidence that they will do so soon, and are humiliated by the long-term necessity to continue large-scale importation of grain. They are acutely aware of the tensions created by Russian domination of what will soon be a non-Slavic majority in their multinational state. They must, in view of the record of the past, expect continued periodic difficulties and eruptions in their East European empire. They are increasingly concerned at the possibility that Japan in association with the United States will devote a larger portion of its enormous economic potential to military purposes. Despite the modest improvements that have taken place in the atmosphere of their relationship with China in the last two years, they are well aware that their fundamental clash of national interests with the PRC endures. And they are deeply chagrined that despite the months of Soviet pressure and the profound divisions of opinion in Western Europe, the Soviet Union has been unable to defeat the European decision to respond to the SS-20 fait accompli with Western nuclear deployments.

Are these difficulties likely to change the combative posture—the "attacking compulsion"—of the Politburo toward the West and the United States?

The advent of Andropov to the General Secretaryship apparently enhanced, at least to some degree, the personal position of certain individuals just outside the policy-making apparatus who have long seemed exceptionally moderate in the Soviet context and who probably all along privately desired that improvement of relations with the United States be given a priority higher than the consensus of the Brezhnev Politburo thought appropriate. I have in mind, in particular, the trio singled out in this connection in Chapter 3: Yuriy Arbatov, Aleksandr Bovin, and Feodr Burlatskiy. These three men, who all were once subordinates or consultants to Andropov in the Central Committee apparatus, appear to share an assumption that the Soviet competition with the United States is a secular great-power rivalry that can be moderated, rather than a sanctified struggle, propelled by the legitimizing myth that underlies the rule of the Communist party in the Soviet Union.

As I have suggested elsewhere, many, many others in and around the ruling Soviet oligarchy do see the struggle against the United States in precisely those latter terms, however. The essential question, therefore, is whether the mix of views in this regard is likely to change significantly within the Politburo in the aftermath of the Brezhnev era.

On the whole, there seems little chance that this will happen. The momentum of Soviet external policy and the continuity of domestic forces, the entrenched influence of the military and the ideologues around the oligarchy, the entrenched external Soviet advantages that Moscow is obliged to defend, and the perceived vulnerabilities of the West all argue against such a change.

So, too, do the consequences of the oligarchy's sense of its own vulnerabilities. The September 1983 Soviet destruction of a South Korean civilian airliner that had strayed over Soviet territory in the Far East provided exceptionally vivid insights into this Soviet mind-set, on two levels. As was frequently remarked in the West, the episode sharply illuminated the fact that the great increases in Soviet military strength over the last two decades have not eliminated the Soviet "fortress mentality," the paranoia over military security that feeds pugnacity and in this case sent hundreds of civilian passengers to their deaths. As Seweryn Bialer has observed, Soviet military expenditures are never sufficient to make the Soviet leaders secure.[33] This will probably remain true for the indefinite future.

Even more revealing, however, was the regime's behavior in the aftermath of the airliner's destruction. The extraordinary contortions of Soviet propaganda in casting about for self-justification, and the resolute refusal of the leadership to admit error or apologize, bespeak a fortress mentality of a more profound kind: the beleaguered pugnacity of a ruling party perpetually insecure as to its legitimacy, despite more than half a century in power.[34] This self-image is also unlikely to change for the foreseeable future, and is therefore unlikely ever to permit the Soviet leaders either to drop the eternal pretense of infallibility or to abandon the eternal search for legitimacy through struggle against external enemies.

It is therefore improbable that the next Soviet leaders will come to see either the possibility or the desirability of abandoning the traditional Soviet offensive political posture toward the United States in the world arena. Still less is this Soviet leadership likely to be able to envision—any more than could its predecessor—any point of lasting political equilibrium with the United States. Those near the leaders who privately disagree with these assumptions are likely to be compelled to dissimulate and take on a different coloration should they wish to remain or rise in positions of influence.

This does not mean that the Politburo will not continue to seek "good" bilateral relations with the United States—as the Brezhnev leadership never ceased to do—in the sense of expanded contacts, credits, trade, and arms control agreements, on the model of what was envisaged in the early 1970s.[35] It is improbable, however, that such "good" relations, should they materialize in the 1980s, will entail any slackening in the ongoing Soviet efforts to weaken the position of the United States at every point in the world where the two powers are engaged. Indeed, it is plausible to suppose that this leadership now hopes, through the slow return of the pendulum of American opinion, eventually to obtain such a bilateral improvement without any such modification in behavior in the world at large.

Such bilateral relations will therefore be pursued in parallel with such phenomena as the continued violation of an arms control treaty through the transfer of mycotoxins to Vietnam for use in Indochina, the continued operations of the Soviet army of occupation in Afghanistan, the continued support of the Vietnamese conquest of Cambodia, the continued effort to promote the erosion of the American connection with Germany and the growth of neutralism in the German body politic, the continued support of Cuban efforts to promote the erosion of U.S. influence in the Caribbean, and the continued interpretation of the famous "Basket Three" of the Helsinki Treaty as permitting the incarceration in psychiatric hospitals of the former members of the Soviet Helsinki Watch Committee.

The underlying reason for my pessimism has been eloquently summarized by Milovan Djilas:

> The importance of ideology for the Soviet leadership—*any* Soviet leadership—is seldom understood in the West. . . . Their rule is anchored in ideology, as the divine right of kings was in Christianity; and therefore their imperialism, too, has to be ideological or else it commands no legitimacy. This is why the men in the Kremlin can lose no territory once acquired, why they cannot abandon friends and allies no matter how objectively burdensome they may have become to them (can you imagine the USSR ratting on the Shah of Iran?), or admit alternative interpretations of the true faith. This is also why it is an unsupportable American hope that the Kremlin may be pressured or humoured into a type of comprehensive detente which would guarantee Soviet moderation in Africa and Asia as part of a SALT settlement, or any settlement. No Soviet leader can do that without abdicating his title to leadership and jeopardising the justification of Soviet rule.[36]

Nothing that has been said here is intended to imply that a civil bilateral relationship with the Soviet Union is unfeasible or that arms control agreements with the Soviet leaders are innately undesirable. On the contrary, a continual search for the possibility that areas of compromisable interest exist is highly desirable, both to preserve and reinforce the Western consensus and periodically to probe the evolution of attitudes within the Politburo.

What is essential, however, is to strive to ensure that this search does not undermine sober expectations about the enduring nature of Soviet competitive urges. Both because of their weaknesses and because of their strengths, the Soviet leaders are likely to continue to be impelled to press outward, responding to their vision of their precarious legitimacy and ever-imperiled security and in the process discovering, as opportunities permit, new advantages that must be defended. It is the responsibility of Western elites to be willing to look steadily at the totality of Soviet behavior, to raise the political costs of venturesome Soviet conduct, to strive as best they can to narrow the avenues of Soviet opportunity, and in general, to so conduct themselves as to encourage the valuable Leninist trait of prudence in the face of adverse circumstances.

Appendix / Selected Chronology of Events, 1964–1983

1964

October	Khrushchev ousted; Brezhnev chosen first secretary.
	PRC explodes its first atomic device.
November	Podgornyy, de facto second secretary, delivers key report to CC plenum.

1965

February	U.S. bombing of North Vietnam begins.
	Kosygin mission to Beijing fails; Mao is implacable.
March	Brezhnev unveils agricultural program at CC plenum.
June	Shelepin-inspired rumors attack Brezhnev.
Summer	Consensus in Soviet leadership, led by Brezhnev, hardens behind all-service long-term military program.
Fall	Soviet Far East buildup against China begins.
September	Former Podgornyy associate Rumyantsev removed as editor of *Pravda*.
December	Shelepin's Party-State Control Commission liquidated; Shelepin loses deputy premiership.
	Podgornyy pushed upstairs to become head of state.

Mao begins Cultural Revolution purges. Mao breaks ties with Soviet party.

1966

April

Brezhnev assumes title of general secretary.

Podgornyy is dropped from Secretariat; Kirilenko enters Secretariat as Brezhnev's chief lieutenant.

1967

April

Defense Minister Malinovskiy dies, replaced by Grechko.

Defense Council nucleus, Brezhnev, Kosygin, Podgornyy, holds meeting with Soviet commanders.

May

Shelepin associate Semichastnyy ousted as head of KGB.

Party Secretary Andropov transferred to be KGB chairman.

June

Arab-Israeli Six-Day War.

Brezhnev confrontation with Shelepin associate Yegorychev at CC Plenum following the war; Yegorychev dismissed as Moscow city secretary.

Kosygin meets with President Johnson at Glassboro.

July

Shelepin demoted from Secretariat to be head of trade union federation.

December

Brezhnev in Prague authorizes replacement of Novotný by Dubček.

1968

Spring–
Summer

Czech crisis. Soviet leadership is divided and vacillates.

August

USSR agrees to SALT negotiations. USSR invades Czechoslovakia.

1969

March

Sino-Soviet border clashes begin on Ussuri River.

April

Greckho threats in Prague finally bring removal of Dubček.

Spring– *Summer*	Extended Sino-Soviet border crisis.
	USSR approaches United States regarding possible Soviet attack on China.
September	Zhou-Kosygin meeting in Beijing defuses border crisis.
October	Brandt becomes chancellor of FRG; rise of *Ostpolitik.*
	Sino-Soviet border talks begin.
	Soviet-U.S. SALT I talks begin.
November	Grechko visits Cuba, prepares 1970 Cienfuegos venture.
December	Brezhnev delivers controversial speech on economy to CC plenum.

1970

January	Clash within Soviet leadership over Brezhnev speech.
Spring	Soviets send thousands of air-defense troops to Egypt.
July	Soviet air-defense deployments bring clash with Israel; five Soviet fighters shot down by Israelis; Soviets pull back combat air patrols.
	Leadership struggle over question of proposed Kosygin resignation. Two plenums of CC held in one month.
August	Soviet-FRG treaty signed.
September	Soviet diplomatic confrontation with U.S. over nuclear submarine base at Cienfuegos, Cuba. Soviets pull back.

1971

Spring	U.S. "Ping-Pong" diplomacy with PRC.
July	Kissinger's initial visit to PRC.
	Soviets hurriedly come to terms on Berlin Quadripartite Agreement.
August	USSR signs Friendship Treaty with India.

November–
December   India-Pakistan War. Soviet airlift to India; fall of East Pakistan. Crisis over Indian intentions toward West Pakistan and possibility of Chinese intervention.

1972

February   Nixon visit to China; Shanghai Communique.

May   U.S. mining of Haiphong.

Fall of Shelest.

Nixon visit to USSR. Signing of SALT I Treaty and Agreement on Basic Principles of Relations.

October   U.S.-Soviet Trade Agreement signed.

1973

Spring   Brezhnev offers private reassurances to Communist audience over tactical purposes of detente.

May   Elevation to Politburo of "national security" triumvirate: foreign minister, defense minister, KGB chairman.

June   Brezhnev visit to United States. Signing of Agreement on Prevention of Nuclear War.

October   Yom Kippur War. Soviet-U.S. crisis over Soviet threat to intervene.

1974

August   Culmination of Watergate crisis in U.S.; Nixon resigns.

October   Brezhnev makes informal commitment to Kissinger over Jewish emigration, to head off Jackson amendment to Trade Act.

November   Brezhnev-Ford SALT negotiations at Vladivostok.

December   U.S. Trade Act passed with compromise negotiated with Soviets over emigration.

U.S. Export-Import Bank Act passed with Stevenson amendment curtailing Soviet credits.

Soviet CC plenum; recriminations regarding detente.

USSR repudiates commitment over emigration.

1975

January	USSR repudiates 1972 U.S.-Soviet Trade Agreement.
April	Shelepin removed from Politburo.
	U.S. debacle ends war in Vietnam.
Spring–Summer	Communist party offensive barely fails to take power in Portugal.
August	Helsinki Conference; signing of Final Act.
	Brezhnev gesture in *Pravda* tacitly endorses Zaradov hard line over Portuguese crisis and the issue of Communist seizure of power.
Winter	Cuba with Soviet assistance begins intervention in Angola.

1976

March	Chernenko enters Secretariat.
April	Defense Minister Grechko dies, replaced by Ustinov.
	Tenth Five-Year Plan adopted, halving planned growth in investment.
	Sharp decline in GNP growth begins.
September	Mao Zedong dies; Chinese reject initial Soviet feelers.

1977

May	Brezhnev replaces Podgornyy as chief of state.
	Podgornyy dropped from Politburo.
Fall	Soviet airlift to Ethiopia inaugurates Soviet-Cuban intervention in Somali-Ethiopian war.

October	Chernenko becomes candidate member of Politburo.

1978

April	Brezhnev and Ustinov tour military facilities in Far East.
	Coup in Kabul brings Communists to power in Afghanistan. Vietnam enters CEMA.
May	USSR begins fortification of "Northern Territories," southernmost Kurils claimed by Japan.
August	Japan signs Friendship Treaty with China, opposed by USSR.
November	Soviet-Vietnamese Friendship Treaty signed.
	Chernenko becomes full member of Politburo.
December	Vietnam launches blitzkrieg into Cambodia.
	PRC and United States announce normalization of relations.

1979

January	USSR establishes high command for Far East.
	Deng Xiaoping visits United States.
	Shah flees Iran.
	Pro-Cuban Maurice Bishop seizes power in Grenada.
February–March	Chinese stage invasion of Vietnam, withdraw.
April	PRC announces intention not to renew Sino-Soviet treaty.
Spring	USSR begins to deploy naval ships to Vietnamese ports.
	Decline of Kirilenko, rise of Chernenko accelerate.
June	U.S. and USSR sign SALT II treaty at Carter-Brezhnev summit.
July	Somoza falls in Nicaragua, replaced by pro-Cuban Sandinista regime.
November	Khomenei regime takes U.S. embassy personnel hostage; Soviet radio applauds.

December	USSR invades Afghanistan, deposes Communist leader Amin.
	NATO adopts "two-track" decision for missile deployment in response to SS-20.

1980

January	U.S. imposes grain embargo on USSR.
July– August	U.S. boycotts Olympic Games in Moscow.
August– September	Polish disturbances bring fall of Gierek, rise of Solidarity.
Fall	Offensive of pro-Cuban guerrillas begins in El Salvador, supplied through Nicaragua.
October	Kosygin resigns as premier, replaced by Tikhonov.

1981

April	Reagan administration cancels grain boycott against USSR.
Summer	Growth of U.S. friction with PRC over Taiwan.
	Rise of "peace movement" in Western Europe.
September	General Jaruzelski becomes first secretary of Polish party.
December	Jaruzelski imposes martial law in Poland; decline of Solidarity.
	Corruption scandal emerges in Moscow involving Brezhnev's daughter.

1982

January	Death of Suslov.
May	Andropov returns to Secretariat from KGB.
Spring	USSR and PRC begin small steps to improve bilateral relations.

June	Reagan administration attempts to impose boycott on European sale of U.S. compressor components to USSR, seeking to block gas pipeline deal.
	Israel advances in Lebanon to Beirut.
August	U.S. and other Western powers send peacekeeping force to Beirut.
	U.S. and PRC announce joint communiqué on Taiwan issue.
Summer	Rise of "freeze" movement in United States.
October	Brezhnev addresses special gathering of top military commanders.
November	Brezhnev dies. Andropov chosen general secretary.
	USSR and PRC open series of semiannual consultations.
	U.S. abandons attempt to prevent European sale of gas pipeline compressor parts to USSR.

1983

March	Ustinov reveals that Andropov is chairman of Defense Council.
June	U.S. relaxes restrictions on technology sales to PRC; Sino-U.S. relations improve.
	Andropov acquires title of chief of state. Romanov is transferred from Leningrad to Secretariat. Rise of Andropov's alliance with Gorbachev.
August	U.S. signs "boycott-proof" long-term grain agreement with USSR.
September	USSR shoots down Korean civilian airliner near Sakhalin.
	U.S. Defense Secretary Weinberger visits Beijing.
October	Ultra-Marxist group kills Bishop, seizes power in Grenada.
	U.S. and Caribbean states invade Grenada.
December	NATO begins deployment of long-range missiles; USSR suspends INF negotiations.

Notes

Introduction

1. Robert Legvold, "The Nature of Soviet Power," *Foreign Affairs* 56 (October 1977), 65. These words were written a year before the Soviets signed the treaty with Hanoi that immediately unleashed the Vietnamese blitzkrieg against Cambodia, and two years before the Soviet invasion of Afghanistan.
2. Ibid., p. 69.

Chapter 1 / *Soviet Postulates, Concerns, and Priorities*

1. Kirilenko address to 12th Hungarian Party Congress, *Pravda,* March 25, 1980.
2. Ibid.
3. Brezhnev TASS interview, *Pravda,* January 13, 1980.
4. See Nathan Leites, *The Operational Code of the Politburo,* The Rand Corporation (New York: McGraw-Hill, 1951), p. 31.
5. Brezhnev election speech, *Pravda,* February 22, 1980; Brezhnev TASS interview, *Pravda,* January 13, 1980.
6. This central purpose has been defined succinctly by Galina Orionova, a defector who has worked in Moscow's USA Institute, as the determination "to extend Soviet power, by detente or any other means, wherever or whenever such expansion is neither too costly nor too dangerous." See Nora Beloff, "Escape from Boredom: A Defector's Story," *Atlantic Monthly,* November 1980.
7. *Pravda,* February 19, 1980.
8. A number of statements by Politburo members in February 1980 indicated their confidence that the correlation of forces was changing to their advantage: "The capitalist world is in a fever. . . . Among the many signs of an exacerbation of the general crisis of capitalism, particular importance is being assumed by the obvious decline of the neocolonialist system" (M. A. Suslov, speech to Polish party congress, Moscow radio, February 12, 1980). "Socialism's positions in the world are steadily strengthening. The change in the correlation of forces in favor of socialism has created favorable conditions for the growth

of the people's liberation struggle. Major victories have been won in recent years by the forces of national liberation and social progress in the countries of Asia, Africa and Latin America. The progressive changes in the world and the growth of real socialism's strength and influence are provoking frenzied resistance from imperialist reaction" (M. A. Suslov, election speech, *Pravda,* February 21, 1980). "The source [of U.S. policy] is U.S. reactionary imperialist circles' discontent with the strengthening of the socialist community, the growth of revolutionary processes and the upsurge of the anti-imperialist struggle. The very course of world events does not suit them" (A. P. Kirilenko, election speech, *Pravda,* February 20, 1980).

9. "Even its [the U.S.] position as leader of the capitalist world has been considerably undermined. . . . The changes in the position of the USA's allies are not just derivative of the intensifying trade, economic and monetary financial rivalry among the major capitalist powers. As a result of the positive changes in international relations, the USA's partners have acquired much greater scope for foreign policy maneuvers and for ridding themselves of the USA's much too rigid tutelage" (L. Vidyasova, "U.S. Imperialist Foreign Policy and the Modern World," *International Affairs,* January 1980).

10. "Representatives of U.S. political and military departments say that the changes that have occurred in Asia, Africa and Latin America over the past few years, especially in countries like Angola, Ethiopia, Afghanistan, and South Yemen, and recently also in Iran and Nicaragua, have 'upset the balance of forces' to the detriment of the United States. They regard these rapid changes as a 'looming tragedy' for the West. This 'tragedy' is exacerbated, from the standpoint of U.S. politicians, by the energy and raw material crises" (ibid.).

11. V. Rut'kov, "The Military Economic Might of the Socialist Countries—A Factor in the Security of Nations," *Kommunist Voruzhenikh Sil,* no. 23, December 1974, 19–20.

12. "Certain leaders who hold high posts in Washington . . . close their eyes to the fact that alignment with China on an anti-Soviet basis would rule out the possibility of cooperation with the Soviet Union in the matter of reducing the danger of a nuclear war and, of course, of limiting armaments" (*Pravda,* June 17, 1978). The Soviets never specified the degree of U.S. association with China that would trigger this effect; the Politburo itself probably remained undecided in this regard.

13. See Leites, *Operational Code of the Politburo,* p. 90.

14. To take an extreme example: the Soviet media in recent years have given support to a long-established Cuban campaign of denunciation, conducted in the UN and elsewhere, of the U.S. relationship with Puerto Rico. On December 18, 1979, less than two weeks before the invasion of Afghanistan, *Pravda* depicted the United States as having hastily dispatched military forces to this island "in recent days" to put down "the Puerto Rican people's protracted struggle" and to safeguard the use of the island's "advantageous strategic location in the Caribbean." *Pravda* condemned in advance the results of any new plebiscite the United States might hold in Puerto Rico, depicting any such vote, regardless of the outcome, as intended "to perpetuate the present situation." In view of the obvious parallels between this largely fictitious representation of the U.S. position in Puerto Rico and the actual Soviet position

at the moment in Afghanistan, it is conceivable that the timing of the article was not fortuitous and may have been intended to imply that American complaints about Soviet actions in Afghanistan could only be hypocritical. Whatever the tactical purpose, however, the article is striking testimony to Soviet attitudes regarding the legitimacy of a U.S. sphere.

15. B. Pvadyshev, "Opponents of Detente from Miami," *Za Rubezhum,* no. 45, October 30, 1975, 15–16.

16. "In Teheran, struggling and enthusiastic young people occupied the building of the U.S. Embassy, this center of corruption and anti-Iranian conspiracies, in this way they reflected the anti-imperialistic feelings of our homeland's people" (Baku [clandestine] National Voice of Iran Radio, November 5, 1979). "The task which the provisional government could not and did not want to implement . . . the enthusiastic and struggling young people of our country implemented with boldness and sacrifice. By occupying the espionage nest of the U.S. in Teheran . . . they proved to the world the conspiracies and intrigues of U.S. officials." (Baku [clandestine] National Voice of Iran Radio, November 10, 1979). See *National Voice of Iran: November 1978–November 1979,* Foreign Broadcast Information Service Special Report, December 10, 1979, pp. 286, 290. Such statements are far more characteristic of "unofficial" radios broadcasting under Soviet control from the USSR or Eastern Europe than of Radio Moscow or other media explicitly identified with the USSR, which tend to be more circumspect. Both classes of Soviet propaganda are, of course, equally instruments of Soviet policy.

17. *Pravda,* March 18, 1980.

18. Immediately after the fall of Somoza, the Soviet press exulted in unusually strong terms, asserting that U.S. influence over Latin America was decaying rapidly and that Cuban influence was growing, as demonstrated by the U.S. inability to get OAS support to head off a Sandinista victory, as well as by the "ever-increasing participation of Latin American countries in the nonaligned movement." The Soviets noted that "the United States had traditionally regarded Latin America as some kind of 'internal security zone' of its own," and expressed gratification that "the Americans are feeling increasingly uncomfortable in their 'internal security zone'" (*Sovetskaya Rossiya,* July 20, 1979). Almost immediately, shortly before the announcement of the establishment of Soviet diplomatic ties with Nicaragua, the Soviet press began eagerly to anticipate the prospects of the revolution in El Salvador (*Pravda,* July 17, 1979).

19. Leites, *Operational Code of the Politburo,* p. 79. Alluding to Soviet policy of the last decade in the Third World, the former USA Institute staff member Galina Orionova thus comments that "the Soviet government behaves like any ordinary Soviet consumer. He grabs anything which happens to be on the counter, even if he doesn't need it, knowing that tomorrow it may no longer be available" (Beloff, "Escape from Boredom").

20. See, for example, statements by Boris Ponomarev on April 25, 1978 (TASS, April 25, 1978), and by Kirilenko on February 27, 1979 (*Pravda,* February 28, 1979).

21. See Thomas A. Wolfe, *The SALT Experience* (Cambridge: Ballinger, 1979), pp. 107, 111.

22. L. I. Brezhnev, "The Great October Revolution and the Progress of Mankind," Radio Moscow, November 2, 1977, cited by Raymond L. Garthoff, "Mutual Deterrence and Strategic Arms Limitation in Soviet Policy." *International Security* 3 (Summer 1978). Garthoff cites a number of other such Soviet assertions made in recent years.

23. See Leites, *Operational Code of the Politburo,* pp. 88–89.

24. See Henry Kissinger, *White House Years* (Boston: Little, Brown, 1979), pp. 179, 187, 836, 1053.

25. See Leites, *Operational Code of the Politburo,* pp. 82–84, 41–42. "To seek unilateral concessions from the Soviet Union by pressing as hard as possible on the 'Chinese lever,'" one leading Soviet specialist insisted in the fall of 1979, "is completely unrealistic" (V. B. Lukin, "Washington-Beijing: Quasi Allies?" *USA: Economics, Politics, Ideology,* no. 12, 1979).

26. *Pravda,* April 3, 1971.

27. A. Grechko, "The Leading Role of the CPSU in Building the Army of a Developed Socialist Society," *Voprosy istorii KPSS,* May 1974.

28. *Krasnaya Zvezda* (Moscow), March 15, 1980.

29. See Alexander Yanov, *Detente after Brezhnev: The Domestic Roots of Soviet Foreign Policy* (Berkeley: Institute of International Studies, University of California, 1977).

Chapter 2 / *The Political Mechanics of the Brezhnev Regime*

1. This point is of central importance. The ambiguity of some Western writers about the boundaries of such referents as "elite," "leadership," or "oligarchy" has the unfortunate effect of promoting a similar ambiguity about the locus of power in the Soviet Union. The best available critique of this practice has been made by Myron Rush in a review essay on Seweryn Bialer's *Stalin's Successors: Leadership, Stability, and Change in the Soviet Union* (New York: Cambridge University Press, 1980). Rush writes, "Is there a gradation of power, then, in which the power of junior oligarchs does not exceed that of powerful non-oligarchs? Is the power structure formless and diffuse so that the Soviet oligarchy—like the 'elites' in studies of the American power structure—has vague boundaries, making it impossible to tell who belongs and who does not? It would be strange if this were so in such a highly authoritarian political system, but this view is implicit in [Seweryn] Bialer's study, and he nowhere discusses the problem explicitly. Given the diffuseness of power in Bialer's model of the Soviet political system, it is not surprising that he believes the oligarchy to be readily accessible to lower-ranking political leaders—what he calls the Soviet 'elite'—and subject to pressure from the groups they represent" (Myron Rush, "The Soviet Military Build-Up and the Coming Succession," *International Security* 5 (Spring 1981), 171).

In this book, I have sought to avoid use of the term "elite" because of the misleading connotations it has acquired. I employ the terms "oligarchy" or "leadership" to refer to the members of the party Presidium (Politburo) and Secretariat, the term "party aristocracy" to refer to the next few hundred officials in the hierarchy, and the term "party baronage" to refer to the oblast party first secretaries and those republic first secretaries who are not members of the Politburo. The boundaries of other groups alluded to should be apparent in the context.

2. Grey Hodnett, "The Pattern of Leadership Politics," in Seweryn Bialer, ed., *The Domestic Context of Soviet Foreign Policy* (Boulder: Westview Press, 1981), pp. 87–118. In this important paper, Hodnett in part builds upon the position laid out by T. H. Rigby a decade earlier (T. H. Rigby, "The Soviet Leadership: Towards a Self-Stabilizing Oligarchy?" *Soviet Studies* 22 (October 1970), 167–191).

The picture of relationships within the oligarchy I present in Chapters 2 and 3 is broadly consistent with the views regarding this oligarchy offered by both Rigby and Hodnett, although there are some important differences. Three of these are of general significance: (1) I submit, for reasons amplified in the text, that Rigby greatly overstates the seriousness of any private commitment Brezhnev and his colleagues may have made after removing Khrushchev to allow the ventilation of major policy differences at Central Committee plenums (Rigby, p. 187); (2) I also contend that Rigby overestimates the political importance of the domestic functions of the Soviet president, and underestimates the importance of his foreign policy/defense functions; and (3) I argue that both Rigby and Hodnett somewhat overstate the relative importance of the Presidium of the Council of Ministers, which in the Brezhnev regime was not really a "key organ of power" comparable in significance to the party Politburo and Secretariat, as Rigby suggests (p. 176). In the hierarchy of power relationships throughout the Brezhnev era, the top government organ was much weaker, was in most respects in a dependent position, and was largely removed, in practice if not in name, from authority over foreign, internal security, and defense policy. (Rigby later partly acknowledges this; see his excellent paper "The Soviet Government since Khrushchev" in the Australian journal *Politics* 12 (May 1977), 15). This is not to belittle the functional importance of the Council of Ministers as the Politburo's primary vehicle for running the economy. As I note later, Brezhnev spent most of his years as party leader vainly attempting to gain personal control of the Council of Ministers in order to assert personal control over the economic machinery.

3. By far the best-known apparent exception was the Central Committee plenum of June 1957, which defeated and expelled from the leadership Khrushchev's opponents V. M. Molotov, G. M. Malenkov, and L. M. Kaganovich after they had allegedly assembled an "arithmetical majority" against Khrushchev in the party Presidium. Yet even this well-known story should be treated with reserve. First, there is strong reason to believe that this plenum was a rump session of only one hundred members, heavily weighted with Khrushchev supporters who were brought to Moscow in Marshal G. K. Zhukov's military aircraft while others were left behind. Second, there is also reason to suspect, as Robert Conquest suggests, that in the maneuvers immediately preceding the plenum Zhukov and KGB chief Serov strongly and successfully pressured the vacillators N. A. Bulganin and K. Ye. Voroshilov to desert Molotov, Malenkov, and Kaganovich and thus to restore Khrushchev's Presidium majority for the management of the plenum and the dictation of its decisions (Robert Conquest, *Power and Policy in the USSR* [New York: St. Martin's, 1961], pp. 312–313). Finally, it is noteworthy that Khrushchev's supporter M. A. Suslov was selected

by the Presidium to "present information about the sessions of the Presidium" to the plenum after Khrushchev and Molotov had spoken. This selection of speakers was apparently the final act of the Presidium before the plenum. The fact that a Khrushchev agent was delegated to tell the plenum the tale of the challenge to Khrushchev strongly suggests that Khrushchev's Presidium majority had by then returned. See the account in the June 1965 issue of the dissident journal *Political Diary* (*Politicheskiy dnevnik* [Amsterdam: Alexander Herzen Foundation, 1972], pp. 106–108). In sum, there are grounds for concluding that even this plenum acted in obedience to the will of a Presidium majority, and was orchestrated to reflect a decisive event that had already occurred.

4. Jiri Valenta considers the expanded Central Committee plenum held during the evolving Czech crisis in July 1968 to be another exception to this norm. He cites the parading of testimony about the Czech danger by a wide variety of speakers as an instance of Soviet "enlargement of the decisionmaking circle," and contends that the plenum was the scene of "pressure" exerted on the Presidium by lower-ranking ideologues sympathetic with the extremist views of Ukrainian first secretary P. Y. Shelest (Valenta, *Soviet Intervention in Czechslovakia, 1968* [Baltimore: Johns Hopkins University Press, 1979], pp. 60–63). This view appears somewhat dubious, in part because it underestimates the degree to which many, if not all, of the non-Politburo speakers were influenced by what they perceived to be Brezhnev's wishes. The notion that figures such as the head of the Writers' Union imagined that they were summoned to speak in order to express their own views—much less to put pressure on the leadership—is at odds with the realities of Soviet politics. In fact, such people almost certainly took their cues from the very tough domestic ideological line publicly espoused by Brezhnev since late March 1968. More important, Valenta's suggestion ignores the mechanics of how speakers are designated at a CC plenum. It was surely the central party Secretariat, dominated not by Shelest in Kiev but by Brezhnev, Suslov, and Kirilenko in Moscow, which organized this expanded plenum.

5. *Political Diary,* April 1970 issue, in *Politicheskiy dnevnik* collection, pp. 657–658. This journal was published during the first six years of the Brezhnev era by intellectuals who in some cases appeared to have good contacts within the Soviet regime. Although some of the statements and rumors reported in *Political Diary* are unverifiable, many are quite plausible, and in some cases have been supported by subsequent evidence. Two such cases are cited in notes 8 and 15 of this chapter.

6. In July 1955, Molotov found himself isolated when he took to the floor of a Central Committee plenum his disagreement with the party Presidium's decision to restore party relations with Yugoslavia. He was said to have been "unanimously condemned" for this conduct by an unpublished plenum resolution, which was itself cited in the resolution issued upon his fall two years later (*Pravda,* July 4, 1957).

7. Werner G. Hahn, *The Politics of Soviet Agriculture, 1960–1970* (Baltimore: Johns Hopkins University Press, 1972).

8. *Political Diary,* June 1965, carries this entry: "Many comrades think an intensification of national trends can be observed in the Ukraine. National attitudes find their reflection in the activity of some governmental and even

party organs, and these attitudes are extensively held among some members of the Ukrainian intelligentsia." The article goes on to give examples, including the "great difficulty" USSR Gosplan had in coordinating plans with Ukrainian officials, who "declare openly that they are being robbed" (*Politicheskiy dnevnik,* pp. 90–91). For the subsequent evolution of this problem, see Grey Hodnett, "Ukrainian Politics and the Purge of Shelest" (Paper delivered at the annual meeting of the Midwest Slavic Conference, Ann Arbor, Michigan, May 5–7, 1977).

9. *New York Times,* June 15, 1973.

10. Alain Jacob in *Le Monde,* February 12, 1974, cited in Hodnett, "The Pattern of Leadership Politics," p. 101. Jacob also attributes to "most trustworthy sources" the view that "it is highly improbable that an important decision or a piece of information of major interest is not circulated either for opinion or simply as information to all members of the Politburo within twenty-four hours." This statement is surely far too sweeping to be taken literally. It seems likely that some items of sensitive information were distributed to Brezhnev alone; thus on one occasion, according to Kissinger, at a 1971 meeting with Brezhnev in Moscow, Brezhnev "proudly" showed Kissinger a cable from Hanoi "to demonstrate that he alone was listed on the distribution" (Henry Kissinger, *White House Years* [Boston: Little, Brown, 1979], p. 1145). It is equally plausible to suppose that other items were normally sent only to the full Politburo members of the Defense Council (that is, to Brezhnev, Kosygin, and Podgornyy); and still others, to the Moscow-based Politburo members alone. In sum, the Brezhnev Politburo's treatment of the dissemination of information was probably characterized by collegiality in some spheres and hierarchy in others.

11. Merle Fainsod, *How Russia Is Ruled* (Cambridge: Harvard University Press, 1963), p. 338. On the relations between the Secretariat and the Central Committee Presidium (Politburo), see Fainsod, pages 220–221, 338–340. Regarding these matters, and many others, Fainsod's depiction of the inner mechanics of Soviet reality in Khrushchev's time has not been rendered obsolete by the modifications introduced during the Brezhnev era.

12. Brezhnev stated at the 25th Party Congress that the Secretariat had "constantly occupied itself" with, among other things, "questions of the selection and assignment of cadres." This occupation lies at the heart of oligarchic politics. Below the very top party echelon, a party committee's exercise of *nomenklatura* authority to select or confirm is often complicated by a multiple subordination of the posts to be filled, particularly when these are industrial or other economic positions. Consequently, it is frequently necessary to coordinate personnel decisions vertically with both higher party echelons and the ministries concerned (Jerry F. Hough, *The Soviet Prefects* [Cambridge: Harvard University Press, 1969], pp. 29–30, 115–116, 150–155, 163–164, 167–168; William J. Conyngham, *Industrial Management in the Soviet Union* [Stanford: Hoover Institution Press, 1973], pp. 278–279; Fainsod, *How Russia Is Ruled,* pp. 224–225, 151–156).

In contrast, in the case of appointments generated at the top—in the central Secretariat and the Politburo—it is evident that the norm is *horizontal* coordination, that is, vetting of appointment decisions among those fellow oligarchs whose interests are particularly affected. In some areas—notably in the appointment of oblast party officials—this task was evidently routinized and simplified and strife minimized after October 1964 by the tacit understanding to avoid politically motivated changes and to promote from within the local party structure (the so-called policy of stability of cadres). Nevertheless, it is likely that in other cases under the Brezhnev regime, the nature and extent of such coordination was itself often politically determined by the balance of forces in the oligarchy. The political aspect of cadre selection was most vividly illuminated on those exceptional occasions when the interests of a member of the leadership were transparently attacked by a leadership appointment. One such case, for example, was the July 1970 designation of V. V. Fedorchuk to be chairman of the Ukrainian KGB, after which, as Grey Hodnett and others have noted, he immediately began to act in a manner harmful to the interests of Shelest, the Ukrainian party boss and Politburo member. This decision was almost certainly coordinated between KGB Chairman Andropov and Brezhnev and approved by either the party Secretariat or the Politburo (more likely the former), without respect for the wishes of Shelest and his Politburo associate Podgornyy.

13. See Lilita Dzirkals, Thane Gustafson, and A. Ross Johnson, *The Media and Intra-Elite Communication in the USSR*, R-2869, (Santa Monica: The Rand Corporation, Sept. 1982), pp. 13–19.

14. Trapeznikov was several times rejected by the membership of the Academy of Sciences in his attempts to achieve the status of academician, but he eventually succeeded. Clearly, the party leadership did not consider it expedient to apply excessive pressure on his behalf. *Political Diary* relates that early in the Brezhnev regime, Trapeznikov made a prolonged effort to reintroduce Stalin's works in the social science teaching syllabus; this effort was defeated after strong resistance from many leaders of institutes and universities. It is evident that on this and other matters he sought, at least in the first half of the Brezhnev regime, to press into policy a line that went beyond the leadership consensus (*Politicheskiy dnevnik,* pp. 119–121).

15. *Political Diary* reported in the summer of 1965 that Kosygin had "recently" renewed an effort he had made immediately after becoming premier to remove the central party apparatus from Soviet economic affairs; he complained he could not function effectively under the existing "dual" system of economic supervision. He was again unsuccessful (*Politicheskiy dnevnik,* pp. 50–51). The credibility of this report of abortive attempts early in the Brezhnev era to get rid of the Party's economic departments has been enhanced by rumors of renewed lobbying in Moscow to the same end in 1983, early in the Andropov era.

For attempts to correlate the various departments of the Central Committee with the ministries and other institutions each supervises, see Abdurakham Avtorkhanov, *The Communist Party Apparatus* (Chicago: Henry Regnery, 1966), pp. 201–204, and Jerry F. Hough and Merle Fainsod, *How the Soviet Union Is Governed* (Cambridge: Harvard University Press, 1979), pp. 412–417.

16. I here exclude the Department for Cadres Abroad, which is concerned with problems of personnel not policy, and the International Information Department, established late in the Brezhnev regime and designated to carry out sophisticated external persuasion on behalf of Soviet policy, not to help in policy formation.

17. Leonard Schapiro, "The CPSU International Department," *International Journal* 32 (Winter 1966–1967), 41–55. See also Elizabeth Teague, "The Foreign Departments of the Central Committee of the CPSU," Radio Liberty Research Bulletin Supplement, October 27, 1980.
18. Schapiro, "CPSU International Department," p. 44.
19. See Barbara L. Dash, *A Defector Reports: The Institute of the USA and Canada,* Delphic Associates, May 1982, and Benjamin Fischer, "The Soviet Political System and Foreign Policy-Making in the Brezhnev Era," an authoritative unpublished manuscript prepared for a project of the Columbia University Research Institute on International Change.

    As in bureaucracies in other countries, while some of this background material produced by the *institutchiki* for the Central Committee is read and absorbed, much of it is apparently unread by the ostensible consumers. Galina Orionova feels that the competition for the attention of the Central Committee recipients is too fierce to make success likely; they are innundated with "tons of papers" which "just physically can't be read by the International Department because they have too many." She quotes a remark attributed by an acquaintance to M. V. Senin, head of the East German Sector of the Central Committee's Socialist Countries Department: "We are sitting here and writing and thinking this and that and we just don't have the time and it goes into the waste paper basket." Orionova's overall impression is that occasionally, on "urgent topics," a commissioned report may be "read and appreciated," but that more commonly, "this influence is nominal" (Dash, p. 220). It is likely that the International Department and the Socialist Countries Department devote attention more consistently to the work of the so-called consultants to these organs, experts who apparently perform tasks within the departments on an ad hoc basis (Fischer).
20. Fischer, "Soviet Political System"; Dash, *A Defector Reports.*
21. Valenta, *Soviet Intervention,* pp. 125–126.
22. Kissinger, *White House Years,* pp. 138–141, 523–526. As earlier noted, on one occasion Brezhnev is said to have shown Kissinger a cable from the Soviet embassy in Hanoi, supposedly distributed to Brezhnev alone among the Soviet leaders (see note 10).
23. Edward L. Warner, *The Military in Contemporary Soviet Politics* (New York: Praeger, 1977), pp. 48–49.
24. "Secret Speech of Khrushchev Concerning the 'Cult of the Individual,' Delivered at the Twentieth Congress of the Communist Party of the Soviet Union, February 25, 1956," in *The Anti-Stalin Campaign and International Communism* (New York: Columbia University Press, 1956), p. 83. Khrushchev asserts that the "importance" of the Politburo was reduced and its work "disorganized" by Stalin's creation of various commissions within the Politburo, and observes that as a result "some members of the Political Bureau were in this way kept away from participation in the most important state matters."
25. See Douglas F. Garthoff, "The Soviet Military and Arms Control," *Survival* (November–December 1977), 246.
26. There is a strong impulse in the oligarchy to spread responsibility for difficult decisions, and to evade decisions when all relevant actors are not committed. Penkovskiy quotes Marshal S. S. Varentsov regarding one incident in Khrush-

chev's time at a meeting of the Supreme Military Council: "Once during Khrushchev's absence Marshal Biryuzov raised the question of additional funds for missile tests in a Council meeting. Suslov and Mikoyan, who were present at the meeting, failed to solve the problem. Varentsov said afterward: 'They started beating around the bush and kept talking, but never reached a decision. If Stalin were alive, he would have given the word and the whole thing would have been resolved then and there' " (Oleg Penkovskiy, *The Penkovskiy Papers* [New York: Doubleday, 1965], pp. 234–235). This tendency is likely to have become more marked during the Brezhnev era.

27. Ibid., pp. 233–234, 299–300. I concur in Edward Warner's judgment that the statements regarding the Supreme Military Council that are attributed to Penkovskiy are probably authentic, and also probably well grounded in authoritative statements made to Penkovskiy by his friend Marshal Varentsov (Warner, *The Military in Contemporary Soviet Politics*, p. 35). See also Thomas Wolfe, *The Soviet Military Scene: Institutional and Defense Policy Considerations*, R-4913-PR (Santa Monica: The Rand Corporation, 1966); Malcolm Mackintosh, "The Soviet Military: Influence on Defense Policymaking," *Problems of Communism*, September–October 1973, p. 3; Vernon V. Aspaturian, "The Soviet Military-Industrial Complex: Does It Exist?" *Journal of International Affairs* 26, no. 1 (1972), 11–12. Wolfe (pp. 11–12) quotes a Soviet source as charging that Marshal Zhukov had sought to usurp control over the Supreme Military Council "despite the fact that it included members of the Party Presidium as well as military and political leaders of the army and navy" (Yu. P. Petrov, *Partinoye stroitelstvo v sovetskoy armii i flote, 1918–1961* [Moscow, 1964] pp. 305–306.)

28. Between 1965 and early 1967 there was evidence suggesting that some elements of the Soviet military leadership were pressing for a modification of party-military joint organizational arrangements at the highest level to enlarge the military voice and to reduce the likelihood of repeating what Chief of Staff M. V. Zakharov called the "very expensive" and "irreparable" damage done by Khrushchev's management of military affairs (*Krasnaya Zvezda*, February 4, 1965). In the January 1966 issue of the restricted Ministry of Defense publication *Voyennaya mysl'*, now publicly available in the West, Colonel General N. Lomov called for the creation of a "single military-political organ" which would "unite" the political and military leadership both in wartime and "in times of peace," and which would give due weight to professional military expertise. A year later, Major General V. Zemskov stated that in the event of war supreme authority would be vested in special "military-political organs" which "are already now being created" (*Krasnaya Zvezda*, January 5, 1967). Twelve weeks later, on the day Defense Minister Malinovskiy expired, Lt. General I. Zavyalov again cited the need for a "collective organ" of national defense leadership premised on the "unity" of political and military leaders (*Krasnaya Zvezda*, March 31, 1967). One may therefore speculate that one of the compromises reached in response to this pressure was the revamping of Khrushchev's Supreme Military Council into a Defense Council in which civilian political representation would be both somewhat reduced and given more formal and institutional definition. One may further speculate that this process may have been completed during the transition between Malinovskiy's

death and Marshal Grechko's appointment as minister of defense in April 1967.

29. Fischer, "Soviet Political System"; Raymond L. Garthoff, "SALT and the Soviet Military," *Problems of Communism,* January–February 1975, p. 29. Although Garthoff's listing of the Defense Council's members under the first Brezhnev era arrangement seems likely to be correct, his nomenclature is probably partly mistaken; he refers to this institution as the "Supreme (or Higher) Defense Council," a hybrid name halfway between Khrushchev's "Supreme Military Council" and Brezhnev's "Defense Council." The correct title was confirmed when the Soviet press began publicly to refer to the existence of the body in the spring of 1976 (*Krasnaya Zvezda,* April 17, 1976).

30. Fischer, "Soviet Political System"; Garthoff, "SALT and the Soviet Military."

31. Fischer, "Soviet Political System"; Hodnett, "The Pattern of Leadership Politics," p. 103. In 1976, after Andropov had headed the KGB for a decade, the Soviet Military Encyclopedia stated that he "takes active part in building the Soviet Armed Forces" (*Sovetskaya voyennaya entsiklopediya* [Moscow, 1976], I, 193). This would appear to imply at least occasional participation in the Defense Council.

32. The change was thus away from a system of de facto representation of the four most senior political figures to a system of strict *ex officio* representation by designated office. This process of formalization was carried a step further in 1977, when the new USSR constitution gave the Presidium of the Supreme Soviet nominal responsibility to "form" the Defense Council and to "confirm" its membership. This is, of course, a ritual function, not a real one.

33. *Krasnaya Zvezda,* April 6, 1967. Thereafter, the Soviet press began to publicize joint appearances by the Politburo members of the Defense Council at defense installations and exercises. In late May 1967, Brezhnev, Kosygin, Ustinov, Defense Minister Grechko, Military-Industrial Commission chairman L. V. Smirnov, and other military and industrial leaders thus made an inspection visit to the Northern Fleet and the military-industrial facilities in the north (*Pravda,* June 4, 1967). In October, Brezhnev, Kosygin, Podgornyy, and Ustinov were photographed with Ukrainian and military leaders outside Kiev reviewing the troops that had taken part in the "Dnepr" exercises (*Pravda Ukrainy,* October 3, 1967).

34. *Pravda,* October 28, 1982.

35. Benjamin Fischer, writing in early 1979, shortly before Ryabov was removed from the Secretariat, states that Ustinov as Defense Minister had "apparently" continued to some extent to retain his old function in supervising defense production, and that "the pattern of public appearances suggest that he shares part of his responsibilities with Ryabov" ("Soviet Political System"). I shall return to this question in Chapter 5.

Chapter 3 / *The Politburo as Battleground*

1. *Political Diary* asserts that at this plenum, Suslov was designated "to give an account of the Presidium's deliberations" (*Politicheskiy dnevnik* [Amsterdam: Alexander Herzan Foundation, 1972], p. 108).

2. *New York Times,* October 22, 1964; *Washington Post,* October 22 and November 30, 1964; Michel Tatu, *Power in the Kremlin: From Khrushchev to Kosygin* (New York: Viking, 1970), pp. 416–417.

3. See Grey Hodnett and Peter J. Potichnyj, *The Ukraine and the Czechoslovak Crisis* (Canberra: Australian National University, 1970), pp. 22–23; Grey Hodnett, "Ukrainian Politics and the Purge of Shelest" (Paper delivered at the annual meeting of the Midwest Slavic Conference, Ann Arbor, Michigan, May 5–7, 1977), pp. 74–77, 84.

4. See Edward Crankshaw in *Observer,* London, November 22, 1964, and June 20, 1965; *Economist Foreign Report,* November 19, 1964; Victor Zorza in *Guardian,* November 20, 1964.

5. One notable example was the case of N. I. Savinkin, who was acting chief of the Administrative Organs Department of the Central Committee for almost four years after the fall of Khrushchev before his position as chief was legitimized (*Pravda,* May 5, 1968). The difficulty in securing his confirmation no doubt arose from the sensitive role of this department, which oversees the armed forces, the KGB, and the MVD. Even more striking was the impasse in the next decade over the Propaganda Department of the Central Committee. Between April 1970, when V. I. Stepakov was summarily removed from this post and presently exiled to a diplomatic post in Yugoslavia, and May 1977, when Yevgeniy Tyazhelnikov was appointed, this department was also run by its ranking first deputy chief, since the oligarchs could not agree on a replacement. Thus for seven of Brezhnev's eighteen years as party boss—about 40 percent of the Brezhnev era—the Soviet propaganda apparatus, although supervised from on high by a party secretary, performed its day-to-day duties without a formal head.

6. See Leonard Schapiro, "The General Department of the CC of the CPSU," *Survey,* Summer 1965, pp. 53–65.

7. Edward Crankshaw, *Observer,* June 20, 1965.

8. For a useful discussion of this 1982 process after the fact, see Joseph Kraft, "Letter from Moscow," *New Yorker,* January 31, 1983. I will address these events in Chapter 5.

9. TASS, December 9, 1965.

10. Victor Zorza, *Washington Post,* December 10, 1965.

11. *Political Diary* subsequently asserted that the leadership decision to remove Semichastnyy, "an old friend of Shelepin's and a like-thinker," was taken by seizing an occasion when Shelepin was in the hospital and could not attend the Politburo session. The journal also notes that Brezhnev had taken Shelepin with him on a visit to Eastern Europe the previous month, and speculates that this may have been done to safeguard the leadership "from any accident" (*Politicheskiy dnevnik,* pp. 243–244).

12. *Khrushchev Remembers: The Last Testament* (Boston: Little, Brown, 1974), pp. 30–34, 43, 51.

13. Ibid., pp. 31, 34.

14. Ibid., pp. 219–230; *Khrushchev Remembers* (Boston: Little, Brown, 1976), pp. 515–517. See also Carl A. Linden, *Khrushchev and the Soviet Leadership, 1957–1964* (Baltimore: Johns Hopkins University Press, 1966), pp. 90–91, 114–115, 190; Tatu, *Power in the Kremlin,* pp. 69–79.

15. *Pravda,* July 4, 1965.
16. The U.S. Defense Department document *Soviet Military Power* (Washington, D.C.: U.S. Government Printing Office, 1981), p. 27, states that "some 30 divisions" were added to the Soviet ground forces between 1967 and 1981. In the same period, the size of all Soviet divisions at full strength was increased by some two thousand men; of course, however, many Soviet divisions are not at full strength (p. 28). A CIA analysis concludes that in 1971–1980 alone, total Soviet military manpower increased by 400,000 men, and the Soviet ground forces by 250,000 (*Soviet and U.S. Defense Activities, 1971–1980: A Dollar Cost Comparison* [CIA National Foreign Assessment Center, SR 81–100005, January 1981], p. 9). It seems likely that when the ground force increase of the years 1965–1970 is added, the total is considerably greater, since this is the period when the bulk of the anti-China buildup occurred.
17. Before the "all-service" buildup was agreed upon, the Soviet tank forces commander Marshal P. A. Rotmistrov attacked "views which have slipped into the press that allegedly 'the queen of the battlefield—the land forces—is relinquishing her crown to the rocket weapons'" (*Pravda,* April 15, 1965). This was an allusion to a statement made by deputy chief of the General Staff S. M. Shtemenko in *Nedelya,* February 7, 1965. In the May issue of *Voyennaya mysl',* Defense Minister Malinovskiy also responded to Shtemenko, asserting that "we consider it premature to 'bury' the infantry, as some people do." It seems clear that these polemics reflected the tugging and hauling over resources that went on within the military as well as outside it during the first four months of 1965, until the broad expansion of the conventional forces became settled policy.
18. *Soviet and U.S. Defense Activities, 1971–1980: A Dollar Cost Comparison,* p. 9.
19. Throughout the bulk of the Brezhnev era Kosygin was, on the whole, the most consistent Politburo supporter of expenditures for the consumer, and in 1965 he more than once appeared to line up with Podgornyy on this issue. In July 1965, however, he made a public obeisance to the emerging consensus on defense spending which Podgornyy was apparently unwilling to make, asserting that "in the current situation" it would be against the national interest "to economize on defense" despite the "certain advantages" that would result if "very large sums" could be diverted from defense to "other branches" of the Soviet economy (*Pravda,* July 12, 1965).
20. *Pravda,* May 22, 1965.
21. *Pravda,* June 3, 1965.
22. Cairo Middle East News Agency, December 28, 1964.
23. *Pravda,* July 25, 1965.
24. One such proposal championed in various forms throughout the Brezhnev era by a number of writers and officials—notably former Politburo member Gennadiy Voronov—involved the so-called 'unregulated link.' This concept involved allowing small farming teams to manage allocated land and equipment on a long-term basis, operating without detailed work orders from above and receiving pay in proportion to the effectiveness of results. The "unregulated link" is the closest approximation that has appeared in the Soviet Union to the steps some other Communist countries have taken to relax central controls

over agriculture—steps that in the last decade have gone furthest in China, which has adopted a "household responsibility system" that has virtually decollectivized agriculture and restored the private peasant farm in all but name. Although the link is said to have produced good results in places where it has been authorized, there are doubts as to its general applicability in the Soviet Union because of the shortage of the skilled labor and agricultural machinery essential to its success.

The hostility Brezhnev and others showed toward the link was primarily political, not economic, and centered on their fear of loosening political controls over the countryside and their horror of tampering with the legacy of Stalin's collectivization. In this regard, Brezhnev was probably strongly influenced by the reactionary views of his personal staff aide V. A. Golikov. However, in its last two years, when it found itself under the pressure of agricultural disaster, the Brezhnev leadership's ideologically motivated resistance to the "unregulated link" weakened (See Keith Bush, "Soviet Agriculture: Ten Years under New Management," Radio Liberty Research Paper, August 21, 1974, pp. 31–32; Paige Bryan, "Investment and Planning: Soviet Agriculture's Performance and Outlook, 1971–72," Radio Liberty Research CRD 50/72, February 24, 1972, pp. 5–6; Foreign Broadcast Information Service Analysis Report, "Soviet Agricultural Policy: End of the Big Investment Era?," FB 80–10039, October 14, 1980, pp. 12–13; "Decentralization, the Private Sector, and the Soviet Agricultural Crisis," Radio Liberty Research RL 398/82, October 1, 1982).

25. M. Elizabeth Denton, "Soviet Consumer Policy: Trends and Prospects," in JEC Compendium, *Soviet Economy in a Time of Change*, (Washington, D.C.: U.S. Government Printing Office, 1979), I, 772–773, and Table 4, p. 768.

26. In the wake of a record 1966 harvest, in 1967 there was a reallocation of some resources away from agriculture and to all the major competing sectors, but particularly to defense (Keith Bush, "Soviet Agriculture: Ten Years Under New Management," p. 3; Werner G. Hahn, *The Politics of Soviet Agriculture, 1960–1970* (Baltimore: Johns Hopkins University Press, 1972), pp. 189–206). But despite large shortfalls, Bush notes that "very large gains were recorded" in agricultural investment accomplished, while on the output side, "Brezhnev aimed at a 25 percent increase in 1966–70 and attained a 21 percent growth" (pp. 3, 4).

27. Keith Bush, "Is the Ninth Five-Year Plan Consumer-Oriented? " Radio Liberty Research, CRD 139/71, April 8, 1971, p. 7. Bush suggests that the Soviets count investment in one or another enterprise under the heading of investment for Group A (producer goods) or for Group B (consumer goods) depending on "the destination of the greater part of their output." This would appear to imply some Soviet mislabeling of the investment used to produce consumer goods in heavy and defense industry; in other words, some understatement of investment for Group B.

28. Denton, "Soviet Consumer Policy," p. 767.

29. Particularly notable was the unusual article published by the Politburo's overseer of agriculture, Dmitry Polyanskiy, in *Kommunist* no. 15, 1967, arguing against the diversion of funds from agriculture. See the discussion in Hahn, *Politico of Soviet Agriculture*, pp. 195–196.

30. Denton, "Soviet Consumer Policy," p. 767. It is noteworthy that although the language used by Brezhnev at the 24th Party Congress in 1971 in alluding to

such matters as the rates of growth of "Group A" and "Group B" seemed somewhat more promising for consumers than the language he had used at the 23rd Party Congress in 1966, consumers fared better between 1966 and 1970 than they did thereafter.

31. See Myron Rush, "Guns over Growth in Soviet Policy," *International Security* 7 (Winter 1982/1983), 167–179; Abraham S. Becker, *The Burden of Soviet Defense: A Political-Economic Essay,* R-2752-AF (Santa Monica: The Rand Corporation, October 1981); and Becker, *Guns, Butter and Tools: Tradeoffs in Soviet Resource Allocation,* P-6816 (Santa Monica: The Rand Corporation, October 1982). Writing in the mid-1970s, as this secular trend was becoming apparent, Abram Bergson concluded that "given competing defense and consumption requirements, Brezhnev apparently feels unable to afford accelerated industrialization even at a reduced pace" (Bergson, "Russia's Economic Planning Shift," *Wall Street Journal,* May 17, 1976). I shall return to this issue in Chapter 5.

32. *Pravda,* September 9, 1965. As Michel Tatu observes, this final Rumyantsev statement as editor of *Pravda* was itself a much more cautious and hedged version of an extremely liberal article he had published on the same subject seven months earlier (*Pravda,* February 21, 1965). It was, in effect, a rearguard action, taken at the close of a period in which Brezhnev had been consolidating his strength (Tatu, *Power in the Kremlin,* pp. 467–474).

33. In a December 1964 press conference in Cairo, Shelepin expounded on the "many obstacles" that stood in the way of peaceful coexistence between the Soviet Union and the United States, including but not limited to what he described as "U.S. plots" against Vietnam, Cuba, and the Congo (Cairo Middle East News Agency, December 28, 1964).

34. During a visit to Leipzig at the beginning of March 1965, Kosygin told Western newsmen that he had sent a letter to President Johnson proposing a summit meeting (*New York Times,* March 2, 1965). He is also reported to have remarked that "it would be very pleasant" if Johnson were to visit the USSR. These statements were not carried in the Moscow media.

35. TASS had attacked the conduct of the "representative of the DRV" at a World Youth Forum held in Moscow in mid-September 1964 (TASS, September 18, 1964). To the best of my knowledge, on no other occasion, before or since, has the USSR explicitly criticized Vietnam.

36. *Pravda,* January 30, 1966.

37. *Pravda,* May 9, 1965.

38. *Politicheskiy dnevnik,* p. 51; Tatu, *Power in the Kremlin,* pp. 479–487.

39. *Pravda,* March 31, 1966. According to *Political Diary,* the initial post-Khrushchev effort to restore Stalin's works to the teaching syllabus was not defeated until October 1966. In that same month, a Moscow conference of ideological officials heard prolonged praise and defense of Stalin by Georgian party Secretary D. G. Sturua, seconded by Azerbaydzhan party Secretary Kurbanov. But while most of the other speakers also took a very harsh line, insisting on a tightening of ideological discipline in a manner that suggested nostalgia for Stalinist verities, they avoided pronouncing the magic name. Party Secretary P. N. Demichev reminded the gathering that the party line on the Stalin issue was now the compromise position embodied in the Central Committee resolution

of June 30, 1956: that is to say, a position requiring decorum (*Politicheskiy dnevik,* pp. 119–126).

40. Addressing Brezhnev rhetorically in 1977, Boris Rabbot, the exiled former assistant to the fallen liberal *apparatchik* Aleksey Rumyantsev, asserted that "the worst enemy of new ideas in the social sciences was—and is—one of your closest friends, the head of the Central Committee's science department, Sergey Trapeznikov" (*New York Times Magazine,* November 7, 1977, p. 8). For accounts of some of Trapeznikov's activities behind the scenes, see *Politicheskiy dnevnik,* pp. 119–121, 663. On his early association with Brezhnev in Moldavia, see John Dornberg, *Brezhnev: The Masks of Power* (New York: Basic Books, 1974), pp. 108–109. On his 1965 public defense of Stalin's actions in the 1930s and his attack on the rehabilitation of Stalin's victims, see Tatu, *Power in the Kremlin,* p. 483.

41. One of Golikov's most noteworthy efforts in this direction was an article he coauthored with two others in the April 1972 issue of *Voprosy istorii KPSS,* whitewashing the historical record of collectivization, absolving Stalin personally of any errors, and attacking Soviet writings that had taken a more critical view. On another occasion, according to *Political Diary,* he and Trapeznikov wrote a private memorandum to Brezhnev attacking as "revisionists" the speechwriters who had prepared a moderate draft for a Brezhnev address to be delivered in April 1970 (*Politicheskiy dnevnik,* p. 663).

42. Jiri Valenta, *Soviet Intervention in Czechoslovakia, 1968* (Baltimore: Johns Hopkins University Press, 1979), pp. 125–126.

43. Pavlovskiy was commander in chief of Soviet ground forces at the time of both operations. On his past association with Brezhnev, see Dornberg, *Brezhnev,* p. 126. On his designation to command the 1968 invasion of Czechoslovakia, see Valenta, *Soviet Intervention in Czechoslovakia, 1968,* pp. 108, 146, 148. On his mission in Kabul in the period leading up to the 1979 invasion of Afghanistan, see Stephen T. Hosmer and Thomas W. Wolfe, *Soviet Policy and Practice toward Third World Conflicts* (Lexington, Mass.: Lexington Books, 1983), p. 113; also *Washington Post,* September 5, 1979.

44. *Pravda,* September 17, 1974. See the discussion of this episode in Chapter 4.

45. On Yepishev's personal associations with Brezhnev, see Dornberg, *Brezhnev,* p. 127; also, Alexander G. Rahr, "A Biographic Directory of 100 Leading Soviet Officials," Radio Liberty Research Bulletin, February 10, 1981, p. 31. In his capacity as chief of the Main Political Directorate of the Soviet Army and Navy, Yepishev joined in the reactionary chorus of Stalinist party functionaries attacking the liberal intelligentsia. According to *Political Diary,* he played such a role at the Moscow conference of ideological officials held in October 1966, and there revealed that he had banned subscriptions to the subversive literary journals *Novyy mir* and *Yunost'* for all Soviet military personnel and military establishments (*Politicheskiy dnevnik,* p. 122).

46. Notably, deputy heads of the International Department R. A. Ul'yanovskiy and K. N. Brutents. Brutents' role in the department expanded in the Brezhnev era in parallel with the expansion of the role the Soviet Union (and the department) played in the Third World; he was a department "consultant" in the late 1960s, head of a "group of consultants" in the early 1970s, and a deputy chief of the department since the middle 1970s. It is noteworthy that

the moderate Alexandr Bovin, who was also identified as leader of a group of consultants in October 1969, thereafter moved in the other direction, losing his official connection with the department while Brutents was ascending the ladder. The thrust and tone of Brutents' many published articles are in striking contrast to those of Bovin's writings. (See Elizabeth Teague, "The Foreign Departments of the Central Committee of the CPSU," Radio Liberty Research Bulletin Supplement, October 27, 1980; CIA National Foreign Assessment Center, *Directory of Soviet Officials, Volume I: National Organizations,* CR 78–14025, September 1978.)

47. Rahr, "Biographic Directory," p. 29; Warner, *The Military in Contemporary Soviet Politics* (New York: Praeger, 1977), p. 46; Dornberg, *Brezhnev,* p. 124, 154.

48. *Khrushchev Remembers,* p. 519.

49. On December 1, 1966, at an awards ceremony in Novorossiysk, Kirilenko praised Brezhnev's war record during the defense of Novorossiysk, and the next day *Pravda* and *Krasnaya Zvezda* carried articles doing the same. This was the first time since Khrushchev's fall that the central press had praised the war record of any member of the oligarchy.

50. Colonel General G. Sredin, "Istochnik sily i mogushchestva," *Voyennyy Vestnik,* no. 10, October 1977, p. 10.

51. Rahr, "Biographic Directory," p. 29.

52. *New York Times,* March 4, 1965.

53. In a 1963 speech to industrial and construction workers, Khrushchev complained about the "shortcomings" of defense industry enterprises, noted that the secrecy of their work prevented public criticism, and insisted that "certain undisciplined people working in the defense industry must not be allowed to take advantage of this." Noting that Dmitry Ustinov had been responsible for defense industry and had now been appointed chairman of the Supreme Council of the National Economy (Supreme Sovnarkhoz), he demanded that Ustinov do something about the problem he was alluding to. He then went on ostentatiously to deny allegations he attributed to the Western press that Ustinov's appointment meant "that the Soviet Union was going to militarize the country . . . and will now produce nothing but rockets" (Moscow Radio Domestic Service, April 26, 1963). After Khrushchev's removal, there were no further public allusions to shortcomings in the work of either Ustinov or the defense industries.

54. TASS, March 26, 1965. Ustinov was simultaneously promoted to candidate membership in the Politburo.

55. On Brezhnev's wartime association with Grechko, see Dornberg, *Brezhnev,* pp. 76–77; Rahr, "Biographic Directory," pp. 30–31.

56. As we shall see in Chapter 5, this relationship became increasingly important toward the end, as Brezhnev's health and his political leverage over his associates began to collapse together. One of the striking features of the important speech delivered by Brezhnev to a military gathering a month before his death was his effort to derive personal backing from Ustinov.

57. See Dornberg, *Brezhnev,* p. 214.

58. See, for example, Victor Zorza in *Washington Post,* July 2, 1967; also *New York Times,* June 29, 1967.

59. Dornberg, *Brezhnev,* considers this thesis equally plausible.
60. *Economist,* January 6, 1968. Along the same line, the knowledgeable British observer Malcolm Mackintosh points out that in July the Moscow Air Defense District Military Council held a special meeting attended by Yegorychev's successor V. V. Grishin, and that the district then launched a lengthy air defense exercise. Mackintosh therefore surmises that Yegorychev, speaking as a member of this military council, had complained at the plenum that Soviet air defense systems were unready for war (Malcolm Mackintosh, "The Soviet Military: Influence on Foreign Policy," *Problems of Communism,* September–October 1973, p. 6). Mackintosh goes on from this to conclude, however, that Yegorychev was prompted to say this "by members of the military" who "considered the policy pursued by the Soviet government in the Middle East crisis too risky." This seems less plausible, particularly since most Soviet official comment after the plenum implied defensiveness about the opposite contention—that the Soviet Union had not taken enough risks for the Arabs (See Christian Duevel, "Soviet Party Press Attacks Left Opposition," Radio Liberty Research CRD 433/67, August 1, 1967).

The most likely conclusion, therefore, is that Yegorychev, who had visited Egypt shortly before the hostilities, wished that the Soviet Union had been able to take more forthright steps during te fighting, and was complaining that Brezhnev's allegedly inadequate military preparations had deprived the country of this capability.
61. TASS, July 11, 1967.
62. *Moskovskaya Pravda,* July 2, 1967.
63. *Radyanska Ukrainia,* June 29, 1967.
64. It has been suggested that personal relations between Novotný and Brezhnev had been severely strained since 1964 as a result of Novotný's exceptionally angry reaction to Khrushchev's ouster (according to one rumor, he hung up the phone on Brezhnev), and that this circumstance helped to influence Brezhnev not to intervene to save him in December 1967 (Dornberg, *Brezhnev,* pp. 182, 219–221.) Obviously, however, a more important factor was Brezhnev's misreading of Dubček and of the forces brewing in the Czechoslovak Party.
65. See A. Ross Johnson, Robert W. Dean, and Alexander Alexiev, *East European Military Establishments: The Warsaw Pact Northern Tier* (New York: Crane Russak, 1982).
66. *Pravda,* March 30, 1968. See Christian Duevel, "Brezhnev Exhorts 'Monolithic Unity' and 'Iron Discipline,' " Radio Liberty Research CRD 155/68, April 3, 1968; Dornberg, *Brezhnev,* pp. 222–223. *Political Diary* records the fierce threats made at the same Moscow city party meeting by others amplifying Brezhnev's words—by President of the Academy of Sciences M. V. Keldysh and Secretary of the Moscow Writers Union Mikhalkov in particular (*Politicheskiy dnevnik,* pp. 300–303).
67. See Valenta, *Soviet Intervention in Czechoslovakia, 1968,* pp. 79–82; Michel Tatu, "Intervention in Eastern Europe," in Stephen Kaplan, ed., *Diplomacy of Power* (Washington, D.C.: Brookings Institution, 1981), pp. 227–228; Hodnett and Potichnyj, *The Ukraine and the Czechoslovak Crisis,* pp. 77–89.
68. This is the judgment cumulatively rendered by *The Military Balance* (International Institute for Strategic Studies) issues for 1968 through 1983. In this

series, estimates of the Soviet forces stationed in European Russia at first decline, with the dispatch of five divisions to Czechoslovakia, and then gradually climb back to a point higher than before.

69. Dornberg, *Brezhnev*, pp. 238–240; Tatu, "Intervention in Eastern Europe," pp. 238–239.

70. For a detailed discussion of the background and evolution of this crisis, see Harry Gelman, *The Soviet Far East Buildup and Soviet Risk-Taking against China*, R-2943-AF (Santa Monica: The Rand Corporation, August 1982), pp. 28–52.

71. Ibid.

Chapter 4 / *The Evolution of Soviet Behavior in the 1970s*

1. Lyndon Johnson, *The Vantage Point* (New York: Holt, Rinehard, & Winston, 1971), p. 481.

2. Ibid., p. 484.

3. *Pravda*, June 19, 1968.

4. *Pravda*, June 28, 1968.

5. On the other hand, two months later, extraordinary circumstances led the Soviets to unbend; after months of stonewalling on the date to begin the strategic weapons talks, on August 19, 1968 they abruptly cabled an invitation to Johnson to visit Moscow in October. (Johnson, *Vantage Point*, p. 487.) This shift in priorities was obviously evoked by the decision the Politburo had just taken to invade Czechoslovakia two days later, and was calculated as a preemptive more to try to offset the expected reaction in the West. It is unlikely, however, that under these conditions they thought it likely that the American president would accept. Nor did this invitation presage an imminent Soviet shift to the detente strategy of multiple negotiations on a broad front with the United States. As Henry Kissinger testifies, throughout 1969 and well into 1970, Soviet policy remained "immobile"; and "as far as the Soviets were concerned, 1969 was a flight from concreteness" (Henry Kissinger, *White House Years* [Boston: Little, Brown, 1979] pp. 147, 159).

6. Erwin Weit, *At the Red Summit: Interpreter behind the Iron Curtain* (New York: Macmillan, 1970), pp. 139–140.

7. TASS, May 30, 1967. On May 23, a Soviet government statement on the crisis, released the day after Nasser's declaration of the closure, failed to mention it.

8. Kissinger, *White House Years*, pp. 567–593.

9. *Peking Review*, January 7, 1966.

10. Mohammed Heikal, *The Sphinx and the Commissar* (New York: Harper & Row, 1978), pp. 174–176; Nadau Safran, *From War to War* (New York: Pegasus, 1969), pp. 274–276.

11. Heikal, *Sphinx and the Commissar*, pp. 176.

12. Johnson, *The Vantage Point*, p. 302.

13. State Department spokesman statement of December 13, 1967 (Associated Press, December 13, 1967).

14. Kissinger, *White House Years*, p. 585.

15. Ibid., pp. 635–652.

16. Credible American newspaper reports later alleged the Soviet Ambassador N. M. Pegov had privately assured the Indian government that a Soviet fleet was now in the Indian Ocean and that the USSR would not "allow" the United States to intervene on behalf of Pakistan (*Washington Post,* December 21, 1971).

17. Kissinger, *White House Years,* pp. 183–184.

18. Ibid., pp. 178–179.

19. Ibid., p. 179.

20. For a description of these demands, see Harry Gelman, "Outlook for Sino-Soviet Relations," *Problems of Communism,* September–December 1979, pp. 50–66.

21. *Izvestiya,* May 16, 1974.

22. John Newhouse, *Cold Dawn: The Story of SALT* (New York: Holt, Rinehart & Winston, 1973), p. 189. See also Kissinger, *White House Years,* pp. 547–548.

23. Kissinger, *White House Years,* pp. 810–823.

24. Ibid., pp. 906–913. For a critique of certain of Kissinger's contentions about the chances of Chinese and Soviet military action in this crisis and the effects of U.S. policy, see Harry Gelman, *The Soviet Far East Buildup and Soviet Risk-Taking against China,* R-2943-AF (Santa Monica: The Rand Corporation, August 1982), pp. 60–63.

25. Nixon, *Memoirs,* pp. 883, 1030; Kissinger, *White House Years,* pp. 1226–1227; Kissinger, *Years of Upheaval* (Boston: Little, Brown, 1982), pp. 223, 294–295, 1173–1174.

26. Nixon, *Memoirs,* p. 1030. Nixon implies that this proposal was dismissed outright. Kissinger, on the contrary, reports that Nixon instructed him, in the presence of the Soviets, to consider the idea of such a treaty for subsequent exploration with the Soviets. He maintains that he was adamantly opposed and that Nixon, soon to be overwhelmed by the Watergate crisis, never referred to the matter again. It is extremely unlikely that this notion would have been considered long by either man in any case, since as Kissinger points out, such a treaty would have had the "clear implication that the United States was giving the Soviet Union a free hand to attack China" (Kissinger, *Years of Upheaval,* pp. 1173–1174).

27. For an eloquent presentation of this view, see William G. Hyland, *Soviet-American Relations: A New Cold War?* R-2763-FF/RC, (Santa Monica: The Rand Corporation, May 1981).

28. Although not explicitly stated, this assumption is evident in Kissinger's discussions in both volumes of his memoirs concerning U.S. relations with the PRC and the USSR during the Nixon administration.

29. In August 1971, speaking to the Yugoslav ambassador in the wake of the announcement of Nixon's forthcoming trip to China, Brezhnev asserted that "now it has become clear that there will be no sensation and that much time will elapse before a really new type of relations between Peking and Washington emerges." He is said to have added that "the Americans, regardless of all Nixon's demagogy and maneuvers, know very well that China is not, and cannot be, a real partner of the United States in the modern world. This role can only be filled by the Soviet Union" (Slobodan Stankovic, "Micunovich Describes Yugoslav-Soviet Disagreements," Radio Free Europe Research Back-

ground Report 187, September 20, 1982). This statement was obviously to some degree self-serving and probably reflected, in August 1971, as much of hope as of conviction. Within the following year, however, Brezhnev is likely to have grown somewhat more confident in this judgment.

30. See Grey Hodnett, "Ukrainian Politics and the Purge of Shelest" (Paper delivered at the annual meeting of the Midwest Slavic Conference, Ann Arbor, Michigan, May 5–7, 1977), pp. 53–55.

31. This contrast in perspective was first made manifest in contrasting passages in the speeches made by the two men at the 23rd Party Congress. For an excellent discussion of the evolution of this issue, see Bruce Parrott, "Soviet Technological Progress and Western Technology Transfer to the USSR: An Analysis of Soviet Attitudes," (Paper prepared for the Office of External Research, Bureau of Intelligence and Research, U.S. Department of State, July 1978).

32. Kosygin insisted that "it would be short-sighted not to use the latest foreign scientific and technical achievements . . . and take every opportunity to buy licenses" (*Sovetskaya Belorossiya,* February 15, 1968). Brezhnev replied that "certain officials clearly underestimate" Soviet technological achievements, and "are inclined to exaggerate the achievements of science and technology in the capitalist world" (*Pravda,* March 30, 1968). See Parrott, "Soviet Technological Progress," pp. 7–10. The explicitness of this polemical exchange was quite unusual for the Brezhnev era.

33. *Finansy SSSR,* no. 3, 1969, p. 16, cited by Keith Bush, "The Eighth and Ninth Five-Year Plans for Soviet Agriculture: Part I," Radio Liberty Research CRD 260/70, July 13, 1970.

34. *New York Times,* April 14, 1970.

35. Some members of the leadership were resentful of the heightened propaganda attention given consumer welfare in the early 1970s, despite the lesson provided by the popular explosion in Poland late in 1970. Belorussian party First Secretary P. M. Masherov, who became notorious for this point of view, complained in November 1971 about "exaggerated" propaganda for material incentives, and warned against encouraging "petit-bourgeois tendencies toward acquisitiveness" (*Sovetskaya Belorossiya,* November 13, 1971). In the same period Ukrainian party boss Shelest also found it intolerable that "in some places it is becoming the style, as it were, to speak exclusively about benefits," and insisted that "these are harmful consumerist tendencies" (*Kommunist Ukrainy,* no. 12, 1971, p. 15, cited in Hodnett, "Ukrainian Politics and the Purge of Shelest," pp. 60–61).

36. *Izvestiya,* January 15, 1970.

37. *Kazakhstanskaya Pravda,* April 17, 1969.

38. V. P. Nikolayeva, "V. I. Lenin and the Organizational Bureau of the Central Committee of the RKP[b] [1919–1920]," *Voprosy istorii KPSS,* no. 9, 1969, p. 40.)

39. Although unpublished, the gist of this speech was provided in a *Pravda* editorial a month later (*Pravda,* January 13, 1970). It was also widely discussed within the party, and the essence of Brezhnev's assertions about the economy was soon leaked to the West (*New York Times,* January 17, 1970).

40. *Partinaya zhizn,* no. 4, February 1970. See Christian Duevel, "CPSU Central Committee Decree Aggravates Party-Government Relationship," Radio Liberty

Research CRD 82/70, March 12, 1970; T. H. Rigby, "The Soviet Government Since Khrushchev," *Politics* 12 (May 1977), 13.

41. TASS, June 1, 1970; Christian Duevel, "Brezhnev Personally Intervenes in USSR Government Session," Radio Liberty Research CRD 202/70, June 3, 1970.

42. *Politicheskiy dnevnik* (Amsterdam: Alexander Herzen Foundation, 1972), pp. 657–658. A slightly different version, provided to Western news services by "reliable communist sources in Yugoslavia and Czechoslovakia," said that the letter had criticized both Brezhnev and Kosygin (Reuters, March 11, 1970).

43. Ibid.; John Dornberg, *Brezhnev: The Masks of Power* (New York: Basic Books, 1974), pp. 244–245.

44. Lenin, said Brezhnev, "regarded factionalism and group action in the Party as the greatest evil which had to be fought resolutely and relentlessly" (TASS, April 21, 1970).

45. Dornberg, *Brezhnev,* p. 248. See also Christian Duevel, "Marginal Notes on a Soviet Leadership Crisis," Radio Liberty Research CRD 272/70, July 23, 1970.

46. Brezhnev repeated this statement for the last time at the first of July's Central Committee plenums, only eleven days before the issue was decided otherwise (*Pravda,* July 3, 1970).

47. Duevel, "Marginal Notes."

48. In April 1971, Brezhnev supporters V. V. Shcherbitskiy, premier of the Ukraine, and D. A. Kunayev, first secretary of the Kazakhstan Party, were promoted from candidate to full Politburo membership, and Central Committee Secretary for agriculture F. D. Kulakov was elevated directly to full membership. In April 1973, the first purge of major Brezhnev opponents occurred, when full Politburo members Gennadiy Voronov and Petr Shelest were ousted from the party leadership. The political position of both of these men had effectively been crushed in the previous year, however.

49. Between 1971 and about 1974, this offensive against Kosygin's position included an unsuccessful campaign to get the oligarchy to approve the creation of a State Council, a new organ to which, according to the *Le Monde* correspondent Alain Jacob, all Politburo members would be co-opted (*Le Monde,* November 21, 1971). Brezhnev, of course, planned to become the head of this State Council. Apparently he intended to secure a powerful new vehicle for authorized intervention into the economy over the heads of the Council of Ministers, thus enabling him to circumvent the effect of the prohibition against his becoming premier. It is also likely that the leadership's impasse over this project became another reason for the long delay in completing agreement on the draft of the new Soviet Constitution (Christian Duevel, "A USSR State Council?," Radio Liberty Dispatch CRD 355/71, November 22, 1971; TAN-YUG Domestic Service, Belgrade, November 20, 1971; Duevel, "Tsedenbal Elected Head of State—At Last," Radio Liberty Dispatch RL 193/74, June 21, 1974).

50. In an election speech delivered in Moscow on June 12, Brezhnev made a region-by-region tour of the horizon of Soviet foreign policy (TASS, June 12, 1970).

51. See Newhouse, *Cold Dawn,* pp. 156–157; Kissinger, *White House Years,* pp. 535, 547.

52. In March 1971, at the 24th CPSU Congress, Brezhnev held out the prospect that a successful SALT outcome would free "considerable means" for "constructive goals." Two years later, in a Budapest television interview, Arbatov alluded to the ABM treaty as having provided such savings, but also hinted at a desire for more such budget dividends. Responding to remarks by the interviewer about Hungarian concern over the tangible economic benefits of East-West military agreements, Arbatov said that "this impatience is characteristic not only of Hungarians. Other people ask the same thing" (Hungarian television, August 5, 1973). Although the longing in such quarters for major resource transfers from the military was never reflected in Politburo behavior, some Soviet defense officials were apparently concerned about the possibility, and were determined to ensure that such views did not influence the decision makers. In 1972, one military writer attacked as "insufficiently mature and shortsighted politically" unidentified people who supposed that successful implementation of peaceful coexistence might "permit a slackening in our military preparedness" (*Krasnaya Zvezda,* July 21, 1972).
53. In a 1971 Supreme Soviet election speech, Brezhnev stated quite frankly that the United States could not expect from arms control "renunciation of the already adopted programs" (*Pravda,* June 12, 1971).
54. Edward Warner and Thomas Wolfe agree that at the outset, the Soviet military was "wary" of the SALT process; indeed, Wolfe feels that the military "had been reluctant to enter the talks at all." By the conclusion of SALT I, however, Warner believes that except for the PVO-Strany (National Air Defense Forces)—for whom the ABM treaty was a blow—"the rest of the military establishment is likely to have been solidly in favor of the accords," and indeed, regarded them with "satisfaction." Moreover, in his view, by the spring of 1977, "the Soviet military, despite its traditional misgivings about arms control," was likely to see "the extended SALT negotiations as a generally successful venture," since "the arms accords they have yielded appear to legitimize the strategic arms competition without interfering significantly with the vast majority of their own highly valued weapons programs." Similarly, Wolfe concludes that "it seems hardly disputable that . . . the military leadership has exerted a strong, conservative influence on the negotiations, and that the political leadership—whatever its own bent may have been—has tended to eschew agreements that, in the judgment of the military professionals, might adversely affect the Soviet military posture" (Edward L. Warner, *The Military in Contemporary Soviet Politics* [New York: Praeger, 1977] pp. 245, 249–250, 258–259; Thomas W. Wolfe, *The SALT Experience* [Cambridge: Ballinger, 1979], pp. 75–76).
55. See Kissinger, *Years of Upheaval,* pp. 122–123, 287.
56. On this subject, see Marshall Brement, *Organizing Ourselves to Deal with the Soviets,* P-6213 (Santa Monica: The Rand Corporation, June 1978), pp. 8–9.
57. See *Soviet Strategy and Tactics in Economic and Commercial Negotiations with the United States,* CIA National Foreign Assessment Center, ER 79-10276, June 1979.
58. *New York Times,* June 16, 1978.
59. In this connection, see the remarks by Marshall Brement, a former political counselor in Embassy Moscow, *Organizing Ourselves,* pp. 7, 14, 17–20, 28–29. See also the comments of former Ambassador Malcolm Toon, *New York Times,* October 17, 1979.

60. See the description of the political circumstances surrounding the creation of the "back channel" in Kissinger, *White House Years,* pp. 130–141.

61. The testimony of Orionova is again relevant here: "In my case, I belonged to the Foreign Policy Department and it was particularly difficult to work because my deputy director was Zhurkin who . . . was a very, very sensitive person. He was really sensitive to where the wind blows and one day the wind blows in one direction and the second, in another direction. So one day he will put his signature and the second day he will ask you to the office and ask: 'What did you write?' He did not know what to do" (Barbara L. Dash, *A Defector Reports: The Institute of the USA and Canada,* Delphic Associates, May 1982, p. 191.)

62. See note 30, Chapter 1, and note 19, Chapter 2.

63. On the mechanisms and procedures used by Soviet authorities to organize and operate this policy-rationalizing function of the institutes in contacts with foreigners, see Dash, *A Defector Reports,* pp. 159–178. Barbara Dash summarizes the details Orionova provides as follows: "Increasingly . . . American visits have been utilized as an opportunity for imparting certain official Soviet views to Americans in a position to disseminate them on any level. Such considerations in fact seem to form the basis of most recommendations to the Academy of Sciences for potential visitors. . . . Often several institutes will consolidate their efforts to influence visitors in a particular direction. . . . To this end, there is considerable preparation in advance of a foreign guest's arrival. Instructions originating at lower levels of the Central Committee's International Department or sometimes the KGB will filter down through the Institute from Arbatov or the executive secretary to department heads and researchers. In some cases, briefings may be held at the Foreign Ministry, as for a foreign conference, or department heads may consult their deputy director" (pp. 163–164).

64. See, for example, *New York Times,* January 3, 1980.

65. For a fairly frank Soviet discussion of one aspect of this process, see Yu. I. Nyporko, *Konstitutionnyye vzaimootnosheniya prezidenta i Kongressa SSHA v oblasti vneshney politiki* (Kiev: Academy of Sciences and Ukrainian SSR, 1979).

66. See the accounts of this interchange with the USSR in the *Washington Post,* December 31, 1979, and *New York Times,* January 1, 1980.

67. *New York Times,* January 11, 1980.

68. Between the spring and fall of 1974, this mixture of motives thus produced an extraordinary alliance of left and right to attack the administration's strategy for economic dealings with the Soviet Union. The *New York Times* declared that "the genuineness of the Soviet interest [in detente] has been cast increasingly in doubt by Moscow's attitudes in Europe and the Middle East. However valuable a mood of reduced tensions between the two superpowers, political atmosphere is not something to be bought by economic transactions that cannot be justified on their own merits" (*New York Times,* March 14, 1974). As the struggle in parallel developed in the summer, Senators Jackson, Ribicoff, and Javits were the primary figures who used the Jackson amendment to the Trade Act as a negotiating lever to exact large concessions from the Soviets on Jewish emigration, while Senators Sevenson, Church, and Schweiker simultaneously pressed their campaign to ban credits for Soviet energy development from the

Export-Import Bank bill. It appears to have occurred to neither the attacking senators nor the defending administration that success for Mr. Stevenson's campaign could affect the viability of the deal being sought by Mr. Jackson.

69. Senator Stevenson's efforts were given considerable impetus in Congress by the Eximbank's announcement, on May 21, of a huge $180 million loan to the USSR at a bargain interest rate of 6 percent, to help finance a $400 million natural gas and fertilizer plant (*Wall Street Journal,* May 22, 1974). One of the many ironies of these events was that the chairman and president of the Export-Import Bank, whose conduct in approving this generous loan to the USSR without congressional approval greatly disturbed the liberal Senators Stevenson and Church, was William J. Casey, a conservative who seven years later was appointed to a senior post in the vehemently anti-Soviet administration of Ronald Reagan.

70. On December 18, Dobrynin is reported to have visited Kissinger in his office and informed the secretary that the Soviet leadership was angered by the Eximbank credit ceiling just agreed to by Congress. Dobrynin is also alleged to have stated that the matter had been discussed earlier that week during the Party's Central Committee plenum, and that the Soviet leaders had agreed that the United States through this action against Soviet credit had refused to live up to its side of detente (*Washington Post,* December 19, 1974).

71. Kissinger now acknowledges that "a preoccupied Administration was caught flat-footed" in dealing with the Export-Import Bank bill, and explains that "in a big government it is impossible to give equal attention to all issues simultaneously." In hindsight, he now professes to believe that Senator Jackson supported the Stevenson amendment as well as his own amendment because Jackson was really seeking, by hook or by crook, to end all East-West trade, whatever the effects on Jewish emigration from the Soviet Union. This theory implies that Senator Jackson did not really care about the consequences for Jewish emigration. This was not, however, Kissinger's view at the time (Kissinger, *Years of Upheaval,* pp. 996–998).

72. *Washington Post,* December 19, 1974.

73. On December 18, after the House had approved the final version of the amended Export-Import Bank bill but while the trade bill was still in conference, the Soviets published a letter they had evidently been holding in reserve, written by Gromyko to Kissinger in October, and denying that any specific pledges on future emigration policy had been made to the United States. That same afternoon, Dobrynin paid his visit to Kissinger to convey the anger of the Soviet leadership over what had been done to Soviet credits (*Washington Post,* December 19, 1974). Under the circumstances, it seems highly probable that the Gromyko letter would never have been published if the Stevenson amendment had not passed.

74. *New York Times,* January 15, 1975.

75. See Anwar Sadat, *In Search of Identity* (New York: Harper and Row, 1977), pp. 220–231.

76. Ibid., also Mohammed Heikal, *The Road to Ramadan* (New York: Quadrangle, 1975), pp. 155–177.

77. Heikal claims (*Road to Ramadan,* p. 181) that the Soviets "seemed anxious to recover lost ground by speeding up the flow of arms, to such an extent that

I remember President Sadat saying to me one day: 'They are drowning me in new arms.' Between December 1972 and January 1973 we received more arms from them than in the whole of the two preceding years." This is probably somewhat exaggerated. See also Heikal, *Sphinx and the Commissar,* p. 253.

78. Nixon, *Memoirs,* p. 885.

79. The alert of the Soviet airborne units was initally reported in the *New York Times,* November 21, 1973; see the discussion in Nixon, *Memoirs,* p. 937. After the October 1973 war, some Soviet broadcasts to the Middle East are alleged to have acknowledged this alert and to have claimed that the USSR had been prepared to intervene (*Washington Post,* May 2, 1974). Regarding this Soviet threat, see the *Washington Post,* November 28, 1973; Nixon, *Memoirs,* p. 938. Some years later, Mr. Nixon asserted publicly that Brezhnev had informed him that he intended to send two Soviet divisions to Syria and had "invited" the United States to balance that action by sending two American divisions to Israel. When this proposal was rejected, Brezhnev is said to have asserted that he would send the Soviet troops in any case. It was this statement, according to Mr. Nixon, that triggered the worldwide American alert on October 26, 1973 (*New York Times,* December 1, 1978).

80. A TASS statement released some hours after the Nixon press conference mentioned that U.S. alert for the first time, alluded to efforts by unnamed U.S. officials to justify it as a response to Soviet actions, and condemned it as a vain attempt to "intimidate" the Soviet Union (TASS, October 27, 1973).

81. *New York Times,* May 22, 1972.

82. Ibid.; *Washington Star,* May 10, 1972; *New York Times,* May 19, 1972.

83. See Hodnett, "Ukrainian Politics and the Purge of Shelest," pp. 28–40.

84. See the evidence from *Political Diary* cited in note 8, Chapter 2.

85. A somewhat similar view is taken by Hodnett, "Ukrainian Politics and the Purge of Shelest," pp. 27–28.

86. *Le Monde,* January 20, 1972.

87. This appointment was announced in *Pravda,* May 16, 1972. The evidence suggests, however, that Rumyantsev had been removed from his institute, and had ceased to be a vice-president of the Academy of Sciences, by the summer of 1971. See the account by Boris Rabbot, "A Letter to Brezhnev," *New York Times Magazine,* November 7, 1977; also, I. Zemtsoy, "The Fate of Soviet Sociology," *Posev* (Frankfurt), no. 6, 1978, pp. 38–41.

88. *Moskovskaya Pravda,* June 15, 1972.

89. *Pravda,* July 30, 1972.

90. Anonymous samizdat document appended to Christian Duevel, "A High-Ranking CPSU Official Corroborates Sakharov's Warning on Detente," Radio Liberty Dispatch, September 7, 1973.

91. Ibid.

92. Ibid.

93. *New York Times,* September 17, 1973.

94. In addition to such efforts to protect himself by assuring ideologues that detente was only a stratagem, Brezhnev made a few attempts to persuade doubters among his colleagues that the multiplication of contacts with the West brought about by detente was not dangerous to the regime. The most explicit statement he made along this line was contained in his speech in Alma-Ata on August

15, 1973 (*Pravda,* August 16, 1973). After this, as relations with the United States began to cool, he never again made this claim so boldly.

95. Grechko's entry into the Politburo evoked an innovation in Soviet political symbolism a year later. In May 1974, a significant change was made in the open letter that the Soviet leadership traditionally addresses to the Soviet people during Supreme Soviet election campaigns. For the first time in the post-Stalin period, this letter now listed "military units" and "servicemen of the army and navy" as members of the oligarchs' nationwide constituency, as well as the customary "collectives of enterprises, collective farms, state farms, institutions, and educational establishments" (*Pravda,* May 5, 1974).

96. *Pravda,* November 7, 1973; *Pravda,* January 1, 1974.

97. *Trud,* May 9, 1974.

98. A. A. Grechko, "The Leading Role of the CPSU in Building the Army of a Developed Socialist Society," *Voprosy istorii KPSS,* May 1974, pp. 30–47.

99. *Leningradskaya Pravda,* June 12, 1974.

100. *Pravda,* June 5, 1974.

101. *Pravda,* June 8, 1974.

102. Kissinger testified to the Senate on December 3 that Soviet assurances on emigration had been repeated to him on several recent occasions, the last being at the mid-November summit at Vladivostok (Committee on Finance, United States Senate, *Emigration Amendment to the Trade Reform Act of 1974,* Hearing, December 3, 1974 [Washington, D.C.: U.S. Government Printing Office, 1974], p. 52). As noted above, the Soviet public denial and repudiation of these assurances was made on December 18 (*Washington Post,* December 19, 1974).

103. *New York Times,* January 15, 1975.

104. In his Moscow talks with the kidnapped Czechoslovak party leaders after the August 1968 invasion, Brezhnev is said to have assured the Czechs that the support they were receiving from the West European Communists was meaningless, since "the Communist movement in Western Europe . . . won't amount to anything for fifty years" (Zdenek Mlynar in the *New York Times,* February 5, 1979). A somewhat similar statement is attributed to Brezhnev by the Australian Communist Frank Hardy in *Sunday Times,* London, November 3, 1968.

105. On August 25, 1975, the *New York Times* reported that in January 1975 the Soviet Union had sent about $500,000 in political funds to Portugal through a shipping concern in Antwerp. Another source at this time reported estimates that the USSR had poured a total of about $45 million in such funds into Portugal through a variety of channels since the overthrow of the Caetano regime in April 1974 (*International Herald Tribune,* August 25, 1975).

106. See F. Stephen Larrabee, "New Light on the Zaradov Controversy," Radio Liberty Research, RL 413/75, September 29, 1975.

107. *Pravda,* August 6, 1974.

108. See *The Lin Piao Affair,* ed. Michael Y. M. Kau (White Plains: International Arts and Sciences Press, 1975); *New York Times,* July 23, 1972, September 2, 1973.

109. See the discussion of this crisis in Gelman, *The Soviet Far East Buildup,* pp. 53–64.

110. Kissinger, *White House Years,* pp. 906–907. See Gelman, *The Soviet Far East Buildup,* pp. 60–61.

111. For an extended discussion of Soviet behavior before and during the Sino-Vietnamese fighting, see Gelman, *The Soviet Far East Buildup,* pp. 84–105.
112. *New York Times,* March 29 and July 9, 1979; *Philadelphia Inquirer,* May 2, 1980.

Chapter 5 / *Brezhnev's Legacy to His Successors*

1. See Michel Tatu, *Power in the Kremlin: From Khrushchev to Kosygin* (New York: Viking, 1970), p. 398.
2. In September 1976, Christian Duevel noted that it had been expected that Brezhnev would seek to elevate Kirilenko to the position of heir-apparent at the 25th Party Congress earlier that year. Instead, Suslov had emerged in the protocol rankings of the congress as the second man in the hierarchy. Duevel noted that Kirilenko had now turned seventy, and that his chances for securing the succession were gradually slipping away (Radio Liberty Report RL 411/76, "Current Trends in Soviet Domestic and Foreign Affairs," September 10, 1976, p. 2).
   Beginning in 1978, Kirilenko's relative status and future were placed increasingly in doubt by a long series of slights that coincided with the rise of Chernenko and the special media treatment afforded him, obviously at Brezhnev's direction. In the summer and fall of that year, the press began to emphasize Chernenko's joint travels with Brezhnev and even gave him equal billing with the general secretary on occasion. Meanwhile, when Brezhnev in May 1978 published a volume of memoirs about the postwar rebuilding of Zaporozhe, his references to Kirilenko, his deputy in that city at the time, were very terse. During the period of nominations to the Supreme Soviet in the winter of 1978-1979, Kirilenko was no longer publicly described as a "prominent party and state figure," as he had been in former years. In the spring of 1979, the press began to attack an August 1977 government decision, which Kirilenko had endorsed and defended, to continue awarding bonuses to industrial enterprises that failed to deliver contracted goods to industrial customers. Kirilenko's protégé Ryabov was shunted from the party Secretariat to Gosplan in April 1979, and Kirilenko's picture was dropped from the May Day leadership lineup by one Moscow paper (*Vechernaya Moskva,* May 1, 1979). During the 26th Party Congress in February 1981, Brezhnev administered more protocol slights to Kirilenko, while further elevating Chernenko (see Boris Meissner, "The 26th Party Congress and Soviet Domestic Politics," *Problems of Communism,* May–June 1981, p. 5). This incremental change in Brezhnev's attitude toward Kirilenko was apparently accompanied by a decline in Kirilenko's health; both processes reached their climax in 1982.
3. See Myron Rush, "The Soviet Policy Favoring Arms over Investment since 1975" (Paper prepared for the 1982 compendium of Joint Economic Committee of U.S. Congress, *Soviet Economy in the 1980s: Problems and Prospects*).
4. See Yaroslav Bilinsky, "Shcherbytskyi, Ukraine, and Kremlin Politics," *Problems of Communism,* July–August 1983, pp. 1–20.
5. *Soviet Defense Trends,* staff study prepared for Subcommittee on International Trade, Finance, and Security Economics of Joint Economic Committee, Congress of the United States, September 1983. See also Abraham S. Becker, *Sitting*

on Bayonets? The Soviet Defense Burden and Moscow's Economic Dilemma, P-6908 (Santa Monica: The Rand Corporation, September 1983); Becker, *The Burden of Soviet Defense: A Political-Economic Essay,* R-2752-AF (Santa Monica: The Rand Corporation, October 1981); *Boston Globe,* February 16, 1983; *New York Times,* March 3, 1983; *Washington Post,* March 4, 1983; *Los Angeles Times,* March 4, 1983.

6. *Soviet Defense Trends,* p. 2.

7. N. Ogarkov, "Guarding Peaceful Labor," *Kommunist,* no. 10, 1981. See the comments of William A. Hyland, "Kto Kogo in the Kremlin," *Problems of Communism,* January–February 1982, pp. 23–24.

8. *Pravda,* October 28, 1982.

9. Some Western observers, notably Lawrence Caldwell and Myron Rush, maintain that in 1981 and 1982 Ustinov helped Brezhnev to resist the pressures for increased military spending brought by Ogarkov and other marshals. In this view, Ustinov "may no longer have been representing a united military establishment" (Rush, "Succeeding Brezhnev," *Problems of Communism,* January–February 1983, p. 5).

10. It should be noted, however, that in the years of Kosygin's declining health when Brezhnev was grooming Tikhonov to succeed him, Brezhnev apparently experienced difficulty and delays in obtaining Politburo approval of the Politburo rank that Tikhonov's position as first deputy premier should have merited. This was no doubt because of Kosygin's obstruction. Similarly, after Kosygin left office and Tikhonov succeeded him in 1980, Brezhnev never did manage to secure promotion to the Politburo for Tikhonov's successor as first deputy premier, Arkhipov. The fact that Arkhipov was yet another old—and aging—Brezhnev associate apparently made his elevation to the Politburo unacceptable to some of the oligarchs as the succession approached.

11. According to one version, on December 27, 1981, stolen diamonds were apparently found in the possession of Boris Buryatiya, a singer at the Bolshoi theater and intimate friend of Galina Churbanov, Brezhnev's duaghter who was also the wife of the first deputy head of the MVD, which was charged with investigation of the theft. Because of the political sensitivity of the case, the matter was evidently referred to the KGB. Despite his own close association with Brezhnev, First Deputy KGB Chairman Semen Tsvigun is alleged to have arrested, or sought to arrest, Buryatiya without seeking the approval of the party leadership. It seems reasonable to suppose that Tsvigun's superior, KGB Chairman Andropov, played a role in this Tsvigun decision, which in effect pressed home the issue of high-level corruption and was surely intensely embarrassing to Brezhnev. After a stormy interview soon thereafter with party Secretary Suslov, who had wished the matter hushed up and did not wish the corruption issue to become an instrument of factional struggle, Tsvigun died under mysterious circumstances in January 1982. His obituary was signed by Andropov and a few other leaders but not by Brezhnev and Suslov, as protocol would have demanded. Many variants of this tale have appeared in the Western press; see, for example, *Soviet Analyst,* March 10, 1982; Andrew Nagorski, "The Making of Andropov, 1982," *Harper's,* February 1983, pp 23–26; and Sidney Ploss, "Signs of Struggle," *Problems of Communism,* September–October 1982, pp. 43–44. One of the many conclusions that can be drawn from this

episode was that the rats had commenced to leave the sinking ship. Apparently, Tsvigun was, in effect, the first in a series of Brezhnev lieutenants and allies who deserted him in 1982.

12. That is to say: Ustinov, Andropov, and Gromyko; plus Leningrad party secretary Romanov, Moscow party secretary Grishin, and Party Control Commission Chairman Pelshe; plus Shcherbitskiy. It is alleged that opposing this new Politburo majority in early May were Brezhnev and his three closest followers (Premier Tikhonov, Secretary Chernenko, and Kazakh First Secretary Kunayev). This account of the lineup has been furnished by Roy Medvedev, an intellectual camp follower of Andropov's. It does not state what role, if any, was played by Kirilenko, who was in poor health. (Joseph Kraft, "Letter from Moscow," *New Yorker,* January 31, 1983). It should be emphasized once more that this was a *Politburo* showdown; the Central Committee plenum was again the forum in which the result was first announced.

13. Nagorski, "Making of Andropov," asserts that many of the rumors were in fact disseminated by "known KGB informers in conversations with Western diplomats." If so, the apparatus of the KGB was being used for purposes of party factional struggle.

14. *New York Times,* September 5, 1982.

15. Nagorski, "Making of Andropov"; Kraft, "Letter from Moscow."

16. See "Andropov Consolidates His Hold on the Central Committee Apparatus," Radio Liberty Research RL 339/83, September 9, 1983.

17. Gregory Grossman, "The 'Second Economy,' " *Problems of Communism,* September–October 1977, pp. 25–40.

18. In his speech to a November 1982 plenum of the Central Committee shortly after assuming Brezhnev's job, Andropov said that it was time to "take up the practical resolution" of the question of expanding the "independence of associations, enterprises, collective farms and state farms." He asserted, in this connection, that the USSR should "take the fraternal countries' experience into account." He also felt obliged, however, to caution that this had to be done "circumspectly," and there was strong reason to believe that this rhetorical caveat reflected the continued political difficulties of carrying out meaningful reform (*Pravda,* November 23, 1982).

19. For a devastating critique of the often fatuous initial Western reporting on Andropov's personality and background, see Edward Jay Epstein, "The Andropov File," *New Republic,* February 7, 1983, pp. 18–21.

20. Archie Brown, "Andropov: Discipline *and* Reform? " *Problems of Communism,* January–February 1983, pp. 18–31.

21. One of the striking features of Soviet diplomacy in the first six months of the Andropov regime was the use of heavy-handed and counterproductive pressure on West Germany and Japan to defend the Soviet advantages brought by the SS-20 deployments in East and West. In the case of Germany, this took the form of crude and unsuccessful Soviet intervention into the 1983 FRG election campaign. In the case of Japan, it took the form of equally crude and counterproductive rhetorical brandishing of the SS-20 against Japan in reaction to an assertion by Premier Yasuhiro Nakasone that Japan must respond to the Soviet military threat by becoming an "unsinkable aircraft carrier." These Soviet actions surely did not display the adroitness and subtlety expected of

Andropov. This dual episode suggests the paralyzing effect upon the behavior of any Soviet leader of the Politburo dogma that the geopolitical edge established by the SS-20 must be preserved.

22. By the spring of 1983, according to Western press reports, Cam Ranh Bay had become a full-time naval operations base for the Soviet Pacific Fleet, and the number of Soviet naval ships in the port at any one time had risen to twenty—a record level. The base was the site of extensive Soviet electronic surveillance facilities, and Soviet long-range naval reconnaisance flights staged from Vietnam provided extensive coverage of U.S. naval movements in the South China Sea and the Indian Ocean (*New York Times,* March 13, 1983. On the same day the Chinese news agency XINHUA pointedly cited these facts).

23. Thus, in the Soviet view, a continuation of the El Salvador stalemate will preserve and exacerbate divisions within the American body politic as well as friction between the United States and important sectors of the West European and Latin American elite sympathetic to the El Salvador insurgents. Should the United States ever decide to intervene in force to crush the guerrillas—a course rendered unlikely by American public opinion—the Soviet Union would stand to gain enormously from the negative reaction in Latin America and elsewhere around the world. On the other hand, should the United States ever withdraw completely and should the essentially Marxist-Leninist guerrilla groups then come to power, the Soviet Union could expect a regime to evolve that would be permanently hostile to the United States and fundamentally aligned with the Soviet Union and Cuba and the model they represent. In sum, the Soviets are well satisfied with the present American dilemma and trust it will continue indefinitely.

24. The adequacy of the Soviet military services in question is of course another matter. Although Sadat, and possibly Nkomo, may have been inclined to carp, most Soviet clients probably feel that the Soviets render good value.

25. Most notably, through political pressures in Cuba in the early 1960s, in Egypt in 1971, and in Ethiopia more recently. Mengistu, for example, has appeared to be quite suspicious of Soviet intentions.

26. Some observers may feel that South Yemen already belongs in this category. I disagree, and would draw attention to the mistaken view, widespread in 1971, that the enormous Soviet military presence in Egypt, including the stationing of advisers in key positions down to battalion level, had given the USSR such control in Egypt.

27. "We have nothing to take back," Andropov insisted in his speech at the November 1982 Central Committee plenum (*Pravda,* November 23, 1982). There is little doubt that this sentiment enjoys wide support in the oligarchy and the surrounding Soviet aristocracy.

28. In contrast, Lawrence Caldwell and Robert Legvold argue that the Soviet statements alleging that the United States had "brought the world to the brink of a universal nuclear catastrophe" were more than tactical expedients intended to play on the fears of the peace movement in Europe. Although they acknowledge that this has been one Soviet motive for such statements, they contend they that also reflect genuine Soviet alarm, particularly after Defense Minister Ustinov joined Chief of the General Staff Ogarkov in the use of such language in May 1983 (Caldwell and Legvold, "Reagan through Soviet Eyes," *Foreign Policy,* no. 52, Fall 1983, pp. 6–7).

29. See, for example, U.S. Department of State Special Report No. 98, *Chemical Warfare in Southeast Asia and Afghanistan,* March 22, 1982; J. H. Turnbull, "Yellow Rain," *Defence* (Eton, England), 14, May 1983, pp. 265–270.
30. "Convention on the Prohibition of the Development, Production, and Stockpiling of Bacteriological (Biological) and Toxin Weapons and on Their Destruction," April 10, 1972, in U.S. Arms Control and Disarmament Agency, *Documents on Disarmament 1972,* Publication 60, U.S. Government Printing Office, Washington, D.C., May 1974, pp. 133–138. Article VI of this convention provides that any state which feels that another state is violating the agreement may "lodge a complaint" for consideration by the UN Security Council. Experience suggests, however, that overriding political considerations make it unlikely that this procedure will be used against the Soviet Union, a permanent member of the Security Council.
31. In March 1983, Soviet officials in Moscow expressed gratification at the improvements that had taken place in Sino-Soviet relations, and were quoted as adding that this had occurred in part because the United States had made sporadic moves to upgrade relations with Taiwan and that "this silly policy of the Reagan Administration taught China a lesson." As a result, one official claimed, "you are losing and we are beginning to gain" *(New York Times,* March 20, 1983). Although not completely unfounded, these statements are somewhat self-serving and exaggerated. See Harry Gelman, "Soviet Policy toward China," *Survey* 27, Autumn–Winter 1983, pp. 165–174.
32. Seweryn Bialer and Alfred Stepan, "Cuba, the US, and the Central American Mess," *New York Review of Books,* May 27, 1982.
33. Seweryn Bialer, "The Soviet Union and the West in the 1980s: Detente, Containment, or Confrontation?" *Orbis* 27, no. 1, p. 42.
34. Another view is expressed by Caldwell and Legvold: "It [the Soviet Union] has more self-confidence in the face of its internal and external problems, and it finds acknowledging the legitimacy of others' national security concerns easier these days" ("Reagan through Soviet Eyes," p. 17). Would that it were so.
35. On November 21, 1982, the new Andropov regime through an editorial in *Pravda* said that the Soviet Union is "always ready" for "normal and even better, friendly Soviet-American relations," after having first made clear that the USSR would "maintain solidarity" with what it termed the "peoples' struggle for national independence and social progress."
36. G. R. Urban, ed., *Stalinism* (London: Maurice Temple Smith, 1982), p. 197.

Index

259

Library of Congress Cataloging in Publication Data
Gelman, Harry, 1930–
    The Brezhnev Politburo and the decline of detente.

    Includes bibliographical references and index.
    1. Soviet Union—Politics and government—1964–
2. TsK KPSS. Politburo. 3. Detente. 4. Soviet Union—
Foreign relations—United States. 5. United States—
Foreign relations—Soviet Union. 6. Brezhnev, Leonid
Il'ich, 1906–1982. I. Title.
DK274.G37 1984   327.47073   83–45963
ISBN 0-8014-1544-6   (alk. paper)
ISBN 0-8014-9280-7 (pbk.)